Praise for

Children's Ministry and the Spiritual Child

"The tradition continues! I am most thankful that this dialogue on the spiritual life and nurturing of children is ongoing and that this book addresses the broad context and ecology of children's spiritual formation. The focus on listening to children, home and intergenerational church influences, and considering loss in the lives of children helps me see their needs and potentials and our ministry opportunities more fully. The different perspectives stir my thinking, raise critical concerns, and help me learn from those who have given deeper thought to these issues than I have. Children deserve our best in ministry, and I'm glad that the contributors to this book push me to give my best."
—**Kevin E. Lawson**, Global Affiliate Professor of Educational Studies, Talbot School of Theology, Biola University; former chair of the Society for Children's Spirituality: Christian Perspectives (now the Children's Spirituality Summit); and author of *Infants and Children in the Church: Five Views on Theology and Ministry*

"I am amazed and thankful to see compiled in one place this stunning breadth of wisdom for discipling children. *Children's Ministry and the Spiritual Child* is a 'bible,' a dictionary, and an encyclopedia for caring for and cultivating the spiritual lives of children. Every Christian leader who works with children should have it, not on a bookshelf, but on their desk as a partner, as a frequent source of wisdom."
—**Rt. Rev. Todd Hunter**, founding bishop of the Diocese of Churches for the Sake of Others, Anglican Church in North America; and author of *Deep Peace: Finding Calm in a World of Conflict and Anxiety*

"Wow! What a helpful book. What is unique about this resource is that many contributors are primarily thoughtful practitioners (and some also happen to be academics). In other volumes, the reverse is usually true. Okholm and Turner's work is extremely valuable for a person in the trenches of local ministry."
—**Scottie May**, associate professor of Christian formation and ministry emerita, Wheaton College; and coauthor of *Listening to Children on the Spiritual Journey: Guidance for Those Who Teach and Nurture*

"The variety of excellent essays in *Children's Ministry and the Spiritual Child* can guide your thinking and practice of ministry with today's children. Woven throughout the book are words and images that can shape your ministry with children: gentle listening, gentle seeing, welcoming, wondering, nurturing, cultivating, story, presence, mystery, vulnerability, discovery, authenticity, multigenerational relationships, and witness. Let the book's wisdom inform your understanding of children's spiritual growth."
—**John Roberto**, founder and director of Lifelong Faith Associates and author of *Lifelong Faith: Formation for All Ages and Generations*

"Okholm and Turner have curated a refreshing array of authors and writings on pressing contemporary questions and innovative applications related to children's spirituality. The topics covered here carry a consistent theme around the surprising expansiveness of children's spirituality and how adults can both cultivate and be encouraged in their own faith by it. Each chapter presents fresh ideas and connects effective practices for parents, scholars, pastors, and children's workers. I read the book breathlessly, eagerly devouring the ideas and approaches it offers."
—**David H. Scott**, assistant professor of intercultural studies and children at risk, School of Mission and Theology, Fuller Seminary; and author of *Understanding Children at Risk*

"We live in a siloed age. Children get relegated to 'Sunday school' while adults go to 'worship'; the ministry practitioners are in the church while the theologians remain in the academy. What society has cast asunder, this volume joins together, reintegrating psychology with theology, evangelization with catechesis, and experimentation with best practices. If you care about the future of the church and want better for those lambs God has entrusted to our flocks, you need this book!"
—**Dustin Messer**, vicar of All Saints Dallas; lecturer at Reformed Theological Seminary in Dallas; and professor at The King's College in New York

"This is a book worth spending time with. The editors have allowed us to listen in on fascinating conversations about children's spirituality. They've done a great job of inviting new voices to these conversations. A dozen young academics and practitioners and some seasoned veterans bring their insights and fresh ideas to us in this helpful volume."
—**Robert J. Keeley**, professor of education emeritus, Calvin University; author of *Helping Our Children Grown in Faith*; and coeditor of *Bridging Theory and Practice in Children's Spirituality: New Directions for Education, Ministry, and Discipleship*

"As a children's ministry professor, my students learn that children are profoundly spiritual yet lack the spiritual language to describe their experiences with God. *Children's Ministry and the Spiritual Child* acknowledges this reality and invites a conversation between researchers and readers, teaching the reader to talk about the spiritual lives of children, to listen deeply to the spiritual experiences of children, and to trust the work of the Spirit in the lives of children. Children's ministry leaders and students will be empowered by practical wisdom that they can use in any ministry, big or small."
—**Shannon Rains**, associate professor of children's ministry, Lubbock Christian University

"Looking for your next children's ministry read? This book will give you plenty to think about. The authors combine qualitative research and practical ideas to help you reach children and families more effectively. From a strong emphasis on receptive listening, cultivating internal motivation, and building developmental relationships to strategies for responding to difficult behaviors and trauma, each chapter offers connections with scripture and social science research. I especially appreciate the attention to addressing racism and Adverse Childhood Experiences (ACEs) as well as the myriad effects of the global pandemic on family faith practices. There's even a chapter on modeling ministry after Mister Rogers!"
—**Rev. Karen-Marie Yust**, Rowe Professor of Christian Education, Union Presbyterian Seminary; chair of the International Association for Children's Spirituality; and author of *Real Kids, Real Faith: Practices for Nurturing Children's Spiritual Lives*

"Learning about children with children is a major development in theology and missiology. For too long, we focused primarily on a curricular approach that saw children as young ones in need of instruction. Thankfully, the fourteen contributors to this important work concentrate on relating to children through listening, paying attention, and nurturing. In addition, they manage to build a solid theoretical foundation for the practical nature of children's ministry. Contributions address the widespread problems of suffering, abuse, death, and racism with integrity, centering on their impact on the lives of children. The redemptive theme flowing through the book is the realization that children are spiritual beings who relate to God's mercy and grace. The editors invite you to read with the conviction that children's ministry requires learning with children."
—**C. Douglas McConnell**, provost emeritus and senior professor, School of Mission and Theology, Fuller Theological Seminary; and coeditor of *Understanding God's Heart for Children: Toward a Biblical Framework*

"This rich and thoughtful collection explores what it means to cultivate spiritual formation in children in theory and practice. While it examines the foundation of ministry with children in faith communities, through families, and in the midst of adversity, it also speaks to the practical needs felt by children's ministers each and every day. The heart of this resource lies in its ability to simultaneously illuminate the what, the why, and the how of spiritual formation. As a result, this will undoubtedly be a valuable resource for children's ministers and volunteers. Equally important, it should also become an essential read for church leaders and other pastors."
—**Jennifer Schroeder**, instructor of children's and family ministry, Abilene Christian University

Children's Ministry and the Spiritual Child

Children's Ministry and the Spiritual Child

Practical, Formation-Focused Ministry

Edited by
Trevecca Okholm *and* Robin Turner

CHILDREN'S MINISTRY AND THE SPIRITUAL CHILD
Practical, Formation-Focused Ministry

Copyright © 2023 by Trevecca Okholm and Robin Turner

978-1-68426-213-7

Printed in the United States of America

ALL RIGHTS RESERVED

No part of this publication may be reproduced, stored in a retrieval system, or transmitted in any form by any means—electronic, mechanical, photocopying, recording, or otherwise—without prior written consent.

All Scripture quotations, unless otherwise indicated, are taken from the Holy Bible, New International Version®, NIV®. Copyright ©1973, 1978, 1984, 2011 by Biblica, Inc.™ Used by permission of Zondervan. All rights reserved worldwide. www.zondervan.com The "NIV" and "New International Version" are trademarks registered in the United States Patent and Trademark Office by Biblica, Inc.™

Scripture quotations marked (NRSV) are from the New Revised Standard Version Bible, copyright © 1989 National Council of the Churches of Christ in the United States of America. Used by permission. All rights reserved worldwide.

Scripture quotations marked (KJV) are from the King James Version.

Library of Congress Control Number: 2022059583

Cover design by Bruce Gore | Gore Studio Inc.

Interior text design by Scribe Inc.

For information contact:
Abilene Christian University Press
ACU Box 29138
Abilene, Texas 79699
1-877-816-4455
www.acupressbooks.com

22 23 24 25 26 27 / 7 6 5 4 3 2 1

*Dedicated to
the many academicians and practitioners
from around the globe who participated in the
Children's Spirituality Summit in June 2021.
Your commitment to the spiritual formation
of children encourages each of us.
We are stronger together
as we share best practices
for the sake of the children.*

Contents

Introduction: The Story Continues   13
Trevecca Okholm, editor

SECTION 1
The Inner Spiritual Life of the Child: Listening and Paying Attention   17

1. Begin with Listening: Gifts of Eyes and Ears   21
   Lacy Finn Borgo

2. From Faith Transmission to Faith Recognition: Exploring Ways to Help Children Make Meaning from the God They Already Know   37
   Heather Ingersoll

3. Cultivating Curiosity: Water with Wonder, Grow Biblical Literacy   59
   Robin Turner

4. "Kids Today Just Can't . . .": Changing Our Posture and Practices to Welcome All Children   73
   Dana Kennamer and Suzetta Nutt

SECTION 2
Spiritual Nurture as Family Life   89

5. Abbots and Ammas: Formational Family Life toward Common Objects of Love   93
   Jared Patrick Boyd

6. Listening to Children: Race Lessons from My White Grandchildren   105
   Anthony Peterson

Contents

7 Neighborly Advice: Effective Preaching and
   Communication with Postmodern Families 117
   Kevin Johnson

SECTION 3
Communal Spirituality in Church Life: Growing in Ministry with All Generations Together 137

8 Discerning Congregational Change through
   a Nonanxious Intergenerational Model 141
   Joseph P. Conway

9 Why Spiritual Nurture of Young Children Matters 155
   Karin Middleton

10 (Un)Divided Worship: Children Leading and
    Belonging in the Worshiping Community 173
    Edwin (Ed) M. Willmington and Trevecca Okholm

SECTION 4
Coming Alongside Children in Challenging Contexts 191

11 The God of the Child: Trauma and Spirituality 195
    Esther L. Zimmerman

12 Theology and Abuse: Vulnerability in the Midst of
    Religious Institutions 215
    Stacey Wilson

13 Accompanying Children and Teens through Loss 239
    Lacy Finn Borgo

CONCLUSION
Practical Guidance for Implementing Best Practices in Real-Life Ministry 253
Robin Turner, editor

Contributors 263

Introduction
The Story Continues

Trevecca Okholm, editor

The story begins like all good stories do... Once upon a time, back in the last decade of the twentieth century, a group of like-minded folks—academics as well as everyday practitioners in the trenches of children's ministry—began a dialogue about children and spirituality. It was an era when scholars and practitioners alike were beginning to question if the way we were teaching kids about God and forming faith was truly effective. It was a time when many of us who worked with children were beginning to question terms such as *education* and ask ourselves what it means to see children not simply as empty vessels needing to be filled with information but rather as holistic, spiritual beings.

As the story goes, this group had within its ranks a number of highly qualified academics, many of whom are recognized leaders in the field of children's spirituality. They formed an organization and named it the Society of Children's Spirituality: Christian Perspectives (later changed to Children's Spirituality Summit). They decided that this society would not only cater to the work of those in the field of Christian education in universities and seminaries but also invite volunteers and part-time workers from the trenches of children's ministry in local churches to be part of the conversation so that the academics and those practitioners could challenge and inform one another.

For their first gathering—on the campus of Concordia University Chicago in River Forest, Illinois, in 2003—they not only invited academics and practitioners to brainstorm together; the board for the Society of Children's Spirituality also published a book[1] that could be accessible to academics as well as practitioners and bring them into a like-minded partnership for the sake of the children both groups loved so deeply.

This book that you are holding in your hands (or perhaps reading on a screen) is the seventh in a series of books created from the best research on coming alongside children in spiritual formation. The chapters that appear in this book have been gleaned from the many presenters at the 2021 Children's Spirituality Summit. Thus, the goal of this book is to continue the tradition of making the best thinking as accessible and easy to read for busy part-time church volunteers as it is for university students in the classroom.

As general editors for this volume, our hope is that whoever you are and whatever your role, you will find yourself engaged and challenged to think better about children's spirituality.

Section one sets the stage for seeing children as spiritual beings created in the imago Dei (the image of God) and asks and answers questions such as the following:

- How do we engage by listening to children and listening to God?
- Why does it matter what we do in ministry with children?
- What church-based practices are the best predictors of children's religiosity?
- How might we cultivate curiosity with children?
- What are some best practices for growing biblical literacy?

This section also addresses the reality of children with challenging behavior by asking, How might we reframe our posture and practices to be welcoming and engaging of *all* children?

Section two invites us into a deeper understanding of and reflection on the role of home life and significant others in prompting a

---

1 For a list of all six of the previously published conference books, see "Our Books," Children's Spirituality Summit, accessed October 2022, https://www.childrensspiritualitysummit.org/our-books.

child's spiritual life. This engagement expands outward in section three, which considers the communal spirituality of intergenerational church life and gives a broader view of what it can look like to intentionally invite children into an intergenerational community in their local church, where they might find their place of belonging in the rich traditions and influences of the whole body of Jesus Christ.

Given the ongoing challenges of ministry with children in difficult and often unstable contexts, the fourth section of our book is devoted to research and experiences of coming alongside children to assist in opening channels for spiritual flourishing. It returns to section one's theme of listening. Taking time to be present and listen creates sacred spaces for accompanying children and teens through loss.

Finally—in keeping with our passion to make this book accessible and useful for all levels of engagement—we conclude with a short and practical section that addresses *how to get this book off your bookshelf and into the crazies of real-life ministry!* This concluding section of the book is written by my coeditor, Robin Turner, a young mother of two little boys and full-time children's minister who can identify fully with the busyness of life and ministry.

This book is designed to equip those in ministry with children. Our hope is that it may encourage group dialogue among church practitioners and thus benefit the children in local communities. Our hope is also to encourage readers to participate in future Children's Spirituality Summits and become a part of the growing network of like-minded folks who love children and love God and desire to more effectively connect the two.

Oh, and one last thing: at the beginning of each section, we have added a short introduction for the chapters that appear in that section. This is to assist readers with an overview of what to expect and to explain how the chapters chosen for each section fit together in order to best equip and encourage those in ministry with children.

SECTION 1

The Inner Spiritual Life of the Child

Listening and Paying Attention

In the first section of this book, you can expect to be engaged with the *what-ifs* of a child's capacity to be drawn into deeper levels of spirituality and consider the unique ways we might come alongside children to experience ministry *with* and even *by* the children in our midst.

In the opening chapter, Lacy Finn Borgo invites us to breathe in God's presence, light a candle, and as her chapter title suggests, "begin with listening." As you begin reading, you are invited to be present, to experience. Engaging theological perspectives that form the basis of her work, Borgo explains the value of listening to children and helping them bring their experiences out into the open as gifts for both the child and the adult. She follows by instructing us, the readers, in the two movements in listening with children and invites us to practice the gentle-listening art of body, openness, and wonder (BOW). Throughout her chapter, Borgo reminds us that the act of listening truly and deeply creates meaningful spaces for connecting with the children in our care.

After the welcoming presence of Lacy Finn Borgo's introductory chapter, we pivot to Heather Ingersoll's invitation to explore ways of helping children make meaning. This chapter is appropriately titled "From Faith Transmission to Faith Recognition: Exploring Ways to Help Children Make Meaning from the God They Already Know." As the executive director of the Godly Play Foundation, Ingersoll explains to you, the reader, the innate human experience that emerges in early childhood as she addresses the growing body of research on childhood spirituality, providing compelling evidence that the spiritual capacity of children should be taken seriously and confirming how important this research is to the way we come alongside children in the transmission of religious formation. For those readers who might find this chapter a bit challenging to apply to their ministry settings, you will be delighted to discover that Ingersoll addresses some practical things that you can do to train your ministry leaders to do this well.

In Chapter Three, Robin Turner, coeditor of this book, invites readers to consider the value of prioritizing biblical literacy and gift children with the basic skills of navigating the Bible—skills too often lost or never taught to adults in our churches, let alone the children in our midst. In this chapter, titled "Cultivating Curiosity: Water with Wonder, Grow Biblical Literacy," Turner explains, "A foundation of biblical literacy started at a young age equips Christians for a lifetime of formational growth." But how to begin? That's the fun part of this chapter! Turner, a director of family ministries in her local church setting as well as a mom of two young boys, knows exactly how important it is to give readers practical suggestions, models, and tried-and-true practices to engage children in the foundational skills of finding one's way around the Bible. She does it by engaging wonder and cultivating curiosity.

In Chapter Four, "'Kids Today Just Can't . . .': Changing Our Posture and Practices to Welcome All Children," Dana Kennamer, a veteran professor of early childhood education at Abilene Christian University who is also known as "Teacher Dana" to the children in her church, partners with the children's ministry director of her church, Suzetta Nutt, to invite you, the reader, into a conversation about the challenges of ministry with children. Dana and Suzetta address questions such as How do you begin to navigate ministry with children who are impacted by the issues of a rapidly changing world in which we live today? and Can we truly join children in a messy journey and begin to make a difference?

Listening and paying attention to the children in our care is a very good place to begin our conversation on *Children's Ministry and the Spiritual Child*—we hope you agree. As the editors of this book, our hope is that you will also invite others in your network to join you in reading and have conversations about the topics presented by some of the best thinkers in the field of children's spirituality. We encourage this so that together, you might enrich God's love and compassion for the children in your midst.

CHAPTER 1

Begin with Listening
Gifts of Eyes and Ears

Lacy Finn Borgo

> *To listen another soul into a condition of disclosure and discovery may be almost the greatest service that any human being ever performs for another.*
>
> —Douglas Steere

> This chapter is experiential in nature. You, dear reader, are invited to engage with not only your mind but also your heart and body. Go and gather a blank piece of paper as well as a few colored pencils, markers, or any other tools for expression. We will begin and end our time together by acknowledging and honoring the Light of Christ, and a candle will help us do just that.
>
> Take a moment to breathe in God's presence and pace for the next few pages. On your exhalation, breathe out whatever is heavy or distracting within you. Inhale your awareness of God's presence; exhale and rest in God's tender, loving care. Light your candle as a reminder of Christ being with you as you engage.

Listening to Our Childhood Selves

In order to deeply listen to the child before us, it helps to be conversant with our own inner lives. To be a good host to a child's life with God, it helps to have experience hosting your own inner child. In this chapter, you will be invited to engage not only for the sake of children within your social context but also for the child within you. We bring our childhood selves into the lives that we are living with God right now. What you believe about God, your experiences of God when you were a child—they come with you into adulthood.[1]

Let's begin with a very familiar passage of Scripture for those who work with children. In Mark 10, Jesus invites the children to encounter him directly. Allow your imagination—a child's superpower—to be at the service of your life with God. Using imagination helps us engage Scripture with all the dimensions of who we are. And as we still have our childhood selves within us, we have access to this superpower as well.

Take a deep breath and listen in:

> People were bringing little children to him in order that he might touch them and the disciples spoke sternly to them. When Jesus saw this, he was indignant and said to them, "Let the little children come to me do not stop them for it is to such as these that the Kingdom of God belongs. Truly I tell you whoever does not receive the Kingdom of God as a little child will never enter it and he took them up into his arms." (Mark 10:13–16 NRSV)

Invite someone to read the passage to you while you close your eyes. Imagine yourself in the passage. Or read it aloud, pausing along the way to see yourself as one of the children. Notice what words or images in this passage hold weight for you. Using the colored pencils or markers, record what you notice on the paper you have gathered. Let this paper help you enter a sacred space for encountering the God who has longed you into being.

Reread the passage, but this time notice that Jesus's first word in this passage is *let*. See him, hear him say this word, and imagine him looking at you. Again, record your response.

---

1 Rahner, "Ideas for a Theology," 33–50.

Notice that the children are already coming. They don't have to be manipulated, cajoled, or bargained with to move toward Jesus. They are already moving.

Reread the passage one last time, and notice Jesus's offer to gather you up into his arms. Do you let him lay his hands upon your back, on your shoulders? Can you hear him whisper words of life and affirmation into your little ears? Record your response.

Children are having experiences of God. The Eternal One has longed each person into being, and we are wired to long right back. God is meeting children in ways that are unique to children.[2]

South African pastor and spiritual director Trevor Hudson says, "We often ask for the gift of tongues when it might be more helpful to ask for the gift of ears."[3] We often bombard children with our "gifts of tongues," explanations, and information, but I wonder what we might learn if we offered children the gift of our listening presence.

I serve as a spiritual director for children at Haven House, a transitional facility for families without homes. We call our time together *holy listening*. When children first come, I explain that our time together is an opportunity for me to listen to them and for them to listen to God. We listen in many different ways—through art and pictures, movement, and playing with toys. In the beginning, the children are cautious, as if testing the truth of my claim, but soon they grow into this spaciousness, and they feel free to take up the space. If we want to listen to the deep places in a child's life, we must learn to listen to the deep places in our own lives. "Deep calls to deep," as the psalmist says (Ps. 42:7).

---

2 Miller, *Spiritual Child*, 51–53.
3 Hudson, *Holy Spirit Here*, 116.

Touching an Early Experience with God

We often tend to ignore how much of a child is still in all of us.
—Elisabeth Kübler-Ross

Take your pencil or pen in your nondominant hand. Call to mind an early experience of God that happened when you were young. This experience could have happened at church or in nature. Many of our first recalled experiences of God happen in nature. It might be the presence of or a conversation with someone who loved you deeply. Choose one image from that encounter and draw it with your nondominant hand. Take a good four to five minutes and get all the details that you can remember down on your paper. Allow this to be fodder for conversation, for prayer right now. Tune your ear to what God is saying to you and what you are saying to God.

For some of us, our early experiences that have been labeled "God" are nothing like the God that we now know. If you are noticing this disconnection, be gentle with yourself. Set this exercise down and walk away for a bit. Maybe you need to say, "Oh God, this was so hard and so painful." Hear Jesus speaking to your childhood self, saying, "Come to me, even if it was painful. Let me heal what was wounded." Perhaps you notice an invitation from God to share your discoveries with a friend. The Holy Spirit loves to knit souls and stories together in life-giving ways.

Our Spiral Life with God

Our spiritual lives are shaped more like spirals and less like algebraic equations. German theologian Karl Rahner helps us understand that we bring our previous experiences of God throughout our lives into the lives we are living right now.[4] We bring our childhood experiences, our adolescent experiences, our young adult experiences, and our middle-aged experiences into our

---

4 Rahner, "Ideas for a Theology," 33–50.

current experiences. This is just one of the many reasons that children's spirituality is so important.

For children, all the dimensions of the self are connected. Thought, feeling, body, social context, and spirit are all engaged with each experience. What a child thinks and feels is expressed in their body and communicated to their social context. For example, when a child wants something shiny in the checkout line at the grocery store, their desire will be expressed by authentically engaging all the dimensions of the self. It can sound like begging, crying, or impressive child-rationalization gymnastics to unassociated bystanders. Once, I overheard an especially chatty toddler yell to random people passing by the grocery cart, "Hey, how 'bout you spring me out of this thing?"

In contrast, parents have had to separate the dimensions of the self. They might be feeling embarrassment, anger, shame, or guilt. But they will not express this. They will lead with chosen feelings and focus their attention on getting through this situation with their dignity and without the shiny item. This is the journey of maturity. Adults split the dimensions of the self, giving the various dimensions priority over one another. The path of Christ is one where the human spirit connected to the Holy Spirit calls the shots. If we are especially attentive and graced with long lives, the dimensions will come back together again, all in glad submission to spirit connected to Spirit. They are connected in a way that reveals the character of the lives we've lived.

Listening for God

The connectedness of the self can be seen in the expansive consciousness of the child. Children's everyday experience is wide and wonder filled. Their spiritual experience follows suit. When a child experiences God, they engage with all the dimensions of their self. The experience will likely have a bodily component, as children use their bodies to experience the world around them. Jumping on the trampoline, playing with friends, or running in the grass with the family dog can all be ways that children encounter God. It will involve their mind: thoughts and feelings. In feelings of being left out, in laughter at the kitchen table, in the exhilaration of a soccer game won, children encounter God. In experiencing the tender kindness of an English teacher, wrestling with their grandparent, and receiving Communion at church, children encounter God. Children encounter God when they are curious about the world around them and how it works.

These experiences may be conscious or unconscious to the child. They may be aware of God's presence or not so much. They may also be aware but lack the language to share their experiences. Listening to children and helping them bring their experiences out into the open are gifts for both the child and the adult.

There are two movements in listening with children: the movement to recognize and the movement to respond. In recognizing, we make space for the child to acknowledge God's presence with them. In responding, we make space for the child to engage with God's presence. We help children recognize when we ask open-ended questions and then let them speak until they have said all they want to say. We also help children recognize by not limiting their recognition to words. We might invite them to draw or play their experience of God. Remembering that their consciousness is expansive therefore requires of us a bit of dexterity in our listening. We also help children listen to God's presence in their own inner voices—their own wants and desires. Children are bombarded with voices that tell them what to think, how to feel, and what to do. So much so that their own inner voices can become dim and unheard. In listening to a child, we can help them hear themselves too.

Through listening, we also help children act upon what they hear and respond to God's presence. We offer them ways to express gratitude to this God who gave them grandparents, dogs, and soccer games. We can create a space filled with paper, crayons, and markers to draw a prayer expressing the sorrow that they feel from a friend's betrayal, the delight of shared laughter, or the quiet sacredness of Communion. Children may want to respond using their bodies. Swinging, skipping, and singing can all be prayer. When we listen to a child, we can help them choose the way they'd like to respond—the way that is most expressive of who they have been created to be.

I invite you to look back again to the picture of an early experience of God. Was there someone who helped you recognize and respond to that experience? If so, take a moment and give thanks. If not, I wonder, what would it have been like to have a person help you recognize and respond to that recognition?

What Does God Sound Like?

God created children to have an expansive consciousness, and so we can be assured that God is willing and able to meet them in it. God has scattered the seed of connection within our everyday experiences of goodness, beauty, and truth. These three transcendentals resonate in some way with every human being and quicken our longing for God. In the parable of the sower (Matt. 13), we encounter the good farmer who is so generous that he throws seed out anywhere and everywhere. Goodness, beauty, and truth have been extravagantly planted so that every person who has the tiniest bit of "want to" can connect with God.

Let's pause a moment and reflect. Place your pencil or crayon in your nondominant hand again. In your mind's eye, see yourself as a child, think back through your childhood, and notice any experiences of goodness, beauty, or truth. Maybe you are wondering what these transcendentals look like for children.

Goodness is whatever leads to human flourishing. Is there an experience of someone enabling your own flourishing that comes to mind? A kindness or an unexpected gesture of love or support? As Dallas Willard says, "Beauty is goodness made alive to the senses."[5] When we give our children cake on their first birthday,

---

5 Willard, "Discipleship as Life."

and they smash it into their hair and ears as they get the most delicious bits into their mouths, this is beauty—a goodness experienced by all the senses. Truth is whatever in fact is real. Can you remember a moment when you experienced something authentic or when the reality of a situation broke into your life? Once when visiting the zoo, I watched a small child communicate with a young gorilla. They traded hand gestures through the glass, responding to one another. The child turned to his mom and said, "We're talking." It was a moment when one of God's creatures realized the living truth of another.

Goodness, beauty, and truth are not the only seeds of connection God generously scatters. Think back to an experience that captured your sense of wonder. Wonder is a God-given curiosity that grows as we notice the world around us. Through wonder, we gladly give mental space to the unfolding of our awareness of God. How did you wonder about the world as a child? What did your wonder look like? Is there a memory that's coming to you that you can draw and add to your prayer page?

Mystery is a grateful resignation to what we don't know. When as a child did you feel free to not know? All of childhood is not knowing, but is there a memory that comes to mind? Awe is a full-body, reverential experience of our core connection to all creation. Whenever we experience awe, we put our shoulders back, opening ourselves up so that we can take it all in. Franciscan friar Father Richard Rohr talks about seeing a Christmas tree as a child and having a moment filled with awe. Even as his little childhood self, he threw his shoulders back and was just trying to take it all in.[6] Was there a time in your childhood when you experienced awe?

Woven threads of meaning, or when things fit together in unmistakable ways, help us make meaning. Is there a time when, like puzzle pieces, you noticed that events or experiences fit together, and it helped you make sense of something? If so, give

---

6 Rohr, "Apocalyptic Hope."

it a few lines on your page. Tears are also God's seeds for connection. They heighten our awareness of our longing for God's presence, especially when we are children. Our patterns for hiding pain haven't quite become so habitual when we are young. We are more tender to God's presence and our desire for love. Was there a time when pain or loss heightened your sense of God's presence?

Lastly, children have experiences of unity. They are born from unity and learn separateness. Unity is an experience of connection so deep that our preoccupation with ourselves thins or disappears altogether. Can you remember an instance when you lost track of time? Children are famously good at this. Or a time when you felt so close to another living being that you forgot about yourself?

Take a moment and go back through this list of seeds:

Goodness—Do you have a memory of experiencing goodness when you were a child?
Beauty—Can you remember an experience of something that captured your senses?
Truth—When you rummage around in your memory, what has held? Is there a thought, idea, or understanding that has had staying power, even today?
Wonder—How did you wonder about the world as a child?
Mystery—When as a child did you feel free to not know?
Awe—Was there a time in your childhood when you experienced awe?
Nature—What is it like to remember being outside as a child?
Woven Threads of Meaning—Was there a time when, like puzzle pieces fitting together, you noticed that events or experiences fit together, and it helped you make sense of something?
Tears—Was there a time when pain or loss heightened your sense of God's presence or your own tender longing for God?

Unity—Can you remember an instance when you lost track of time or when you felt so close to another living being that you forgot about yourself?[7]

Feel free to stop and draw a picture or add a word to your paper with your nondominant hand. Let your faithful recognizing lead you into conversation with the God who longed you into being. What do you hear from God about your childhood self? What whispers of love and welcome come to you?

Gentle Listening

Here are four simple gentle listening practices that can help us listen to the child before us. We begin by asking open-ended questions. Open-ended questions have no set answers and invite reflection and curiosity on the part of the child and the adult listener. Some examples of open-ended questions might be the following:

When was a time you felt God near?
How has your body felt during the pandemic?
Can you tell a story about when you felt angry, afraid, or confused?
When did you experience something good or beautiful?
What is one thing that you are thankful for?
How does a special person or creature in your life make you feel?
What do you say to God?
What does God say to you?
Where have you seen God's fingerprints?

An acronym that can help us with gentle listening is BOW: body, openness, and wonder. As we BOW to the child before us, we not

---

[7] For more details, see Borgo, *Faith like a Child*.

only have the opportunity to "listen another into a condition of disclosure and discovery, but we have the opportunity to encounter God in the shared experience."[8]

Body—when a child speaks, we want to be sure not to interrupt but to let them speak until they have no more words left. We might ask a few questions that help them say more, like "Can you say more about that?" As they are speaking, we are fully present to them. Being fully present to another looks like making sure that our bodies are communicating with full attention: our hands are free, and our bodies are facing the child. We lower our bodies to be on the same level as the child so that they feel free to fill the space with their thoughts and feelings.

Openness—we check within ourselves for our own openness: Are we open to hearing whatever the child wants to share? Have we suspended our judgment and let our gaze rest on the child as one who is made in the image and likeness of God?

Wonder—how is your inner wonderer? Are you in touch with the ways that God met you when you were a child? Do you have a sacred curiosity about how God might be meeting the child before you?

As the child is sharing, we listen for words or images that are "weighty"—those that have a feeling dimension or the weight of authenticity. If we are listening to the Spirit, we might sense the Spirit calling our attention to something that has been shared. When that happens, we mirror the image or word back to the child. This helps them reprocess what they said; it helps them hear themselves and recognize an encounter with God.

While listening, we also pay attention to similarities, contrasts, or woven threads of meaning. At times, the Spirit speaks in continuities, and we help children see them. Just a reminder that this doesn't mean that we see for them, but we point it out and give the child the chance to see for themselves.

---

8 Steere, *On Beginning from Within*, 198.

Maybe you begin a listening conversation with a child by asking for a story of something beautiful. They tell about seeing a daffodil just beginning to open and the yellow petals peeking out—which shade of yellow is their favorite? You might ask them to tell you how the color yellow makes them feel or what God might be saying to them through the color yellow. On Sunday at church, there is a reading of the story of Pentecost, and when the child hears about the flames that were dancing on the heads of all who were present, he imagines that the flames are yellow and tells you so. You notice the similarity and say something like, I wonder what God might be saying to you through the yellow flames and the yellow flower? These little snippets of conversation help the child stay in conversation with God, who longs to connect with them on an ongoing basis.

Light paraphrasing, like "Are you saying that the color yellow is like God saying, 'I like you?'" and brief summarizing, such as "So when you see the yellow petals on the daffodil and imagine the flames at Pentecost, it reminds you that God likes you," reinforce the child's experience of God. These simple, active listening practices help children have agency in their lives with God. They see that God regards them as worth his time and attention. They learn that God will meet them where they are. We adults have given weight to their experiences, and now, through reflection, this transforms our minds to be able to look for God again.

Gentle Seeing

Since children engage all dimensions of their selves in their lives with God, listening deeply to them involves the eyes also. We need the gift of ears and eyes. We are present to a child when we see them. Children often call out, "Watch me!" It is a cry to be known beyond verbal articulation. Adults quite often communicate through our fleeting and focused glances. It's essential that we reflect on both what we see and also how we see. We ask the Spirit to help us notice how a child might be using their body to try to connect, and we ask for help to notice when a child is using their body to hide in fear. We can ask children where they feel certain emotions in their bodies, even asking them how God is meeting them in their bodies. I once listened with a six-year-old who told me that the sweet taste on his tongue when eating a banana was God saying, "I will keep you healthy." To that I say, "Amen."

Asking a child where they feel God's love and acceptance in their bodies creates another level of awareness that they can savor throughout their lives. We can also take children's bodies elsewhere to notice what catches their attention. Taking children outside into spaces that they haven't experienced helps build their awareness of God. They learn to look—by looking.

How we see communicates so much to children. Do we see children as full participants in the Kingdom of God? Do we nurture unmitigated positive regard for the child in front of us? Do we believe the best, hope for the best, and encourage what at times might be hard to find? Can we look into the eyes of the child in front of us and know that they bear the image and likeness of God? Are we aware that each child is not a mere mortal but an eternal splendor?[9] What practical steps could you take today to sharpen and soften your seeing?

A Warning

To listen wholeheartedly to a child will cost you something. When you are fully present to the child in front of you, you will change. Their experiences of God will touch your own; you will be invited to stretch the boundaries of what you thought about God, yourself, and others. You will be challenged and your faith tried, but all living things grow. You can rest in the reality that the God who longed you into being continues to shepherd your life.

Let's pause together one last time. Look at the paper in front of you with all your drawings and reflections. Let your gaze rest

---

9 Lewis, *Weight of Glory*, 15.

on your childhood self; let the children that are within your social context come to mind as well. Welcome them all at God's generous table. Is there an invitation that is emerging? What might God be inviting you to as you listen with children?

Blessing

Take a moment and go and find a tube of lip balm . . . Trust me on this. This idea comes from children's chaplain Leanne Hadley. When children come to *holy listening* at Haven House, we end our time together with this little ritual. I explain that while this might only look like lip balm, it is indeed Blessing Balm. It is a reminder of all we talked about during our time; it is a reminder that God is always with them, even if they can't see God. It is a reminder that they are loved more than they can ever imagine. Then I ask the child's permission to make a cross, a heart, or a circle on the back of their hand. While giving the blessing, I say something like "Jimmy, God loves you very much. Every time you see this or smell this or think about this, remember to look for the seeds of God's love. They are everywhere." If there is someone near to you, use the lip balm you faithfully found and give them a blessing. Ask them to bless you too.

May you experience children with a renewed heart. May you become increasingly aware of children and greet them in common places like the grocery store or the park. May your deepening sensitivity to childhood experiences change the way you think and the way you live. May you encourage a child's life with God through listening to what is being spoken and also to what is being said. May your life become one of prayer for children as people who are on the margins of society. May you honor the God-given autonomy of children, taking special care not to manipulate or smother them. May you be granted the awe-inspiring opportunity to witness a child's life with God.

> Together we will blow out our candles and remember that we cannot put out the Light, but we do get to witness the transformation of the Light into smoke and particles, and we get to breathe it in, and it becomes part of us.

Bibliography

Borgo, Lacy Finn. *Faith like a Child: Embracing Our Lives as Children of God*. Downers Grove, IL: InterVarsity, forthcoming May 2023.

Hudson, Trevor. *The Holy Spirit Here and Now*. Nashville: Upper Room Books, 2013.

Lewis, C. S. *The Weight of Glory*. Grand Rapids, MI: Eerdmans, 1949.

Miller, Lisa. *The Spiritual Child: The New Science on Parenting for Health and Lifelong Thriving*. New York: Picador, 2015.

Rahner, Karl. "Ideas for a Theology of Childhood." In *Theological Investigations*. Vol. 3, 33–50. London: Cox & Wyman, 1982.

Rohr, Richard. "Apocalyptic Hope: A Special Note from Fr. Richard; My Hope for This Community." Center for Action and Contemplation, April 27, 2021. https://cac.org/a-special-note-from-fr-richard-my-hope-for-this-community-2021-04-27/.

Steere, Douglas. *On Beginning from within and on Listening to Another*. New York: Harper and Row, 1964.

Willard, Dallas. "Discipleship as Life in the Kingdom." Conversatio Divina, October 13, 2010. https://conversatio.org/discipleship-as-life-in-the-kingdom/.

CHAPTER 2

From Faith Transmission to Faith Recognition

Exploring Ways to Help Children Make Meaning from the God They Already Know

Heather Ingersoll

Even before the onset of the COVID-19 pandemic, churches had begun to face an uncertain future regarding regular church attendance as well as limited financial and volunteer resources. Our rapidly shifting world has intensified these trends, and leaders of religious education programs for children must face these unique challenges, helping their congregations make informed decisions about how to support children's spirituality. The question remains, What components are most important for nurturing the spiritual well-being of children in our communities, and how do we go about determining that?

Childhood Spirituality

To begin to make decisions regarding how to support the spirituality of children in our communities, it is important to define what we understand to be childhood spirituality. Children's spiritual lives are intricate and complex; a simple definition may not adequately reflect the multifaceted nature of their spirituality.

Eugene C. Roehlkepartain has argued that it is "potentially counterproductive to propose that a particular definition could adequately capture the richness, complexity, and multidimensional nature of this domain of human life."[1] Similarly, John Chi-Kin Lee posits that spirituality is a multidisciplinary field, not necessarily a discipline, because it must hold space for the wide and varying approaches, perspectives, and paradigms that together bring a holistic picture of childhood spirituality. Within this multidisciplinary and multifaceted discourse, there are several generally agreed-upon characteristics of childhood spirituality.[2]

Spirituality is a salient part of the innate human experience that emerges in early childhood, and therefore, childhood spirituality is innately centered in a child's way of engaging the world.[3] Rebecca Nye describes children's abilities for "spiritual processing" and argues that "it turns out that children, partly by virtue of their distinctive psychological characteristics, have an intriguing rich capacity for spirituality, for a kind of religious knowing and being which is neither contingent on their religious knowledge nor moral accountability."[4] Michael M. Piechowski notes there are examples that "genuine spiritual experiences are accessible to children" and that the quality and depth of such experiences challenge developmental theories that put absolute limits on children's conceptual and experiential capacities.[5]

There is also a general understanding that childhood spirituality has a relational aspect to it, most often encompassing an integral connection with oneself, the natural world, others, and a transcendent being outside ourselves.[6] David Hay and Rebecca Nye experienced the relational aspect of spirituality in the children

---

1 Roehlkepartain and Patel, "Congregations," 324–36.
2 Chi-Kin Lee, "Children's Spirituality," 1–8.
3 Hay and Nye, *Spirit of the Child*. See also Bryant et al., "Child's Right," 305–18.
4 Nye, "Christian Perspectives," 90–107.
5 Piechowski, "Childhood Spirituality," 1–15.
6 Fisher, "God Counts," 191–203.

they interviewed as the child's acute awareness of their connectedness with self, others, God, and the world.[7]

Finally, children's spiritual experiences provide a source of significant meaning for the child. The search for meaning is integral to identity formation, an exploration of existential limits, and an understanding of purpose. Coles notes that children are natural "seekers" or "young pilgrims, well aware that life is a finite journey," who are eager to make sense of it.[8]

Childhood Spirituality and the Church

The growing body of research on childhood spirituality provides compelling evidence that the spiritual capacity of children should be taken seriously in our organizations and communities. Considering that reality, the term *spiritual formation* is quickly becoming common nomenclature for describing the process of Christian education in the church.[9] Johnson argues that the movement from a focus on Christian education to "spiritual formation" provides the impetus for a more holistic understanding of education in the church, particularly with children. Yet the shift in the general language used does not necessarily equal a shift in the paradigms and methodologies that undergird the practice of supporting the spiritual lives of children in the church.

Scholars interested in children's spirituality argue that children have few opportunities to integrate the Christian tradition and language with their spiritual quests in traditional models of Christian education.[10] Rebecca Nye argues that children's capacity for deep reflection is neglected in these programs, where the priority is instilling religious knowledge and morals through a

---

7 See Hay and Nye, *Spirit of the Child*.
8 Coles, *Spiritual Life of Children*, xvi. For more on how a range of experiences can instill meaning in children, see Hay and Nye, *Spirit of the Child*; Berryman, *Stories of God*; and Lin, *Love, Peace, and Wisdom in Education*.
9 Johnson, "Christian Spiritual Formation," 309–31.
10 Bellous and Csinos, "Spiritual Styles," 213–24. See also Berryman, *Godly Play*.

more transactional approach to education.[11] Evidence from church observations and interviews with children led to the conjecture that there is generally a disconnect in the Christian church between children's spiritual lives and programs designed to support children's religious beliefs.[12]

The Danger of Rationalizing Spirituality

The use of the words *know*, *introduce*, or *pass along* in reference to faith indicates that our work in Christian education with children continues to be grounded in an epistemological framework most salient in contemporary public education. When we use the terms *know*, *teach*, or *introduce*, it situates faith as an object to be grasped, much like the way we approach math in our dominant schooling paradigm. Philosopher James K. A. Smith poignantly critiques this approach and reminds readers that detaching knowledge from the body makes the student into a "brain on a stick."[13] Sharon Warner notes that this perspective can "deceive the knower" and lead an individual to believe the fallacy that "detachment from the world [is] necessary for obtaining 'pure and undistorted' knowledge."[14] This leads to methodologies that purposely detach the child's own experience from the process of "teaching them" to "know" God. Equally as problematic in using a schooling paradigm in Christian education with children is a behavioralist approach to "knowing God" that places an emphasis on certain behaviors as signs of one's faith maturity. Children are soon taught to behave in a certain way that has been deemed acceptable by the adults in the faith community. Without a deconstruction of those dominant narratives considering our burgeoning understanding and belief in children's capacity for spirituality, we run the risk of adopting the "next greatest thing" in curricula that may be grounded in a

---

11 Nye, "Christian Perspectives."
12 Bellous and Csinos, "Spiritual Styles."
13 Smith, *You Are What You Love*.
14 Warner, "Epistemology of 'Participating Consciousness,'" 189–205.

pedagogical strategy that negates the role of childhood agency and children's own spiritual experiences as central to their faith development. When we center the child's spiritual autonomy, we can facilitate an approach to Christian education that moves beyond a focus on imparting biblical knowledge or inspiring moral living and adherence to behavioral expectation to what practical theologian Andrew Root refers to as human action that participates in divine action. Root considers this the core of ministry[15]

This confusion about childhood religious experience also shows up in the ways in which children's "religiousness" is understood in research from various disciplines. Take, for example, an influential study out of the University of British Columbia. In 2009, Mark D. Holder, Ben Coleman, and Judy M. Wallace investigated correlations between happiness and spirituality and happiness and religiousness in children ages eight through twelve. Their findings showed a statistically significant correlation between spirituality and happiness but no significant relationship between religiousness and happiness. Mainstream media promoted their study with provocative headlines, like the one stating, "Spirituality, not religion, makes kids happy."[16] However, Holder, Coleman, and Wallace's study, which was published in the *Journal of Happiness Studies*, showed that a child's religiousness was measured by just two factors: how often the child attended church and how often the child prayed or meditated.[17] Researchers often rely on one or two items (frequency of prayer, church attendance, feelings about church) and make inferences regarding children's religiosity and correlations with other markers of well-being.

---

15 Root, *Revisiting Relational Youth Ministry*, 19–20.
16 "Spirituality, Not Religion."
17 Holder, Coleman, and Wallace, "Spirituality, Religiousness, and Happiness," 131–50.

Charting the Depth of Children's Spirituality

The discourse on children's spiritual formation in the church needs both academic pursuits exploring the nuanced realities of children's religiosity considering the understanding of salient characteristics of childhood spirituality and practical pursuits of how to best support the spiritual formation of children in the church. A body of research focused on religious orientation can offer a framework for how we might understand children's religious lives in congruence with the most salient features of childhood spirituality.

In 1950, Gordon Allport began exploring measurements of religiosity in a motivational framework and distinguished certain self-reported religious practices and beliefs as either intrinsic or extrinsic. Building on his work, others developed measurements for understanding the motivations behind religiosity.[18] Similarly, Ryan, Rigby, and King developed the Christian Religious Internalization Scale to measure religious motivation based on self-determination theory, measuring integrated and introjected faith.[19] Integrated faith is an autonomously held belief and practice that is integrated into the value system of the individual. Introjected faith refers to externally oriented beliefs that are practiced due to internal or external pressures. Others adopted this scale to begin exploring religiosity from this motivational framework with adolescents[20] and children[21] to help guide academic and practical understandings of how young people's religious beliefs and practices are central to their identities.

Self-determination theory (SDT) is a multidimensional theory of motivation that explores the catalyst for humans and the process

---

18 Allport and Ross, "Personal Religious Orientation," 432. See also Batson and Ventis, *Religious Experience*; and Maltby, "Internal Structure," 407–12.
19 Ryan, Rigby, and King, "Two Types," 586.
20 Assor et al., "Choosing to Stay Religious," 105–50.
21 Flor and Knapp, "Transmission and Transaction," 627.

by which action becomes increasingly internalized.[22] Furthermore, SDT posits that humans universally have three psychological needs: autonomy, competency, and relatedness.[23] Humans thrive in social situations that provide all three and are most likely to internalize the beliefs and values espoused in a social situation in which they feel a sense of autonomy, competency, and relatedness.[24] Research with children indicates that perceived autonomy, competency, and relatedness in educational[25] and family environments[26] positively relate to self-regulation, school performance and engagement, and other prosocial behaviors.[27]

A small subset of scholars have explored the connection between self-determination theory and religiosity to provide a more holistic understanding of religiosity. Studies like the happiness study referenced previously measure religiosity by the amount of engagement with faith practices. In those studies, a child who attends Sunday school four times a month because their parents require them will have the same "religiosity" as a child who attends Sunday school four times a month because they find it meaningful. A motivational approach to research on religiosity explores *why* one engages in those faith practices. On one side of the motivational continuum, one is externally motivated by a reward or social pressure to engage in a certain practice or behavior. I was externally motivated to memorize scripture as a child when I received a piece of candy after properly reciting a verse. This might be categorized from a research perspective as externally motivated religiosity. On the other side of the continuum, one is internally motivated to engage in a practice or behavior when one finds personal value in that behavior. This is highlighted as internalized religiosity for the purpose of research. This nuanced

22 Deci and Ryan, "'What' and 'Why,'" 227–68.
23 Church et al., "Need Satisfaction," 507–34.
24 Deci and Ryan, "'What' and 'Why.'"
25 Cordova and Lepper, "Intrinsic Motivation," 715.
26 Grolnick and Ryan, "Autonomy in Children's Learning," 890.
27 Connell and Ryan, "Developmental Theory of Motivation," 64–77. See also Crosby and Smith, "Church Support."

approach to religiosity can help us gain a better understanding of if children are internalizing their faith and what methodologies might be most salient in allowing children to find deeper meaning in their faith.

Findings

I analyzed the data to identify any correlations between perceived relatedness in church or perceived autonomy in Sunday school and internalized religiosity or spiritual well-being in relation to God.[28] The statistical analysis revealed a significant relationship between parent religiosity and internalized religiosity as well as a positive relationship between parent religiosity and spiritual well-being in relation to God. These findings confirmed the body of research indicating that perceived parent religiosity is the most salient predictor of children's religiosity.

Additionally, perceived relatedness in Sunday school was positively related to spiritual well-being in relation to God, also confirming research primarily from Crosby, Smith, and Frederick.[29] Finally, there was a statistically significant relationship between internalized religiosity and relationship with God, indicating that internalized religiosity may offer a way to explore the connection between religiosity and spirituality.

Before exploring the potential implications of this study, it is important to name the limitations to ensure that the interpretation of the data does not overinflate the findings. First, the use of convenience sampling and self-reported data should be taken into consideration when exploring the implications of the data, as the results might be different in a broader, more diverse population. Additionally, the correlational design of the study excludes the option of making any causal inferences from the findings. We

---

28 Ingersoll, "Predictors."
29 Crosby, Smith, and Frederick, "Kid-Friendly Church," 87–109.

noticed a relationship between the variables, but we cannot confirm if one variable causes another.

Implications for Future Research

The statistically significant correlation between integrated religiosity and the relationship with God subscale of the Feeling Good, Living Life scale, along with the findings of the few studies on children and adolescents conducted using self-determination theory, indicates that it is worth exploring self-determination theory as a guide for measuring and understanding the nuances of children's religiosity. Though there was no statistically significant relationship between religiosity and perceived autonomy in this study, one issue could have been the use of a measurement designed for a primary school classroom that may have not been appropriate for a Sunday school setting. Given the research on the innate nature of childhood spirituality and the recognition that it is tied to meaning making and identity formation, it is worth exploring potential methods for measuring perceived autonomy in Christian education environments to better explore the value of autonomy-supportive environments in children's religiosity.

My Research Project

In order to determine the effectiveness of self-determination theory as a framework for understanding children's religiosity, I conducted a correlational study on third- to sixth-grade children from various Protestant churches. I sought to determine if internalized religiosity would correlate to the relationship with God subscale of Feeling Good, Living Life—a well-known measurement of spiritual well-being designed for children.[30]

---

30 Ingersoll, "Predictors." For another study that uses a similar methodology, see Fisher, "Feeling Good, Living Life."

Due to the considerable body of literature indicating that parent religiosity correlates with children's religiosity, my study controlled for parent religiosity as measured by the Perceived Parental Religious Intrinsic Value Demonstration questionnaire.[31] Other scales used included the Kids Church Survey,[32] the Teacher as Autonomy Support Scale,[33] the Inventory of Religious Internalization,[34] and the relationship with God subscale of the Feeling Good, Living Life questionnaire.[35]

Practical Implications

This study confirms the evidence that there is a positive correlation between children's perceived parent religiosity and children's internalized religiosity. The body of literature shows that parents support their children's faith through a variety of methods, including having bidirectional conversations about religion,[36] engaging in regular family religious or spiritual practices,[37] and modeling an authentic experience of their own faith lives.[38] Assor and others[39] found that children's perception of the degree to which their parents have internalized their faith is correlated with adolescents' religious internalization. This study used the same measure with children, furthering the results that children's perceptions of their parents' religiosity are important components of the transmission of religiosity in the family.

What does this mean for churches exploring how to best support their children's ministry? Programs can benefit from putting

---

31 Brambilla et al., "Autonomous versus Controlled Religiosity," 193–210.
32 Crosby and Smith, "Church Support," 243–54.
33 TASC, *Two Measures of Teaching*.
34 Flor and Knapp, "Transmission and Transaction."
35 Fisher, "Feeling Good, Living Life."
36 Flor and Knapp, "Transmission and Transaction." See also Okagaki and Bevis, "Transmission of Religious Values," 303–18.
37 Desrosiers, Kelley, and Miller, "Parent and Peer Relationships," 39. See also Francis, "Parental Influence," 241–53.
38 Barrow, Dollahite, and Marks, "How Parents Balance Desire," 222.
39 Assor et al., "Choosing to Stay Religious."

resources toward supporting, educating, and encouraging parents as role models in their children's religious and spiritual lives. Those who want to support parents should first consider how parents talk about faith with their children. This may include helping parents explore how they can authentically model and discuss their religious understandings and practices, educating parents on the value of storytelling and ways to create opportunities to weave family stories with stories of God to "fill a reservoir of meaning,"[40] and finally, encouraging parents to adopt a bidirectional approach to conversations and faith-based practices with children in which children are seen as equal contributors to the dialogue. In other words, encourage parents to have open and honest conversations with their children about faith. Break down barriers that make parents feel anxious about giving their children the "right answers" so parents have permission to not have all the answers or really any answers at all. Help parents see that wondering together about faith, spirituality, and the mysteries of our human experience can be deeply fulfilling and valuable to children as they make meaning out of their own ideas and experiences of God. In guiding parents and caregivers through this, it should be recognized that a more open, wondering approach to conversations of faith with children is often a completely new concept. Church leaders can begin to support parents in this direction by modeling it themselves. If parents see church leaders modeling open conversations with children—where children's ideas and questions are honored, and they are invited to share their honest ideas and perspectives without judgment—parents may begin to feel the freedom to do that themselves.

Christian educators can further support parents in recognizing their children's spiritual capacity and using play, creative expression, and storytelling to make meaning from children's spiritual experiences and questions. In her work *The Gardener and the*

---

40 Berryman, *Stories of God*.

Carpenter, Alison Gopnik[41] writes particularly to help provide an antidote to the "parenting model" of the twenty-first century, which, much like the schooling paradigm, turns parenting into a job that, if done well, will "produce" children and, later, adults with the very specific skills, competencies, personalities, and value systems we want. The promise of this model—that following a particular curriculum or resource will ensure children turn out a certain way—doesn't align with our evolutionary realities as human beings. Inviting parents to recognize that children have agency as spiritual beings and unique ideas, perspectives, and experiences with God will allow parents to broaden their understanding of how to support their children's religiosity. This includes helping parents focus less on a specific desired outcome for the faith of their children and more on creating an environment where children's spiritual capacity is honored and they can make meaning from their own experiences of faith.[42]

What might this look like in practice? Begin by auditing the language you use about children in your programs and your congregation. Watch for phrases that imply that children's faith development is only a transactional experience, such as *helping children know God* or *passing on the faith*. Try out new terms, such as *nurturing* or *cultivating* children's spiritual experiences or experiences with God. Share stories about the children's wonderings, questions, and ideas that you hear and how those point to the depth of children's spiritual probing. Invite parents and caregivers to remember their spiritual experiences as children: What memories are most salient, or what times were most valuable or positive? Give parents the opportunity to think about their unique children and where they come alive and find the most joy. Explore how those two exercises might change the way parents create environments to support their children's spiritual lives. Invite them to find joy and freedom in trying it out.

---

41 Gopnik, *Gardener and the Carpenter*.
42 Barrow, Dollahite, and Marks, "How Parents Balance Desire." See also Batson and Ventis, *Religious Experience*.

Focus on Relationships

Perceived relatedness with both peers and adults in the church was shown to be a significant predictor of a child's relationship to God. In this study, perceived relatedness in the church was measured by a "child's perception that he or she is loved, valued, and supported by (non-family member) peers and adults in his or her church community." Children's ministry leaders should focus the use of limited resources on creating opportunities to build authentic relationships where children feel loved and valued in the community by both adults and peers. Children's programming benefits from being wired for relationship building and opportunities for deeper reflection based on the children's interests. Crosby and Smith posit that leaders hoping to "promote a transformative kind of spirituality" should explore how to create an environment of social support and "be intentional about providing relational—rather than just instructional—opportunities for children in their care."[43]

The first step in making this shift is building a culture of volunteers who recognize that relationship building and time for connection are key to nurturing the spiritual lives of children. In a church setting, where children's programs are often limited to an hour or less, leaders and volunteers feel pressure to get as much content in during that time as possible. The relationship-building activities are left out or relegated to only a short portion of the hour, seen as auxiliary instead of central to supporting the main objectives of the time together. There is evidence that this way of operating might be counterproductive. Take, for example, this quote from a twelve-year-old girl when talking with researchers about when she felt loved in church: "Sometimes when we're doing the talks in [Sunday school] and you're trying to tell them something, they'll say 'not now' so you can't talk right now. You're trying to say your opinion and they won't let you, but sometimes

---

43 Crosby and Smith, "Church Support," 252.

they will let you say your opinion."[44] The researchers noted the "sometimes" feeling valued and loved as important to pay attention to. Help your leaders turn that "sometimes" into a "most of the time" by recruiting and training leaders who are skilled at listening and acknowledging the community of children. Highlight the value of cultivating an environment of shared respect, love, and honesty that values each person and honors their stories within each children's ministry classroom. Often, this will be a better "teacher" than what is written down in the curriculum guide.

What are some practical things you can do to train your leaders to do this well? Help your leaders develop a language of valuing when redirecting. Honoring a circle of children requires recognizing when some children are taking up too much space in the room. Give your adult leaders a toolkit for redirecting stories and questions with value-based statements, like "[Name], your story/question is really important, so when [I've given all the directions], I want to take time to listen to your [story/question]." Ensure that the adults working with children have the skills to be attentive listeners by modeling them yourself, practicing attentive listening with one another, and building a culture of noticing by inviting adults to share one or two things each week that a child said or did and how they recognized that child's contribution.

According to Crosby, Smith, and Fredrick,[45] another important aspect of relationship building among peers in church is the opportunity for unstructured play. They found that children were able to build connections with peers most readily through unstructured time in the classroom or before or after Sunday school or worship. Relationship-building activities in Sunday school curricula are typically designed as structured games or activities to help children get to know one another. While these can be important for community-building characteristics, like learning one another's names, they don't necessarily lead to feelings of being

---

44 Crosby, Smith, and Frederick, "Kid-Friendly Church," 100.
45 Crosby, Smith, and Frederick.

valued and cared for among peers in that community. Offering opportunities for children to navigate those connections through unstructured time will help them build authentic relationships with peers. The environment can help facilitate this time by giving children materials to guide their relationship building, such as art supplies, big pieces of butcher paper, blocks, and game pieces. While less structured time in the classroom may feel frivolous, it can lead to the development of a supportive community that is central to children and their spiritual lives, built on connection with themselves, with others, and with God.

Autonomy Support

The way we approach school-based education should not be the way we approach religious education or spiritual formation.[46] Instead, we should be building practices in our ministry based on holistic perceptions of children in the church as agents in their religious experiences. While the current study did not show a correlation between perceived autonomy and children's religiosity or spiritual well-being with relationship to God, the research guided by SDT offers enough compelling evidence for the value of autonomy-supportive environments to continue to explore autonomy support as an important characteristic of spiritual formation of children. Autonomy support can include giving children meaningful choices regarding the way they spend their time in a program, supporting children's questions and doubts, and inviting children to identify how the story of our faith relates to their everyday lives and their unique spiritual experiences.

While in theory, this all makes sense, it can be a difficult shift to make for most church leaders because we are so used to a schooling approach to our work with children. Begin by making small adjustments and building on them as you go. Provide opportunities

---

[46] For an excellent introduction to the agency of children in their own spiritual formation, see May et al., *Children Matter*.

for children to make meaningful choices by offering unstructured time, as discussed earlier, where children get to choose from a variety of materials and determine what they use and how they use it. A small step in this direction might be shifting from a structured craft to unstructured free art. Instead of giving children one medium—let's say watercolor—and instructing them to paint a picture of the Bible story for the day, give them several types of paint and invite them to paint something from their own lives that reminds them of the Bible story. Build into your gathering time opportunities for children to reflect on the content, ask questions, or wonder about their ideas in an open-ended, nonjudgmental way. Use a curriculum that provides a framework for children to explore the content in their own way and through their lens, ensuring they have an opportunity to make meaning from a story or idea without being guided by a specific agenda. If that isn't part of your current curriculum, supplement by adding a wondering or reflecting time for children to explore, through conversation as a group, what they think about the content, how it connects to something they've experienced, or how it makes them feel. Finally, consider a model of Christian education that is grounded in a pedagogical framework different from the schooling model. Godly Play, a Montessori-inspired method for religious education, offers a solid approach to an autonomy-supportive way of spiritual formation with children that centers the child's own spiritual journey.

Conclusion

This chapter opened with the question, What components are most important for nurturing the spiritual well-being of children in our communities, and how do we go about determining that? Answering the question begins with a review of the salient characteristics of childhood spirituality, which show that spirituality is inherent in the human experience, often framed in relationships, and provides a source of meaning making and identity formation. To build a more holistic approach to spiritual formation with children grounded in the literature on children's spirituality, scholars and practitioners need to reevaluate their understanding of children's religiosity and how we support it. Self-determination theory offers a promising theoretical framework for understanding how we might measure religiosity as central to a child's identity formation. For practitioners exploring how to build social spaces that support the spiritual experiences of children in their communities, autonomy support and social support should be considered valuable components. Instead of looking for resources that are designed to help kids "know" God or "adopt" some sort of subscribed outcome, we should be considering programs and resources that help kids make meaning from the God they already know.

Bibliography

Allport, Gordon W., and J. Michael Ross. "Personal Religious Orientation and Prejudice." *Journal of Personality and Social Psychology* 5, no. 4 (1967): 432. https://doi.org/10.1037/h0021212.

Assor, Avi, M. Cohen-Malayev, A. M. Kaplan, and D. Friedman. "Choosing to Stay Religious in a Modern World: Socialization and Exploration Processes Leading to an Integrated Internalization of Religion among Israeli Jewish Youth." In *Advances in Motivation and Achievement*. Vol. 14, 105–50. Bingley, UK: Emerald Group, 2005.

Barrow, Betsy Hughes, David C. Dollahite, and Loren D. Marks. "How Parents Balance Desire for Religious Continuity with Honoring Children's Religious Agency." *Psychology of Religion and Spirituality* 13, no. 2 (2021). https://doi.org/10.1037/rel0000307.

Batson, Charles Daniel, and W. Larry Ventis. *The Religious Experience: A Social-Psychological Perspective*. Oxford: Oxford University Press, 1982.

Bellous, Joyce E., and David M. Csinos. "Spiritual Styles: Creating an Environment to Nurture Spiritual Wholeness." *International Journal of Children's Spirituality* 14, no. 3 (2009): 213–24.

Berryman, Jerome. *Becoming like a Child: The Curiosity of Maturity beyond the Norm*. New York: Church Publishing, 2018.

———. *Godly Play: An Imaginative Approach to Religious Education*. Minneapolis: Augsburg, 1995.

———. *Stories of God at Home: A Godly Play Approach*. New York: Church Publishing, 2018.

Brambilla, Maria, Avi Assor, Claudia Manzi, and Camillo Regalia. "Autonomous versus Controlled Religiosity: Family and Group Antecedents." *International Journal for the Psychology of Religion* 25, no. 3 (2015): 243–54.

Bryant, Fred B., James Garbarino, Stuart N. Hart, and Kevin C. McDowell. "The Child's Right to a Spiritual Life." In *International Handbook on Child Rights and School Psychology*, edited by Bonnie Kaul Nastasi, Stuart N. Hart, and Shereen C. Naser, 305–18. New York: Springer, 2020.

Chi-Kin Lee, John. "Children's Spirituality, Life and Values Education: Cultural, Spiritual and Educational Perspectives." *International Journal of Children's Spirituality* 25, no. 1 (2020): 1–8.

Chirkov, Valery I. "A Cross-Cultural Analysis of Autonomy in Education: A Self-Determination Theory Perspective." *Theory and Research in Education* 7, no. 2 (2009): 253–62.

Church, A. Timothy, Marcia S. Katigbak, Kenneth D. Locke, Hengsheng Zhang, Jiliang Shen, José de Jesús Vargas-Flores, Joselina Ibáñez-Reyes, Junko Tanaka-Matsumi, Guy J. Curtis, Helena F. Cabrera, Shairul A. Mastor, Juan M. Alvarez, Fernando A. Ortiz, Jean-Yves R. Simon, and Charles M. Ching. "Need Satisfaction and Well-Being: Testing Self-Determination Theory in Eight Cultures." *Journal of Cross-Cultural Psychology* 44, no. 4 (2013): 507–34.

Coles, Robert. *The Spiritual Life of Children*. Boston: Houghton Mifflin, 1991.

Connell, James P., and Richard M. Ryan. "A Developmental Theory of Motivation in the Classroom." *Teacher Education Quarterly* 11, no. 4 (Fall 1984): 64–77.

Cordova, Diana I., and Mark R. Lepper. "Intrinsic Motivation and the Process of Learning: Beneficial Effects of Contextualization, Personalization, and Choice." *Journal of Educational Psychology* 88, no. 4 (1996). http://doi.org/10.1037/0022-0663.88.4.715.

Crosby, Robert G., and Erin I. Smith. "Church Support as a Predictor of Children's Spirituality and Prosocial Behavior." *Journal of Psychology and Theology* 43, no. 4 (2015). https://journals.sagepub.com/doi/abs/10.1177/009164711504300402.

Crosby, Robert G., Erin I. Smith, and Thomas V. Frederick. "The Kid-Friendly Church: What Makes Children Feel Loved, Valued, and Part of a Supportive Church Community." *Journal of Family and Community Ministries* 28, no. 1 (2015). https://www.academia.edu/28663407/

The_Kid_Friendly_Church_What_Makes_Children_Feel_Loved
_Valued_and_Part_of_a_Supportive_Church_Community.

Deci, Edward L., and Richard M. Ryan. "The 'What' and 'Why' of Goal Pursuits: Human Needs and the Self-Determination of Behavior." *Psychological Inquiry* 11, no. 4 (2000): 227–68. https://doi.org/10.1207/S15327965PLI1104_01.

Desrosiers, Alethea, Brien S. Kelley, and Lisa Miller. "Parent and Peer Relationships and Relational Spirituality in Adolescents and Young Adults." *Psychology of Religion and Spirituality* 3, no. 1 (2011): 39. https://doi.org/10.1037/a0020037.

Estep, James Riley, and Lillian Breckenridge. "The Ecology and Social Dynamics of Childhood Spirituality." In Lawson and May, *Children's Spirituality*, 328–46.

Fisher, John W. "Feeling Good, Living Life: A Spiritual Health Measure for Young Children." *Journal of Beliefs & Values* 25, no. 3 (2004): 307–15. https://doi.org/10.1080/1361767042000306121.

———. "God Counts for Children's Spiritual Well-Being." *International Journal of Children's Spirituality* 20, nos. 3–4 (2015): 191–203. https://doi.org/10.1037/0893-3200.15.4.627.

Flor, Douglas L., and Nancy Flanagan Knapp. "Transmission and Transaction: Predicting Adolescents' Internalization of Parental Religious Values." *Journal of Family Psychology* 15, no. 4 (2001): 627. https://doi.org/10.1037/0893-3200.15.4.627.

Francis, Leslie J. "Parental Influence and Adolescent Religiosity: A Study of Church Attendance and Attitude toward Christianity among Adolescents 11 to 12 and 15 to 16 Years Old." *International Journal for the Psychology of Religion* 3, no. 4 (1993): 241–53. https://doi.org/10.1207/s15327582ijpr0304_4.

Gopnik, Alison. *The Gardener and the Carpenter: What the New Science of Child Development Tells Us about the Relationship between Parents and Children*. New York: Macmillan, 2016.

Grolnick, Wendy S., and Richard M. Ryan. "Autonomy in Children's Learning: An Experimental and Individual Difference Investigation." *Journal of Personality and Social Psychology* 52, no. 5 (1987): 890. https://doi.org/10.1037/0022-3514.52.5.890.

Hay, David, and Rebecca Nye. *The Spirit of the Child*. London: Jessica Kingsley, 2006.

Holder, Mark D., Ben Coleman, and Judi M. Wallace. "Spirituality, Religiousness, and Happiness in Children Aged 8–12 Years." *Journal of*

Happiness Studies 11, no. 2 (2010): 131–50. https://doi.org/10.1007/s10902-008-9126-1.

Hyde, Brenda. "Identifying Some Characteristics of Children's Spirituality in Australia Primary Schools: A Study with Hermeneutic Phenomenology." PhD diss., Australian Catholic University, Melbourne, 2005. https://www.semanticscholar.org/paper/Identifying-some-characteristics-of-children%27s-in-a-Hyde/e6eb765b6ee44013b6383931eeb2752e6ef2e262.

Ingersoll, Heather Nicole. "Predictors of Identified and Introjected Religiosity in Upper Elementary Age Children." PhD diss., Seattle Pacific University, 2017.

Johnson, Susanne. "Christian Spiritual Formation in an Age of 'Whatever.'" *Review & Expositor* 98, no. 3 (2001): 309–31. https://doi.org/10.1177/003463730109800302.

Lawson, Kevin E., and Scottie May, eds. *Children's Spirituality: Christian Perspectives, Research, and Applications*. 2nd ed. Eugene, OR: Wipf & Stock, 2019.

Lin, Jing. *Love, Peace, and Wisdom in Education: A Vision for Education in the 21st Century*. Lanham, MD: Rowman & Littlefield Education, 2006.

Live Science Staff. "Spirituality, Not Religion, Makes Kids Happy." Live Science, January 9, 2009. https://www.livescience.com/3198-spirituality-religion-kids-happy.html.

Maltby, John. "The Internal Structure of a Derived, Revised, and Amended Measure of the Religious Orientation Scale: The 'Age-Universal' IE Scale–12." *Social Behavior and Personality: An International Journal* 27, no. 4 (1999): 407–12. https://doi.org/10.2224/sbp.1999.27.4.407.

May, Scottie, Beth Posterski, Catherine Stonehouse, and Linda Cannell. *Children Matter: Celebrating Their Place in the Church, Family, and Community*. Grand Rapids, MI: Eerdmans, 2005.

Myers, Scott M. "An Interactive Model of Religiosity Inheritance: The Importance of Family Context." *American Sociological Review* 61, no. 5 (October 1996): 858–66. http://www.jstor.org/stable/2096457.

Nye, Rebecca. *Children's Spirituality: What It Is and Why It Matters*. London: Church House, 2009.

———. "Christian Perspectives on Children's Spirituality: Social Science Contributions." In Lawson and May, *Children's Spirituality*, 83–101.

Okagaki, Lynn, and Claudia Bevis. "Transmission of Religious Values: Relations between Parents' and Daughters' Beliefs." *Journal of Genetic Psychology* 160, no. 3 (1999): 303–18.

Piechowski, Michael M. "Childhood Spirituality." *Journal of Transpersonal Psychology* 33, no. 1 (2001): 1–15.

Pitel, L., A. M. Geckova, P. Kolarcik, P. Halama, S. A. Reijneveld, and J. P. van Dijk. "Gender Differences in the Relationship between Religiosity and Health-Related Behaviour among Adolescents." *Journal of Epidemiology and Community Health* 66, no. 12 (2012): 1122–28. https://psycnet.apa.org/record/2012-32984-007.

Roehlkepartain, Eugene C., and Eboo Patel. "Congregations: Unexamined Crucibles for Spiritual Development." In *The Handbook of Spiritual Development in Childhood and Adolescence*, edited by Eugene C. Roehlkepartain, Pamela Ebstyne King, Linda Wagener, and Peter L. Benson, 324–36. Thousand Oaks, CA: SAGE, 2006.

Root, Andrew. *Revisiting Relational Youth Ministry: From a Strategy of Influence to a Theology of Incarnation*. Westmont, IL: InterVarsity, 2007.

Ryan, Richard M., Scott Rigby, and Kristi King. "Two Types of Religious Internalization and Their Relations to Religious Orientations and Mental Health." *Journal of Personality and Social Psychology* 65, no. 3 (1993): 586. https://doi.org/10.1037/0022-3514.65.3.586.

Smith, James K. A. *You Are What You Love: The Spiritual Power of Habit*. Ada, MI: Brazos, 2016.

TASC. *Two Measures of Teaching Provision of Involvement, Structure, and Autonomy Support*. Rochester, NY: University of Rochester, 1992.

Warner, Sharon. "An Epistemology of 'Participating Consciousness': Overcoming the Epistemological Rupture of Self and World." *Religious Education* 93, no. 2 (1998): 189–205. https://www.tandfonline.com/doi/abs/10.1080/0034408980930205.

Wilhoit, James C., and John M. Dettoni, eds. *Nurture That Is Christian: Developmental Perspectives on Christian Education*. Ada, MI: Baker Academic, 1995.

CHAPTER 3

Cultivating Curiosity
Water with Wonder, Grow Biblical Literacy

Robin Turner

A few years ago, I asked a pastor what percentage of adults in his congregation he thought could look up a passage in the Bible independently. "Forty percent, maybe?" he guessed. While his guess was based on conjecture rather than research, it reflected his honest assessment that many adults who prioritized taking part in his congregation's worship, learning, and community life simply didn't have the basic skills to navigate the Bible. As a children's ministries director, it reiterated for me that I couldn't merely encourage parents to take the lead in teaching their children how to navigate the Bible, as they might not have the tools to pass on to their children. The obstacles to families participating in Scripture reading or worship together might start with being overwhelmed by the subject matter and confused about how to open a biblical text, not being overwhelmed by schedules or chaos.

The primary goal in growing biblical literacy is knowing God, not academic achievement or knowledge accumulation. By knowing God's story more fully, people can experience God's love more deeply and extend that love to the world more holistically. For children, just like adults, increased knowledge about something leads to a greater capacity to love it. We see this with children who become obsessed with a story or character. When my sister was young, she became obsessed with *The Lion King*. In addition to practically memorizing the film, *Lion King* action figures filled her bedroom, and she pretended she was Simba so often that she wore holes in the knees of her pants. Eventually, she was checking books out of the library on all types of wild African cats and developing an impressive array of knowledge of something no one else in our household had any interest in. As an adult, *The Lion King* still holds a special place in her heart and imagination.

Cultivating curiosity in the lives of children means creating spaces and times for them to encounter the stories of God in winsome, Spirit-led ways; wonder aloud about various aspects of these stories; engage in child-level research in their particular interest areas; and fall gradually more in love with God and God's Word.

What Is Biblical Literacy?

For this chapter, *biblical literacy* is the ability to know enough of the Bible to navigate the text in a meaningful way, ask intentional questions, and draw thoughtful conclusions. It includes the following:

1. The physical text: This involves learning how to look up a Scripture passage in the Bible and locating the book, chapter, and verse.
2. The literary context: This means knowing the various genres of Scripture, such as law, history, wisdom, poetry, prophecy, gospel, or epistle, as well as the basic implications of the genre for how the Scripture passage is read or interpreted. A child can learn that Psalm 23 is poetry about God as a shepherd and that Jesus's statement "I am the good shepherd" is a teaching from a New Testament Gospel (John 10:11, 14).
3. The metanarrative (timeline): This includes considering whether a passage is in the Old or New Testament and how a particular story fits into a larger narrative. For instance, the

story of Rahab and the spies takes place during the Israelites' exploration of the land of Canaan, Jesus calming the storm takes place on the night after he feeds the five thousand, and Paul's shipwreck happens on his way to Rome. Even young children can differentiate whether narratives take place before, during, or after Jesus's earthly ministry.
4. The geography: Where did the story take place, and does the location hold significant meaning or context? Location often held significant meaning for ancient contexts, and early readers would have understood the significance of multiple events happening in the same location separated by hundreds of years. Additionally, geographic context can help children understand the historical veracity of biblical narratives. These stories took place not in a mythical time and world but in a real historical and physical context, a location that exists today.
5. The culture: The secular history surrounding an event, as well as the Jewish and Gentile norms of the time, provides helpful context for the stories. For instance, Jesus calming the storm or walking on water not only showed his power over the physical world but also displayed his supremacy over false gods, who were believed to cause chaos and shipwrecks in the water.[1]

Growing in biblical literacy can mean a lifetime of learning more about each of these areas, and while the depth and breadth of knowledge available in any of these areas far exceed what a children's lesson can cover, children are able to begin to build a context for their own exploration of these areas over time.

Just as a person is able to love something more fully as they grow in knowledge about it, knowledge also has the capacity to compound exponentially. In other words, as a person learns about

---

[1] One wonderful resource for child-sized cultural and literary context is Walton and Walton, *Bible Story Handbook*.

something, they also grow in their capacity to learn about it with greater depth or breadth.[2]

For example, a young child might be told that parts of the Bible were written as poetry. As that child grows older, they might learn that there are various types of poetry in the Bible and that sometimes, poems were composed for specific occasions. This could eventually lead to thoughtful questions about modern interpretations and applications of the poetic texts of Scripture, a desire to compose poetry of worship or lament for modern contexts, or a deeper understanding of a God who values poetry and the arts. These higher-level questions and curiosities are accessible only by starting at a basic understanding of Scripture genres and are reached through gradual growth over time. A foundation of biblical literacy started at a young age equips Christians for a lifetime of formational growth.

Obstacles to Biblical Literacy

Never have so many resources for teaching Bible stories to children been as available as they are today. Large publishing houses create dynamic lines of curricula that cater to church wants and desires; websites allow children's ministry leaders, pressed for ideas, to access countless resources for free; and Bible editions created specifically for children are available across translations with child-friendly notes and winsome designs at relatively affordable prices. Why do these not translate to high levels of biblical literacy?

First, sharing the Bible with children will always mean trying to engage young minds with an ancient text from a foreign culture. Regardless of the race, ethnicity, socioeconomic level, or academic aptitude of a modern child, engaging with Scripture is an inherently cross-cultural activity. Furthermore, the text of the Bible is long and can be complex; reading Scripture is overwhelming to many adults, much less children! Oftentimes, those teaching

---

2 National Center for Education Statistics, "School and Staffing Survey."

children have difficulty navigating the physical text or the cultural context themselves. Prioritizing teaching children to look up Scripture passages or ask thoughtful questions might need to begin with guiding the adult teachers by providing resources for their own learning.

Second, there is a temptation to focus on making the stories of Scripture palatable or applicable at the cost of exploring the depth, richness, and complexity of the text. Many churches feel pressure to engage children with fun activities each week so children or families will desire to return to church often. In order to do this, lessons are often made so accessible that they no longer challenge a child to grow. For instance, a fun-oriented lesson about David and Goliath might include a relay race, tossing "stones" at a paper cutout of a giant, or crafting a slingshot snack out of pretzel sticks, Twizzlers, and M&Ms. At the end of the lesson, children might be encouraged to remember that they can be brave because God is stronger than anything they face. While this is an undeniably fun time, and children have learned a truth about God, they have learned very little about the context of 1 Samuel, God's power over the Philistines, or the Lord's continued providence for the Israelites as they became an established nation. Furthermore, a lesson focused on entertainment typically sparks curiosity about what fun activities or events will be provided at the next gathering to entertain the children, not curiosity about the character of God, the applicability and veracity of Scripture, or the implications of God's call on the life of the child.

Finally, if the church gathering is the primary space and time in which children are equipped to learn how to navigate the Bible, low attendance and a low value of engaging the actual texts of Scripture both impede growing in biblical literacy. Even if a child attends an average of three Sundays a month, they will only spend about thirty-six hours over the course of a whole year in Sunday school, which includes a variety of activities that often have very little to do with building biblical literacy. By comparison, most elementary-age children in the United States receive about 5–6 hours of math and 10–11 hours of English-language arts instruction per week, totaling 175 hours of math and 360 hours of English-language arts![3] Of course, academic skills are vital for children and can augment their growth in biblical literacy, but the quantity, quality, and intention of time devoted to these areas in comparison to the intention often placed on learning how to engage with Scripture can miscommunicate the value of Scripture.

Scripture as Living and Active

For the Christian, the Bible is more than a book. The Word of God is a living and active source of God's presence in the world today. John 1 states that the Word of God is eternal and that Jesus is the Word that became flesh. The author of Hebrews teaches that the Word of God is "alive and active. Sharper than any double-edged sword" (Heb. 4:12). The Word of God will not return empty (Isa. 55:11). The Word of God is "useful for teaching, rebuking, correcting and training in righteousness" (2 Tim. 3:16). In other words, God's Word in any context is dynamic and active, not a mere text to be dissected, dressed up, or droned on about. Too often, the church approaches children's lessons as opportunities to make children aware of Bible stories so that they might be of use someday rather than trusting that God can and will use Scripture in the lives of children while they are still children. Instead, children would benefit from adults who arrive expectant of God's work, challenge them to engage the texts directly, and model using Scripture powerfully.

When working with children, adults can come expectant that God will work through Scripture to teach, comfort, admonish, and engage with children. While children may need help reading or otherwise engaging with texts and certainly need assistance in understanding things like cultural contexts, the truths of Scripture, and the active work of God, Scripture is still able to minister to a child's heart and mind. For instance, a child might need an

---

3 National Center for Education Statistics, "School and Staffing Survey."

adult to read Psalm 23 aloud, may benefit from various visuals an adult uses in presenting the text, and might have questions like "What does it mean to 'anoint my head with oil'?" but none of those scaffolds of adult assistance preclude the ability of God to minister deeply to a child through the imagery of a faithful shepherd offering green pastures, quiet waters, protection from enemies, or a feast. This is not to say that every text is equally accessible to children or should even be shared with children—there are texts in Scripture that are weighty, risqué, or otherwise inapplicable to the lives of most children. While a young child can benefit from learning about the Fall through Adam and Eve's disobedience, many would argue that very young children do not need to read the deeply disturbing passage in the following chapter where Cain kills his brother, Abel.

The second principle for actively engaging in Scripture with children is to open the Bible and directly read the Scripture rather than only reading a retelling or storybook. There are many beautifully written and illustrated children's Bible storybooks available today, and these too can spark wonder that leads to curiosity. However, these tools should be used as supplements rather than primary texts, similar to the way a beautiful illustration might capture the imagination of a child but cannot adequately tell the full or most true account of the story. In some approaches, like Catechesis of the Good Shepherd, Godly Play, and Young Children and Worship, the Scripture is read directly from the Bible after a thoughtful sharing of the story through manipulatives and responses from the children through art. This allows a physical, tactile "hook" for the more complicated and abstract world of the text to hang on. In other contexts, a teacher might encourage children to listen to the text as they illustrate it themselves on paper, or children who have basic literacy might read along with a teacher in their own Bible and mark their questions and areas of wondering as they read. Intentionally incorporating the divinely inspired Word of God rather than just a retelling or reinterpretation acknowledges that ultimately, what matters in a children's lesson is the work of God in and through a child's life, not a child's familiarity with a retelling of an ancient event. The same God who turned water into wine at Cana in John 4 is present through his Word and Spirit in a third-grade Sunday school class, and inviting and engaging with God's presence in that class is vastly more important than merely learning that the story took place and taking home a weekly application point.

Finally, children benefit from adults modeling the power of Scripture. When I was five years old, on my first Sunday visiting a new church, I remember the Sunday school teacher opening up her floppy, leather-bound Bible to our story for the day and exclaiming, "Every time I read God's Word, God shows me something new!" I was highly confused about how her Bible had new words each time she opened it because my Bible storybook at home was the exact same no matter how often I flipped through the pages. My teacher was demonstrating that God was active and at work in her Scripture reading. For children, this active use can be modeled by using Scripture to bless them; turning to Scripture in times of great emotions like fear, anger, joy, or sorrow; and acknowledging personal growth from engaging with Scripture. In my church, each children's class closes with the teacher blessing the children with a verse from Scripture after they line up to rejoin the congregation for the Eucharist.

Sometimes, the Bible is treated as a passive entity to be examined, interpreted, and applied. Instead, Christians believe that the Bible is a primary way that God is teaching, shaping, and equipping the saints for faithful living. It is only considering this acknowledgment that God is at work through the scriptures in the hearts and minds of believers that the Bible should be studied and applied.

The Roles of Wonder and Curiosity

Contemplative and Montessori approaches to sharing Scripture with children have become increasingly popular over the last fifty years through organizations like Catechesis of the Good Shepherd,

Godly Play, and Young Children and Worship. As mentioned before, each of these programs includes a presentation of a biblical text using manipulatives, a time of wondering aloud in community, a time of personal response, and an opportunity to listen to the scripture text read aloud from a Bible.[4] This time of wondering invites children to ask questions about the story and about God—What was God thinking as the story was unfolding? What were the humans in the story thinking or feeling? What might it have been like to be part of this story? What might the real implications of this event have been? What does it look like to apply this knowledge about God's character or God's work in the world in daily life? The wondering questions provide a sharp contrast to the reading-comprehension questions commonly asked in response to church Bible lessons, which tend to focus on determining whether the children remember the important facts and can articulate the potential moral applications of the text.

Wondering unlocks deeper levels of questioning, personal connection, and openness to God's continued work in present-day life; in some cases, this intentional wondering process opens a door that children and adults need to be invited to walk through. In many cases, the greater context of Scripture, centuries of biblical scholarship, and historical and archaeological studies can offer potential answers to these wonderings. Wonder, therefore, is a great mental and emotional activity that can lead children to curiosity that can be explored and investigated to reveal a richer, deeper meaning of a text and the nature of God. As a child probes these questions with age-appropriate tools, their initial curiosity can be satisfied while they continue to discover new questions to investigate. In this way, a child or small group of children begin to take the initiative to grow in their own understanding of Scripture and God rather than merely receiving what a parent or teacher reads or presents to them. Even if a child needs an adult's assistance in utilizing resources to answer their questions, the child's

---

4 Stewart and Berryman, "Part 1: Introduction," 13–54.

curiosity can be the driving force behind learning rather than the teacher or parent working to convince the child of their interest. In this investigative process, children begin taking ownership of a piece of their biblical literacy. When a child wonders something in community or in private, the follow-up response can often be, "I'm going to try to find out!" Certainly, there are some things a reader can wonder about and never know, but in many cases, there are tools to search for meaningful answers.

Prepared Spaces: Tools for Investigation

Church and home contexts vary significantly based on location, economic resources, space, and even factors like whether a church is mobile or has a permanent building. A large, English-speaking congregation in the United States will have more free and inexpensive resources and likely more financial backing to equip children with tools for growing in biblical literacy. Other congregations might need to seek out resources in other languages, tools that can be packed and unpacked on a weekly basis, or budget-friendly options that recognize their congregation's financial constraints.

The first tool for growing biblical literacy is access to a Bible. Ideally, children will have their own Bibles that they can read, mark, and annotate. A child's annotations are typically nothing spectacular! Underlining repeated words, highlighting verses of interest, placing a question mark next to confusing words, and bookmarking special stories are all ways that children develop ownership of their own biblical literacy. I saw a six-year-old scrawling pink highlighter over a whole section of verses, and when tempted to intervene, I caught myself and instead asked her, "Can you tell me about your highlighting?" She replied, "This is my very favorite story in the Bible, and pink is my favorite color. I want to always be able to find the pink page where I can read about how Jesus goes to find the one sheep who's missing." I'm glad her Bible has a pink page, and I believe she will wear out that copy in time for her to have more mature highlighting in her upper-elementary and middle-school years. Scripture is a precious gift, and counterintuitively, the way children actively love something is often to the object's eventual destruction and demise. A well-loved Bible may be marked, highlighted, and dog eared, but when it results from care and not carelessness, it's a beautiful sight.

A second phenomenal classroom tool is a map or set of maps that includes ancient Israel and the surrounding regions of Egypt, Greece, Mesopotamia, and even parts of the Roman Empire. As children become aware of world geography through their academic studies, they can begin locating places referenced in Scripture. Seeing these locations in relation to one another and other regions of the world emphasizes the veracity of Scripture and prompts questions like "How far between?" "What else happened here?" and "Why did they travel there?" Additionally, children begin to weave a web of connections between their academic world and their biblical knowledge and establish relationships among Scriptural events. For instance, an eight-year-old studying ancient Egypt in school might excitedly realize that the events of Exodus took place in the same region and then, at Christmastime, bring a new depth of understanding to the holy family fleeing to Egypt to escape King Herod and eventually returning along the same route that the ancient Israelites traveled during their desert wanderings. Another child might realize for the first time that a significant portion of Jesus's earthly ministry took place in the small towns of Galilee near the shores and on the Sea of Galilee rather than at the hub of religious life in Jerusalem. Upper-elementary-age children seem particularly interested in the distances between towns and villages, gauging how long it would take them to walk the same distance and pondering the types of people who might have traveled between these villages. For children with an interest in history or geography and who think and remember things visually, spatially, or pictorially, a set of classroom maps can be a wonderful rabbit hole of biblical exploration.

Along with maps, Google Earth and Google Images offer digital resources that allow children to see, more clearly than in any other preceding generation, primary sources for biblical studies. In prior generations, children might see a drawing of a Roman coin or pass around a single photograph during Sunday school, but now a Google Image search reveals hundreds of photos of pristine-condition coins from this era, often linked to websites with more information. When reading Jesus's story of the good Samaritan, a child or teacher can pull up a photograph of the geography of the region between Jericho and Jerusalem and see the context Jesus's listeners would have brought to the story. Likewise, Google Earth offers the opportunity to take a virtual visit to survey the Bethlehem hillsides; look out from Mount Tabor, the site of the Transfiguration; gaze from Capernaum across the Sea of Galilee; or explore the ruins of the Colosseum. Each of these virtual visits emphasizes that the Bible is both a supernatural text and a historical text; the places really exist, and the events truly happened. While children's illustrations might help young children understand abstract texts, these phenomenal photographic resources help older children break down preconceived notions of the world of the Bible. While access to these resources requires a screen and an internet connection, the actual resources are free for anyone to use.

Finally, charts listing the books of the Bible and classroom or personal timelines of biblical events help children understand the narrative context of the Scripture passage they are studying. Even a simple poster board with the books of the Bible listed in order and color coded by genre can help children begin to understand how the parts of the Bible fit together and where the story they are reading takes place. A basic timeline of the Bible, with periods of time like "the Patriarchs," "the Desert Wanderings," "the United and Divided Kingdoms," and "the Early Church," can help a child place the story they are exploring in context with other important key events, social and political realities, and the overarching work of God in the world. Creating something like this for a classroom wall with colored paper and then filling in specific stories with smaller index cards allows for a class to work to make their own timeline. Similarly, a class might begin to make individual timelines that each child can create on a sheet of paper and tuck in their own Bible cover, taping extra pieces on the end to lengthen it as necessary.

In the context of Sunday school, teachers can model and teach these tools by beginning each lesson by helping the class locate the text of that week's lesson in the physical Bible, on the map on the wall, and on the timeline. Then as questions and wonderings arise, teachers might either encourage a child to look up an answer during the week and report back or offer to look up the answer themselves and bring more information back to the class the next week. In either case, one necessary ingredient for indulging curiosity is a commitment of time. It takes time to travel down rabbit holes of thoughts and ideas, and the best explorations offer the bandwidth to veer from the current investigation to look at a new point of interest. The unhurriedness of the exploration invites children and adults alike to revisit thoughts and ideas and build both their own understanding and their own list of curiosities and questions.

When children and adults love something, they long to know more about it. And when they know more about it, they can love it more deeply. One of the tasks of Christian education is to foster these loves in relation to God and God's Word, not for the eventual mastery, but for the delight in knowing a God of love more deeply and intrinsically. While every tool might not be accessible to every child, depending on age, ability, or global context, the God of love invites every child into this world of learning and exploration with their own abilities. Ultimately, they are coming to know Godself, not just a text or set of skills. Truly, no child or adult will ever master the sacred texts of Scripture or know so much about God that they no longer need God. Instead, as we come to know God and God's Word more deeply, we will find both our hearts and minds transformed, renewed, and restored by the power of the Spirit leading and guiding us to all knowledge and truth.

Bibliography

Meek, Esther Lightcap. *Loving to Know: Introducing Covenant Epistemology*. Eugene, OR: Cascade Books, 2011.

National Center for Education Statistics. "School and Staffing Survey." Institute of Education Sciences. Accessed April 5, 2022. https://nces.ed.gov/surveys/sass/tables/sass0708_005_t1n.asp.

Stewart, Sonja M., and Jerome Berryman. "Part 1: Introduction." In *Young Children and Worship*, 13–54. Louisville, KY: Westminster John Knox, 1989.

Walton, John H., and Kim Walton. *The Bible Story Handbook: A Resource for Teaching 175 Stories from the Bible*. Wheaton, IL: Crossway, 2010.

CHAPTER 4

"Kids Today Just Can't…"
Changing Our Posture and Practices to Welcome All Children

Dana Kennamer and Suzetta Nutt

During the years of the COVID-19 pandemic, the entire global community faced fear, dismay, and uncertainty over a virus we did not understand. In many parts of the world, this was combined with war, political unrest, hunger, poverty, or racial injustice. As we began working on this chapter, the trauma of COVID-19 seemed to be waning in our city, but the uncertainty of what tomorrow held made everyone, young and old alike, a little bit wary. And we know that in ways we have not yet fully discerned, we have been forever changed.

Our church, probably much like yours, isn't immune to the challenges present in every corner of our world. The children we pastor have also been deeply affected, and we find this wariness reflected in them too. We see how these issues affect our children and wonder how to move forward as we navigate a rapidly changing world.

Children have indeed changed. How could they not be different now than they were a few years ago? It's easy to respond with "Children today just can't" and become frustrated with them, their parents, their schools, or any number of things impacting them. And yet we still hear Jesus call us to let the children come—all children—and join him in the posture of welcome. This is not easy.

We begin by sharing a bit about who we are as we join children on the spiritual journey. We are both in our early sixties and have been engaged with children in our faith communities from the time we were in middle school. We are mothers of adult children with complex stories, and Suzetta is also the parent of a soon-to-be sixth grader.

Dana's official job is serving as a professor of education at a Christian university. Suzetta is a minister at a midsized church. We have worked together in ministry for almost forty years and continue to gather each week with children on Sunday mornings and Wednesday nights.

We have experienced many changes on this journey with children, adapting our approach and learning new things along the way, but we have always been guided by the unwavering belief in the value of children and their capacity to know and experience God.

Change and Our Children

For some time now, we've all observed how children are affected by the changes in our world—the distraction of technology, the pressure of academic testing, the overwhelming and ever-changing demands of family life. In response to these changes, we have often heard repeated, "Kids today just can't." They can't pay attention. They can't sit still. They can't listen. They can't. But what we believe with complete confidence is that children are capable of more than we often think.

The significant changes in our communities, cultures, and families continue to challenge churches to adapt in order to welcome and nurture children on their spiritual journeys. Very few times in history have we experienced changes such as we have all experienced during the years of this pandemic. COVID-19 affected everyone, and we're still discovering the effects of isolation, loss, illness, and social distancing as well as new and confusing rules about how to live in this world together.

Early in the pandemic, Dana was on her university campus, which had been shut down. She left her building to take a break and was surprised to see two dear children from our church playing outside with their mother. The oldest was in first grade and knew not to come toward her. The other, a kindergartner, started running toward Teacher Dana to give her a hug. Suddenly, fear came across his face, and he froze. Next came confusion and then sadness because he knew it was no longer OK to give Teacher Dana a hug. This was a painful experience for both of them. Dana hugged herself and said, "This is hard. I am hugging you, and I love you." He hugged himself as well, and a small smile appeared along with the lingering sadness.

As with all churches, our faith community dealt with many difficult challenges during COVID-19. We had lots of questions and differing opinions about how we should safely gather. Do we wear masks? Do we gather indoors? We were constantly asking the question of how we care for the least of these and love our neighbors. We realized that none of us were completely "OK." This was true for our children as well.

In the midst of this pandemic, the entire globe encountered significant economic impacts, social isolation, and the overwhelming challenges of providing health care resources for all people. In the United States, we were also engaged in hard and often divisive conversations about race, gender, and political viewpoints. Our children were not unaware. They heard the conversations, saw the images on the screens, and sometimes struggled to find a place to ask questions and make sense of the world around them.

In this era, we find ourselves with new questions: What do our children need now? How has the pandemic changed childhood in homes, schools, churches, and the broader community? And yet our guiding principles remain the same—the inherent value of children and their capacity to know and experience God.

The Challenge of Innocence

As a society, we have "overwhelmingly chosen the image of the pure and innocent child" and have idealized children "as precious, delicate, and in need of vigilant and constant care."[1] We try to shield and protect them, and in many ways, this is appropriate, but their emotions are not different from ours. Often, we need to walk alongside them through the hard things and see what God has to teach us as we journey together.

Many contemporary American churches have come to equate faithfulness with being "happy, cooperative, and nice," so nurturing children in faith means socializing them into smiling, happy, compliant little people.[2] When children's emotional responses are less than ideal or, at times, extreme, we respond with disappointment, surprise, helplessness, shock, and even anger. This idealized view of children does not serve us or the children well, particularly in these complicated times.

Think about the children you know. Do they fit this pure, innocent vision, or are they, at times, grumpy and selfish? At other times, do they surprise you with compassion? Sometimes, they make unreasonable demands with an impatience that tests our patience. And then, do they surprise you with their insight, creativity, and joy?

We believe that churches need to ask questions about how to receive the real, not the idealized, children who come to us. Children are both vulnerable and capable. They are joyful and yet observant of the problems of the world. They desperately want to belong and yet often push others away. They ask questions, wanting answers, but are fully capable of living in the mystery. They have things to learn from us about how to live in this world as people of God, and we have things to learn from them. We need a more complex theology of childhood that can hold in tension all

---

1 Miller-McLemore, *Let the Children Come*, 7.
2 Mercer, *Welcoming Children*, 120.

the realities of children's lives.[3] This is the posture that informs our practice with children. It is our calling not to control them but to join them in learning how to submit to God's voice and one another as a community of faith.

What do children learn as they watch trusted adults persist in love and welcome? Children watch us and learn from how we respond not only to them but also to the other children in the room. We have to continually question what the children in our faith communities are learning about God's hospitality and welcome from us as we respond to all the children God has entrusted to us.

A Sometimes Messy Journey

Truly joining children is messy. Some children bring stories that make it seem impossible for them to belong. There are no magic answers, only the commitment to trust that God is at work in the process. This messy welcome can be seen in our journey with our friend David.[4]

David has a complicated life. He is intellectually gifted, but his mind often wanders toward violent stories and images. School is hard for him. He wants to belong but almost always tests people, pushing them away. It is often challenging for him to come to church, and yet it is here that he wants to be. He often says shocking things, like "I hate church, and God doesn't love me. I hate you, and you don't love me."

One Sunday, as Suzetta was sitting in worship, she heard a child screaming outside the sanctuary. She quickly moved into the atrium, trying to find who needed help. Her search led her to the women's restroom, where David was screaming and kicking the wall. He was saying hard words, like "I hate this church.

---

3 Bunge, *More Vibrant Theology*.
4 All children's names are pseudonyms to protect their privacy.

Nobody loves me. God doesn't care about me. Church is stupid." His mother was quietly crying, totally at a loss for what to do.

Suzetta sat down on the floor beside David and asked, "What do you need right now?" He shouted at her, "I just need a place to be alone. It's too noisy here." His mom gave Suzetta permission to take David to a safe place where he could have what he needed, and she was able to get what she needed too—uninterrupted worship knowing her son was safe.

On that day, Jesus was present in solidarity with David and Suzetta. Like the children Jesus met, who could not control their bodies and feelings and who sometimes frightened and confused the people around them, David needed to be seen, heard, and trusted to name what he craved.

That day was the turning point for Suzetta's relationship with David, leading to a change in the way we all welcomed him. Rather than forcing David to participate in ways he is unable, we provide him with the agency to tell us what he needs. If we can accommodate it, we do. It's not perfect. He still has hard days and nights at church, but he is always welcome and loved. He continues to test whether we mean what we say, sometimes pushing us away, asking us again by his behavior to prove that what we are saying is true. It's messy, but we engage in holy persistence, acknowledging that God is in charge of God's relationship with David. And we see glimpses of God's work in this messy journey with our friend.

Later that year at our fall festival, as David and his family were leaving, Suzetta waved at them from a distance. David came running across the field, shouting, "Miss Suzetta! Miss Suzetta!" When he reached her, he flung his arms around her and said, "I love you so much, and I'm so glad I came tonight." She returned his hug and told him how much she loved him. He asked, "Are you glad I came tonight?" She replied, "Yes, David. I'm so glad you were here." He happily ran off to join his family, shouting, "I'll see you on Wednesday."

When Wednesday came, his anger and resistance returned. But it's important to know that his parents don't make him come to church on Wednesdays. Even on those nights when he is hostile and defiant, it is his choice to come. And it is our choice to welcome him with open arms and unconditional love, even though we don't know what the night will hold.

It is true: some kids can't, at least not yet. We are joining God in this process. It is God's work in the child that calls them to God. It's our job to provide a safe, welcoming space for God's transformation.

Behavior as Communication

David reminds us that all behaviors communicate. The children tell us what they need by what they do or don't do. It is our responsibility to first seek to understand what they are saying to us rather than focusing on simple compliance or control.

This requires noticing—a posture of holy curiosity—as we welcome children with challenging behavior. What are the children in your world telling you? Some of the messages we have received from children through their behavior include the following:

- You're asking me to do something that is too hard for me.
- I don't understand what you want me to do or why.
- I'm overwhelmed.
- I'm bored, and this doesn't mean anything to me.
- I need some attention.
- I don't belong here.
- I am so excited that I can't hold it in.
- My body is uncomfortable.
- I'm tired or hungry.
- I don't feel safe.
- I'm embarrassed.
- My heart is heavy and sad.
- I have controlled myself all day and have nothing left.

It is easy to take a dismissive posture toward some of these messages. After all, children still need to behave, don't they? But if we look at this list and are honest, there are times when our own behavior, as adults, has been less than ideal when experiencing these same emotional responses. Sometimes, we just imagine what we would like to do in response, but at other times, fatigue, frustration, or fear get the best of us, and we behave in ways we regret.

Considering Our Posture toward Children's Behavior

Children are not that different from us, but they are not always able to use words to tell us what they need. When we encounter challenging behaviors in children, it can be overwhelming. This almost always signals that it is time to ask questions before we respond.

One important first step is to ask what we mean by *challenging behavior*. Kaiser and Rasminsky[5] offer a very helpful answer. They describe it as a pattern of behavior that

- interferes with a child's cognitive, social, or emotional development;
- is harmful to the child, other children, or adults; and
- puts a child at high risk for later social problems or failure.

Consider this description for a moment. It defines challenging behavior not by what children do but by how the behavior affects what they ultimately need. They need to be safe. They need to belong. They need to have a future and a hope. Our goal is not to simply control children's behavior but to join God in calling them into community with God and God's people. And so we must discern whether our practices align with this purpose.

In our long journey with children, the following are some of the questions we've had to ask ourselves. In this process of

---

5 Kaiser and Rasminsky, *Challenging Behavior*, 7.

spiritual discernment, we have not always liked the answers to our questions but are called again and again to take the posture of welcome modeled by Jesus. We have come to understand that welcome is the only posture! Perhaps some of our questions can guide you as you reflect on your gathering spaces and practices:

- Do our gathering spaces mirror our values of engagement, spiritual formation, and relationships?
- Does everyone belong, and does everyone feel that they belong? Have we made this clear by our responses to all the children in the room?
- Has something changed in our space that is triggering the children or making them uncomfortable?
- What do I notice as children enter? Do they come in easily or with anxiety? Are they tired, stressed, confused, or sad? What reassurance can I offer?
- Is the behavior I am seeing typical or out of the ordinary?
- Are our expectations for our own comfort or familiarity?
- Are we responding to the current needs of the children?
- Has something happened in our broader community that we need to hold in mind as we welcome the children?
- Have we clearly communicated what we need to do in our space to take care of one another and why it is important?
- Have we gotten caught in a negative way of thinking about a specific child? If so, how does that impact our relationship with the entire class? What can be done to break this negative posture?

These can be hard questions to ask. And questions continue to emerge with each new group of children we welcome. As an experienced children's minister, Suzetta has watched this dance of change many times. Children today are different than they were even ten years ago, and every child who comes to us has their own unique needs.

Consider some of the following descriptions of some of the children we love and their unique needs. Do you know children like this? Does your own childhood story resonate with one of these descriptions?

- I am bored! You are asking me to do what I can't because my body is uncomfortable, and this is all too easy for me.
- I don't belong here because you don't have anything to teach me. I have my own ideas.
- My friends seem to be farther along than I am. I just feel behind all the time.
- Life has wounded me, and I am striving for approval.
- It's hard for me to feel comfortable with you. I am nervous and easily embarrassed.
- You need to pay attention to me because I am absolutely adorable!
- It's hard knowing I can be a leader, but sometimes I just want to be cool.
- I'm good at getting others to laugh, and that makes me feel important.
- Yes, I am brilliant, but I don't know how to make friends. I am awkward and often on the outside.
- My life has completely changed, and I do not know how to be anywhere right now.
- My overwhelming shyness looks like withdrawal. But I am watching everything.

All children need the adults in their world to see them as they are and accept them without reservations or conditions, no matter how much they seem to be communicating the opposite. We have to be willing to change. Many changes we have discovered to be helpful are not earth-shattering but relatively easy to undertake. One such change is the simple but powerful transformation of our collective language.

The Formative Power of Language

In the book of James, our tongues are compared to the rudder of a ship—small but powerful in setting the course of the journey. And so it is with our words that we determine our direction, shape our communities, and form our attitudes. The language we use with and about children matters. Does our language communicate respect? Does it point us toward one another and to God? Does it guide us in creating safe and inclusive spaces where all voices are valued? Over the years we have developed a language of community that we use in our gatherings with children. These simple phrases have been deeply formative for us all.

When God's People Gather . . .

We use this phrase to remind ourselves that we are God's people gathered. When God's people gather, we listen to one another, we welcome one another, we hear God's story, we pray, we help one another, we sing. This simple phrase, used in various aspects of our communal time, affirms again and again that we are the people of God, and so what we do is holy and important—a reminder the grown-ups often need as much as the children.

How Do We Take Care of One Another When . . . ?

Instead of asking children to name the rules for our time together, we want to all think about how we take care of one another in our gathering spaces. How do we take care of one another when we gather around God's story today? How do we take care of one another as we go to the prayer wall? How do we take care of one another as we share materials during response time? These conversations create an atmosphere of invitation, with a posture of welcome and inclusion, rather than simply restating rules.

This was an important question for us when we returned to our children's ministry spaces. Dana asked some of the children how we could take care of one another when we came back together as a group after the pandemic. Two fourth-grade girls provided some important insights to guide us as we welcomed one another back:

Nikki reminded Dana that returning sometimes felt weird and awkward: "No offense to the teachers, 'cuz I know you are a teacher, but I felt embarrassed." She also reminded Dana that like many others during the pandemic, she had experienced significant loss. Nikki was still grieving the deaths of her dog and her grandmother, and she knew she was not alone in this. She suggested, "Well, maybe have a section where you can still listen, but you are only by one person, or less people." This space, she said, would allow you to cry or laugh or respond however you needed without worrying about what people thought.

Emily reminded us that just hopping right back into "normal" wasn't realistic. She told Dana that it won't be normal, so we need to be careful about what we expect of one another: "What is important not to do is like, 'Hey, do you want to do this? Do you want to do that? What do you want to do?' You just don't need to force kids but encourage them. That's how I always felt when I was younger—people were just not letting me do what I needed to do. You know, just letting me choose and take my time."

Every time we engage with this question, the children affirm for us that they have wisdom to share as we learn how to take care of one another.

This Isn't Working for Us. I Wonder What We Can Do That Will Help Us?

As we work together to be a community, the language of *us* is critical. When we encounter a challenge as a group, we make sure to name that the challenge is with the process or structure and not with the children. As we engage in these conversations about whether our structure is working and what approaches we might try to help us, we are learning together the process of communal discernment. Faith community is not always easy. True community requires listening to one another not with blame but rather with true hospitality, receiving one another as Christ receives us. These conversations help us all learn how to better be God's people gathered.

This Is Hard. God's People Can Do Hard Things.

Hard things include coming to church when we are tired or just wanted to continue playing at home. Sometimes it is very hard to calm our bodies for story or prayer. Waiting our turn or sharing materials is hard. It is hard for all of us to know how to respond to change, loss, or disappointment. During the pandemic, this phrase became part of the language of the whole church. Gathering in strange ways, wearing masks, we reminded one another again and again that God's people can do hard things.

Get Your Mind, Your Heart, and Your Body Ready To . . .

Learning to love God with our hearts, bodies, and minds is not easy for any of us but is often especially hard for children. We all need space to get ready. As we enter God's story or join together in prayer, we repeat these words: get your mind, your heart, and your body ready. We model our own process of getting ready to receive what God has for us. It is not perfect, but it is amazing to see how these words call the children to consider if they are ready for the holy work we are doing together.

What Helps You When . . . ?

It is critical that when we ask this question, we commit again to the posture of respectful listening. Children may need guidance and prompting to help them think about what they need, but our goal is to discover with them how we can help them. While this is sometimes a question for an individual child, we often ask it when gathered as a group.

On Wednesday evenings, our kindergarten through fifth-grade children gather in prayer using our prayer wall—a wall-sized chalkboard where we write and draw our prayers together. It is a time to practice the spiritual disciplines of prayer and coming to quiet. And so we ask the children, "What helps you come to quiet when we go to the prayer wall?" As various children and adults respond, we all learn from one another in the holy discipline of being present and still before the Lord.

Is It Silly or Serious?

We have all loved children who enjoy giving silly answers to serious questions. They are funny and creative and still need to learn when silly helps us hear from God and one another and when it does not. So we offer the child a way to evaluate and regulate their own behavior. Living in a community is complicated, and self-awareness is an essential skill to learn. Silly or serious? They know we are not angry but asking them to consider how they use their words. When we ask, "Silly or serious?" they often give a smile and a shrug and decide to wait until a more appropriate time.

And then sometimes, our silly friends have truly serious things to share, so this question leaves space for them to let us know when this is the case. One night we checked with one often-silly friend, and he assured us that it was serious. It was. He shared with the group that his grandmother's dog was run over and killed. He loved that dog. His sadness was so overwhelming. As he shared, the rest of the room—children and adults alike—received his sadness and provided a space for his fears and confusion.

What Is Important About . . . ?

When children respond to this question, they remind themselves and one another why our spiritual practices matter. We are not simply hearing stories and singing songs. We are God's people gathered, and God is at work in and among us. Children want to do important things. Yes, they enjoy having fun, but they also long for meaning—to be part of the real work of their church.

Again, this question guides us as we go to the prayer wall: What is important about the prayer wall? The children name the things that they want to remember. It is our time with God and God's time with us. The prayer wall is like the heart of our church. It doesn't matter if you know how to spell or write correctly. Draw a picture, because God knows. We can see one another's prayers and pray for them too. We are practicing the spiritual discipline of prayer and stillness. It helps us remember that God always sees us.

There have been times when the prayer wall held the names of children with cancer—some who eventually died and others who got well. The children pray consistently for people without homes or food. Hard, personal family struggles are named on the wall. Often, one child will simply write, "Our enemies." Their prayers are real, and the wall provides a space for their worries and fears—something we all need. It is important and they know it.

Guided by the Ultimate Goal

When we encounter challenges with children, the first question often asked is, "What do we do about this?" Our sense of urgency makes us want to fix things. But we have found that there are no quick fixes if our goal is to welcome children as Jesus did. Jesus was fully present with those who struggled. His posture was one of joining, inviting, listening, and seeing. And so we use strategies, provide experiences, and create structures with the ultimate goal in mind—that the children know they are loved and are able to participate in the community of God's people as we take the journey of faith together.

Bibliography

Bunge, Marcia. *A More Vibrant Theology of Childhood*. Waco, TX: Center for Ethics at Baylor University, 2003.

Kaiser, Barbara, and Judy S. Rasminsky. *Challenging Behavior in Young Children: Understanding Preventing and Responding Effectively*. New York: Pearson, 2017.

Mercer, Joyce Ann. *Welcoming Children: A Practical Theology of Childhood*. St. Louis: Chalice, 2005.

Miller-McLemore, Bonnie J. *Let the Children Come: Reimagining Childhood from a Christian Perspective*. Minneapolis: Fortress, 2019.

SECTION 2

Spiritual Nurture as Family Life

Countless resources are available to families seeking to raise their children to know and follow Jesus, many of which are adapted to highly specific life stages and family or cultural contexts. For children's ministry leaders, this breadth of information means quality resources are often available to pass along to families. But what does it mean to equip families in our congregation beyond passing resources along? How can we encourage the diverse families who walk through the church doors each week? The chapters in this section look at preparing nuclear families to embrace the support that the church offers through the intergenerational network of the church family.

In Chapter Five, "Abbots and Ammas: Formational Family Life toward Common Objects of Love," pastor and father Jared Patrick Boyd writes of how ancient spiritual mothers and fathers can inspire today's parents to live spiritually authentic and vulnerable lives marked by prayer, questions, and faith in such a way that children are invited to watch the parent's growing relationship with God. A home marked by intentional honesty, a pursuit of knowing

God's love more deeply, and attentiveness to the working of the Holy Spirit will shape a family more than any program or curriculum. For the children's ministry leader, Boyd's writing offers a perspective of equipping families to see God's work throughout the everyday, ordinary moments of family life rather than focusing on adding layers of activities.

In Chapter Six, "Listening to Children: Race Lessons from My White Grandchildren," Anthony Peterson, an African American grandfather, shares wisdom from his experiences talking about race with his White and biracial grandchildren. Peterson acknowledges the layers of difficulty in talking about race and racism in our current age and writes from a perspective of love and intentionality as he listens to his grandchildren, challenges their presuppositions, and encourages them in loving and race-conscious conversations. Readers outside of the United States can glean wisdom from how Peterson uses stories, personal experiences, and patience to gently address difficult and often emotionally charged conversations. Ministry leaders in all contexts can read with attentiveness to how to facilitate friendship and learning across generations.

In Chapter Seven, "Neighborly Advice: Effective Preaching and Communication with Postmodern Families," Kevin Johnson uses his research on the work and guiding principles of Fred Rogers to explore how the church can listen to and learn from children as a means for the whole congregation to grow. In many congregations, only people with children under the age of twelve have any regular interaction with the children's ministry. This can leave families with children isolated to only interact with one another, and it costs those without children in their homes the opportunity to interact with and learn from children. By thinking of the church as an integrated, intergenerational "neighborhood" of mutual dependence and transformation, with children as active and vital participants in community life, the whole church family can thrive together.

For the Christian family, growing together in Christ is not a solo or isolated activity; it's a process that takes place by the guidance of the Holy Spirit in the context of the church. Within that spiritual web of support, children are invited to grow, question, explore, and serve. The whole faith community is charged with caring for their nurture and guidance, and their presence has the opportunity to minister beyond the walls of their home or the context of their school or Sunday school classroom. By remembering that family life is best supported within the context of church-family life, ministry leaders can care for and equip each unique family represented in their congregation with a spirit of hospitality and the love of God.

CHAPTER 5

Abbots and Ammas

Formational Family Life toward
Common Objects of Love

Jared Patrick Boyd

In the fourth century, there lived a woman who significantly shaped the lives of her younger brothers. In turn, they would grow up to have roles in shaping all *our* lives. When one of her brothers died, their mother's grief was so great that she—the eldest of ten children—assumed the role of matriarch. She was a mother, in so many ways, to those around her.

She was known as Macrina the Younger in the written works of her brothers Basil of Caesarea and Gregory of Nyssa, who wrote theological works, founded monasteries, served as bishops, and helped form and articulate the creeds that still hold our dispersed traditions together. She herself founded a monastery of women and there became the Amma, which means *mother*. She was the spiritual mother of women, living in prayer and devotion to God alongside them, in front of them, and in some ways, *for* them as much as for herself. Mothers, you know this life of devotion.

Macrina's model of spiritual motherhood took hold. Throughout the region of what is now Turkey, little communities of women, led by a spiritual mother, emerged to do the work of spiritual formation and cultivate a life together, learning to love God while also learning to love one another. And the same thing was happening for the men. They began to live in new ways and with deeper practices of devotion to prayer. Modeling their lives within the *prophetic* tradition, they moved outside the city—sometimes deep into the desert—to practice an unusual way of life. This fourth- and fifth-century migration to the desert birthed Western monasticism.[1] Organized in community by a variety of people, most notably Saint Pachomius, this way of life was further codified when Benedict of Nursia's rule of life became widely adopted. Western monasticism informed the way brothers and sisters lived in community. It sought the right balance between solitude and togetherness, between work and prayer, and between the contemplative life and the active life.

Not always knowing how to live this way of life, the fledgling monastics sought fathers—men who became known as the Desert Fathers—to show them the way. The men called their community leader Abbot, which means *father*. Fathers, you know what it is like for younger people to ask for help and seek to model their lives after yours.

I find it intriguing that at its very beginnings, a tradition steeped in deeply formational practices—one that birthed Jesuits, Franciscans, and Dominicans—began as a community of people being given a father or being given a mother. Mothers and fathers—this is the model of spiritual formation the early church gave to us. When the church birthed communities of formation, they modeled their ways of life after the roles that a father and mother are meant to play in one's life. The people who came to live alongside these spiritual mothers and fathers were formed in up-close encounters with authentic lives on display in front of them.

In the *Sayings of the Desert Fathers*, readers can find a report of holiness and piety.[2] However, we can assume that under the harsh and rigorous conditions of poverty and manual labor, there were moments of impatience, seasons of conflict, periods of weariness for the fathers, and pressures of leadership on the mothers.

---

1 A classic text providing a history of early monasticism is Chitty, *Desert a City*.
2 Ward, *Sayings of the Desert Fathers*.

I'd like to invite you to consider that your role as a father or your role as a mother of young children might simply rest on living an authentic and vulnerable life of prayer, struggle, doubt, and faith and a willingness to share the growing love of God within you. This could very well be the main curriculum for your children's formation. Simply put, the spiritual formation of our children has to do less with what curriculum we use or which developmental strategy we adopt than with our willingness to live a life with God that is vulnerable and on display in front of them.

Our children, with their little watching eyes, observe that life is about learning how to pray, not so much because we tell them, but because every morning when they crawl out of bed, they find you sitting in your red chair by the window with a candle lit, crying out to God for strength to be the father you long to be. And when your child wakes up too early and interrupts that precious time, it is your turn to learn that what first felt like a disruption is actually an encounter with God in the form of a sleepy-eyed three-year-old who crawls into your lap to teach you the contours of the Father's love for you.

Our teenage girls and boys learn that life is not meant to be centered around one's own needs not because we read this to them from a book. They learn it in our authentic display of faith and vulnerability. They learn that life is meant to be lived in service of others simply by watching the way that our lives are oriented toward the love and service of others. They have seen us live this way, and they have been along for the ride in this way consistently, albeit imperfectly, over time.

Our kids know the love, grace, and forgiveness of God primarily through witnessing the ways we receive the grace of God into our own lives and then allow that grace to spill over onto them—restoring them when they lose their way rather than punishing them. They know forgiveness because they practice it around the dinner table in hard conversations, over tears, maybe even after a little bit of raised voices—not because this is what we wish for our family life but because it is the reality of family life.

We create an environment gracious enough to hold raised voices, tears, unmet expectations, deep feelings, and anger. They learn forgiveness because they see mom and dad ask for it in all the little and big ways we fail—thanks to our impatience, hard-heartedness, selfishness, or lack of attentiveness.

In his book *Domestic Monastery*, Catholic theologian Ronald Rolheiser shares a vignette from the life of Carlo Caretto, one of the great contemplatives of the twentieth century. Caretto, who lived more than a dozen years in the desert as a hermit, remarked that his mother, who spent more than thirty years raising children, was more of a contemplative than he was. She seemed to pray just as well, if not better, than he did. And she was more patient. Rolheiser concludes that her life as a mother—filled with interruptions and very little space both physically and mentally—did as much inner formational work for her as solitude in the desert had done for Caretto.[3]

So often we hold up professional contemplatives, religious leaders, pastors, priests, bishops, clergy, elders, and Sunday school teachers—however you name such people within your own tradition—as those most formed in Christ's likeness. We look to these people to equip us with a top-notch spiritual resource within our own homes. But what if the resource was there all along in the everyday stuff of life?

This is, of course, not a dismissal of those resources spiritual mothers and fathers have to offer us. I myself have devoted a portion of my work to this end—to equip the saints with spiritual formation resources—and it's the reason you're reading the words on this page. I simply find it inspiring that those of the tradition that's taught us so much about the formation of our spiritual lives into the way of Jesus—this contemplative tradition of monks and nuns—have, from the very beginning, said to one another, "We need a mother. We need a father."

---

3 Rolheiser, *Domestic Monastery*, 17.

As a father or mother, your impact on the spiritual formation of your child has the potential to be greater than anyone else's. If we can choose to live in vulnerability, with our life in God on display, we can experience the gift of helping our kids learn how to love some of the same things we love about the scriptures, prayer and service, and the way of Jesus.

If you are not a parent, you may wonder if this message is for you. It is. Everything on these pages about mothers and fathers is also applicable to you. The apostle Paul experienced the power and privilege of this role—of serving as a father—when he wrote to the church at Corinth and to his spiritual son Timothy. Even if you had ten thousand tutors into the way of Christ, there are not many fathers; there are not many mothers (1 Cor. 4:15—paraphrase). Mothers and Fathers: we need you. The older I get and the more I reflect on how people change and are formed in partnership with the Holy Spirit, the more convinced I am that what people long for most are fathers and mothers—spiritual fathers and mothers who can show them the way of Christ up close.

I will highlight three simple things our kids need to see in us in order for their lives to lean toward the work of spiritual formation: first, our kids need to watch us grow and change; second, they need to see us yield to the way of Jesus; third, they need to hear our questions more than our answers.

Growing and Changing

Last summer, my family had a fun conversation about the sounds of footsteps in our one-hundred-year-old house. Some of the people in our house are loud walkers. One of my daughters has a particular cadence when she walks downstairs; we always know it's her. Most of the time, it's lovely and endearing, but some of the time, it wakes people up because she is usually the first one awake. This conversation led to a recollection of the way I walked through the house ten years ago, when my body was full of unprocessed grief, pain, frustration, loneliness, impatience, and disappointment. My teenage children can recount to me the cadence of my footsteps when I was impatient with them at ages seven, six, and four.

This was an opportunity to say something significant about the work of God's love in my life over the past ten years. Just a few years ago, hearing my child tell me she remembers feeling anxious at the sound of my footsteps would have sent me into a place of shame. But God is healing me of shame. So instead, I got curious. I brewed her a cup of tea and asked her to tell me more about it. And I got to share more of my story and what I was facing ten years ago—the job I hated, the grief I was working through, and the anxiety I held about whether or not there would be enough money. I shared with her about the way I have been able to process my grief in counseling and with spiritual direction and how I have learned to trust over time—by noticing all the ways that God provides for our family—that there will be enough money.

My daughter remarked that she can see the ways I have changed over the years; she can see more joy and laughter. She experiences me as lighter. "Oh, that's God's healing work in me," I said. "That's just what happens—the Holy Spirit does this strange work of transformation in us as we partner with the presence of God in our lives."

In terms of spiritual needs, our children need to see tangible places of growth in our lives. They need to see we are not hiding from the reality of who we are and who we long to be and how we are trusting God will close the gap for us. There is an often-quoted phrase, I think from the legal tradition, as it relates to reciprocity: *you cannot give away what you don't have*. In order to pass along to the children in our lives the work of God in the world, that work of God has to first do its work *in us*. Only then can we have the authority to say to our confused teenager, lonely middle schooler, or anxious fifth grader, "I know a little something about this." If it's weariness, show your child the way to the one whose burden is light. If their heart is broken, tell them about the one who wipes away tears. If they are afraid, share a story about when your own life felt like a small boat in a giant storm: there was only one person with me in that moment—and he was sound asleep, filled with peace in the bow of the boat (see Matt. 8:23–28).

That we can only give away what we have is one of the greatest gifts of mothering and fathering. It serves as somewhat of a hunger cue; a cue for us to hunger and thirst for only what God can give us. Only God can give us everything we need. Only God can give us what is needed to be a mother or a father. I believe that our children need to watch this process unfold. They need to be able to watch us grow in the process, drawing strength and love from God. And I believe we need to be willing to let them see us in the process.

Yielding to the Way of Jesus

Our children need to see how we yield to the way of Jesus. In Sunday school, most children learn a story about a short man climbing a tree in order to see Jesus pass along the way (see Zacc.; Luke 19:1–10). Certainly, one lesson of this story is the way Jesus sees this man and insists on staying with him, even though no one else in the town liked him. We love this story because the children we tell this story to are often little and can feel unseen.

But what we often leave out of the story we tell our children is how after meeting Jesus, that short man gave half of what he owned to the poor and paid back four times all he had stolen. What we leave out of the story is that an encounter with Jesus compelled this man toward justice, beginning with rectifying the injustice of his own way of life. He yielded to the yoke of the rabbi Jesus, to the way of Jesus. This act of yielding and surrender had a great personal impact: it brought salvation to his entire household.

What would it look like in your family to tell your own version of this story? Around the dinner table, you remark, "I met Jesus in a fresh way this past season, and I'm trying to sort out what God is asking of me, but kids, I think I'm being invited to carve out a little of my free time to be more present to our neighbors."

As you're finishing up a playdate at the park, you say to your kids, "Dad got a promotion, which means his job will give him more money, but we don't really need the money. We're wondering how we, as a family, can live in a way that blesses someone else right now; we'd like to pray together about this."

While driving to soccer practice, you say, "Hey, there is a single mom a few streets over, and we've learned her car has just died. We want to let you know we sense God asking us to give this car to her, or buy her a car, or let her borrow our car."

After losing a job when money is already tight at home, you remind your kids that Jesus taught us to pray, "Give us enough bread for today" (Matt. 6:11—paraphrase).

When your children watch you walk out a posture of *yielding* to Christ in real time, it's akin to a young man going into the desert to weave baskets next to a man he calls Abbot. The young man moves into a cave because the man living in a cave is said to know and live the heart of God. The young man might as well weave baskets next to him to see if he can learn a thing or two.

The young ones in our lives walk next to us, watching for real-life, individual examples of transformation and radical obedience to the way of Jesus. The beauty of Zacchaeus's story is that it wasn't a workshop about divesting wealth and working for justice that produced change in him; rather, it's just a story of a small little man whose life got wrecked by the presence of God one day. Jesus walked by and invited him to live his life in a particular direction—and he said, "Yes."

Being mothers and fathers means we vulnerably display the real-time work of the Spirit in our lives—for the sake of his glory, for the people who live right next to us, and for the benefit of everyone. Being mothers and fathers means allowing our children to see the process of yielding our lives to the way and teachings of Jesus.

Asking More Questions

Every healing moment of Jesus begins with a question. Jesus was so much more interested in asking questions than he was in giving answers, not because the answer wasn't important, but because the way to the answer is through the vulnerability and confrontation a good question can bring.

> "Why are you crying, Mary?" This is the first question Jesus asks after the resurrection.
> "Will you also leave me?" He asks of his disciples when some begin to walk away.
> "What do you want me to do for you?" He says to the blind man Bartimaeus on the side of the road.
> "How long has he been like this?" Jesus asks the father of a sick child.
> "Do you love me, Peter?"
> "Philip, do you believe that the Father is in me?"
> "What are you discussing?" He says to the couple on the way to Emmaus.

Jesus asks questions—good ones at that—because it creates connection and draws people deeper into their own thinking, thus fostering self-awareness. More than almost anything else, Jesus is interested in what people are thinking and feeling. We give our questions to one another as gifts. As poet Denise Levertov says, asking questions is like handing someone an unhatched songbird egg to attend to and keep warm.[4] Children need to hear our questions.

These are the kinds of questions I ask my teenage girls:

> How are your friends?
> What are you most excited about these days?
> Are you worried about anything?
> Do you need anything?
> You seem a little sad; what are you sad about?

---

4 Levertov, *Sands of the Well*, 18.

We ask questions because we believe there are parts of us that have yet to be revealed. When once unknown and hidden things are brought to light, the work of God that can only be done in relation to one another can begin.

Our children need to hear our questions because it helps expand their visions of themselves and of God. They need to know there is more in them than they have the capacity to be aware of. They need to know there are parts of them that have yet to be shared with the world. Our questions also help them trust there are ways we can love them beyond what they know how to ask for. Finally, thanks to our limitations as imperfect vessels, they will learn we will never be able to fully comprehend the depth and breadth of who they are. For that degree of knowing, they'll need an infinite God with unlimited capacity to love.

Embracing Our Roles as Mothers and Fathers

What is the goal of embracing our roles as mothers and fathers? What is the purpose of recognizing we play the most important role in the spiritual formation of our children? Why must fulfillment of these roles include a willingness to live in vulnerable ways before our children? Why must our children get to watch us grow in our own formation journeys? Why must we live in ways that put on display our willingness to yield to the way of Jesus? Why should our children experience the gift of our good questions more than the declaration of our answers? What is all this *for*?

In Oliver O'Donovan's book *Common Objects of Love*,[5] he writes that the basic sense of what it means to love something is to give it your attention, which then reinforces the love. He is drawing on the work of Saint Augustine. If I say I love my wife, it means I give her the focus of my attention (the thoughts, affections, and resources of my being). And as I give her the focus of my attention,

---

5 O'Donovan, *Common Objects of Love*, 15–16.

I am also participating in the act of learning how to love: loving reinforces the act of loving.

If we pay attention to the growth of our lives rather than the perfection of our lives, and if we help our kids pay attention to the ways we are growing in our lives with God and in living in the way of Jesus, our children will grow up not with the heavy yoke of perfection but rather with a love for the process of growing. If we pay attention to the act of yielding—even ever so incrementally—to the work of God's Spirit in our lives, and if we do this in front of our children, we are teaching them to love yielding to God and to give the bulk of their attention to it.

And if we give attention to the goodness of questions and teach our children to hold them, receive them as the gifts they are, and hand them as gifts to others—questions about their faith, about Scripture, about what it means to love justice—then we are teaching our children how to love questions and the invitational space questions create for relationship.

What makes healthy formation possible is the ability to point to the common objects of our love. What things will we give our focus and attention to? Whatever those are for you and whatever those are for me will be the things that our children learn how to love. And this will shape them far beyond anything else.

Bibliography

Chitty, Derwas J. *The Desert a City: An Introduction to the Study of Egyptian and Palestinian Monasticism under the Christian Empire*. Oxford: Blackwell, 1999.

Levertov, Denise. *Sands of the Well*. New York: New Directions, 1998.

O'Donovan, Oliver. *Common Objects of Love: Moral Reflection and the Shaping of Community*. Grand Rapids, MI: Eerdmans, 2002.

Rolheiser, Ronald. *Domestic Monastery*. Brewster, MA: Paraclete, 2019.

Ward, Benedicta. *The Sayings of the Desert Fathers: The Alphabetical Collection*. Kalamazoo, MI: Cistercian, 2004.

CHAPTER 6

Listening to Children

Race Lessons from My White Grandchildren

Anthony Peterson

When my granddaughter June was four years old, she could tell you Marshall wears red and rides in a fire truck.[1] Skye wears pink and flies through the air. Rubble wears yellow. Rocky wears green. Chase wears blue. Tracker wears dark green. She would even tell you that Everest wears teal. June knew that Zuma wears orange. But Zuma is the only *PAW Patrol* pup that she referred to by his color, not just the color of his clothes. Zuma is a chocolate lab, and June says, "He's Black, like Peepaw."

June was communicating her confusion without even knowing it. Just as she was learning her colors, she was learning that skin color is different: when it comes to skin color (or fur color), brown is black. When we teach that confusion, we also teach children that race matters. Even when we pretend that it doesn't.

The way forward to clear up the confusion on skin color and race is to talk about it. But many of us are reluctant to even begin those conversations. Do we start with unconscious bias; microaggressions; institutional, systemic, and historical racism; White privilege; White fragility; or intersectionality?[2] Or are there other

---
1 Whitney, "New Pup."
2 These terms and many related words are defined in ICMA, "Glossary of Terms."

entry points for those who are serious about engaging with race and racism? All those topics are important. They are important to me as an African American encouraging race talk, and they are important for progress on race. But often, those conversations take place among people who are already engaged, already familiar with a particular lexicon or a particular setting.

This chapter is about everyday conversations—those conversations that try to avoid race at all costs. The discussion is intentionally oversimplified. I use *race* in the most popular sense of the word. I refer to race as if it is mainly about skin color, when I know clearly it is not. In the context of this discussion, it might seem that race problems are mainly about people who are called Black and people who are called White, when we know they are much more complicated than that. This is an intentionally simple starting place. In the fifteen years since I first began leading workshops on diversity, I have noticed that many people do not know how to talk about race in their everyday lives. The simplicity offers a starting place and carries through in the practice of telling stories. I begin with my own stories of my grandchildren: June, Charlie, Renay, Anna, and Lynn. But we all have race stories that shape our ideas, beliefs, and attitudes. Tapping into those stories can be a powerful starting point for race talk and antiracism.[3]

My own race talk became more personal when I started paying attention to race conversations I have had with my White grandchildren. My wife (who is White) and I have twelve grandchildren, and ten of them are White. Seven of them have lived in our home with us, so I have had many interesting experiences. In 2014, I shared some of those stories on a TEDx stage. Since then, that talk, "What I Am Learning from My White Grandchildren: Truths

---

3 "Anti-racism: The active process of identifying and challenging racism, by changing systems, organizational structures, policies and practices, and attitudes, to redistribute power in an equitable manner," according to the International City/County Management Association. ICMA, "Glossary of Terms."

about Race," has been viewed almost four million times.[4] Some of those stories are retold here.

As I write, it is the first anniversary of the day the world first heard about the George Floyd murder in 2020. But 2014? When it comes to our racial climate, it seems like a lifetime ago. Among other things, we have had the election of 2016 and then the election of 2020. I thought there was a great need for these race conversations back in 2014. I was trying to encourage those conversations. Now it's a matter of *how* to have those conversations. I think story is one of the best ways there is.

Race-Conscious Talks with My Grandchildren

Charlie was five years old when he asked his Aunt Kimberly the question, "Lyly, am I Black or am I White?" Lyly's response was a little simplistic. She said, "Well, your mommy is White, and your daddy is White, so you are White." Charlie was not satisfied with that answer. He said, "Well when I grow up, I'm gonna be Black." Charlie was not confused by his basic colors. So why would a five-year-old ask such a strange question? He already knew that race mattered. And at five years old, he had already attached value to race. According to Dr. Nathalia Gjersoe of the University of Bath, at as early as three months, infants begin making distinctions based on skin color. In a short time, young children learn more about those distinctions. They begin to put meaning to them. Some studies have shown that three- to five-year-olds begin to sort themselves and those around them into racial categories, even if they do not have the language to express these.[5]

---

4 Peterson, "What I Am Learning," 18:56. The talk was given in 2014 to encourage race conversation years before the discussions of 2020, which were sparked by the killings of Ahmaud Arbery, Breonna Taylor, and George Floyd. Even before those tragedies, millions of viewers were embracing the need for race conversation.
5 Gjersoe, "How Young Children Can Develop Racial Biases."

When June and Charlie's cousin Porter was four years old, he loved the human body. It was more than the typical four-year-old obsession with body parts—there was a time when he started instructing me in anatomy. He told me all about the respiratory system: the parts that the lungs and the diaphragm play. And he told me all about the digestive system: what the esophagus, the stomach, and the large and small intestines do. And he told me that the brain is the control center for the entire body. I was getting a little bored with the lecture, so I stopped him and said, "Porter, what color is my skin?" Without even looking at me, he said, "It's black." Then I asked him, "What color is your skin?" There was a long pause. And then he said, "Gray?" Gray.

If we pay attention, we can catch our children midindoctrination. Porter had figured out that my brown skin is supposed to be called *Black*, but he had not yet been schooled in what to call the color of his own skin. And he had not been told why we call this brown *Black* and that pinkish color *White*. This is obvious to us. Yet from a very early age, when our children are just learning their colors, they pick up that skin color is different from all other kinds of color, and we don't tell them why.

In her book *Raising White Kids: Bringing Up Children in a Racially Unjust America*, Dr. Jennifer Harvey encourages parents of White children to take advantage of these moments to promote what she calls "race consciousness." For her, race-conscious parenting involves "noticing and naming race early and often."[6]

Seven-year-old Anna spotted Dr. Harvey's book when I was preparing for a workshop. She giggled, "Peepaw, people sometimes have funny names for books. This book is called *Raising White Kids*. That's funny!" I tried practicing what Dr. Harvey suggested. "Do you know why that book was written?" I asked. Anna shrugged. "Well," I tried to explain, "because a lot of White people think of themselves as normal and of everyone else as different. They don't think about being White. I know you think

---

6 Harvey, *Raising White Kids*, 42.

about it because you have a Black grandfather, and we talk about being Black and White. Plus you go to a school where there are a lot of brown people and only a few White kids. So you can see yourself as normal and as different. And you can see your friends as normal and as different. But a lot of White people can only see themselves as normal and everyone else as different. That's why there's this book."

Perhaps the most controversial story I tell from my TEDx talk is one involving Renay. It is about the night in 2014 that June was born. June's siblings—then ten-year-old Charlie, six-year-old Renay, and three-year-old Anna—were staying the night with me while their parents and grandmother went to the hospital for the birth. The next morning, I got up and viewed pictures of the baby on my tablet. Renay woke up and joined me, but then she wanted to look up pictures from the Disney animated movie *Frozen*. She stumbled upon an image of her favorite character, Elsa. *This* Elsa had a dark brown face. Renay was not having it: "What?! That's not Elsa! She's Black! It's ugly!" What would you say? What would you do? She was sitting there practically in my lap. I sat there . . . frozen. I could ignore it. I could "Let it go! Let it go!" I could get angry and say, "Don't say that about Black people!" But I love our Renay, and I decided that I wanted to hear more. "So you think Black skin is ugly?" I asked. Still enraged, she said quickly, "Yes." And then just as quickly, she said, "Well not *your* skin. But Elsa is not supposed to be Black." What sounded like a racist sentiment—"White skin is beautiful, Black skin is ugly"—was nothing of the sort. Not only was the particular artistic rendering of Black Elsa not well done, but also, I had to venture into the discomfort to find out what she really meant: "I have seen this movie dozens of times, and Elsa has White skin and a long, blonde side-braid. That's how I know she's Elsa. Unless it's coronation, when she wears her hair up." Perhaps the most important lesson Renay taught in that moment was that our ethnicities are essential to our identities, even for animation characters. What followed was a truthful and loving race conversation that involved Renay, her ten-year-old brother, and her three-year-old sister—three White children and their Black grandfather.

Recent studies show where children get their racial messages. One group of six researchers aggregated their disparate ethnographic work to analyze children and race.[7] Several of them are part of the Motherscholar Project, researchers who intentionally bring their mothering into their studies.[8] Some of them recorded observations of their own children. I have not found a corresponding Grandfatherscholar Project, but I use some of that same methodology. Through analyzing their aggregated work, these six researchers generated propositions about how children learn race. The first proposition is, "Racial identity and racial (dys)consciousness are learned over time and across multiple spaces, therefore... racial literacy requires reflection or memory work over both time and space."[9]

Race Myths and Children

Researchers Erin Winkler and Maggie Hagerman provide insight into children's race understanding by dispelling myths. The first myth is that race socialization is "all about what parents say."[10] Winkler and Hagerman insist that actions speak louder than words. Children model what they see. They also model what they hear or do not hear. When race is silenced in their worlds, they learn racial silence. Hagerman, author of *White Kids: Growing Up with Privilege in a Racially Divided America*, emphasizes the messages parents send in choices about neighborhoods, schools, churches, and friendships. Parents do a lot to create their child's racial contexts, and children derive racial meaning from parental decisions.

---

7 Nash et al., "Critical Racial Literacy," 256–73.
8 See the website for the Motherscholar Project: http://motherscholar.org/.
9 Nash et al., "Critical Racial Literacy," 256–73.
10 Hagerman and Winkler, "Kids Learn about Race."

The second myth is that "families control what their children learn."[11] These researchers remind us that children, like all of us in the United States, live in a racialized society. Children are actively navigating racial messages from media (books, cartoons, music, movies, games, social media), peers, schools, appointments, stores, travel, neighborhoods, regions, and various activities. They are trying to figure out the "rules" of racial behavior.

Winkler and Hagerman describe a third myth: "Race comprehension is something that just happens to kids."[12] In truth, children navigate messages from a variety of sources. They are actively, not passively, learning race. And the learning is comprehensive. But children do not always interpret messages the way adults intend.

In 2014, Ali Michael and Eleonora Bartoli described what they found in a study of White parents and their White adolescent children. They interviewed the parents and children both separately and together.[13] They found that the parents reported teaching their children, "Do not be racist. Do not talk about race. Do not use the word 'black.' And do not notice racial differences." They wanted to teach their children that everyone is the same and that racism is bad. And they defined racism as "overt, violent, and, for the most part, obsolete."

But the messages the children reported were conflicting and incomplete. They described learning from their parents, "Everyone is the same. Race is superfluous. And hard work alone determines where you get in life." They also reported views they had learned about certain racial groups, including the beliefs that Black people are poor, Black people are lazy, Black neighborhoods are dangerous, and Black people are physically stronger than White people. These messages reveal that race does matter. Incidents like the murders of George Floyd, Breonna Taylor, and Ahmaud Arbery gain global attention, and our children, who have been taught to be color-blind, are left blindsided. But these incidents give us the

11 Hagerman and Winkler.
12 Hagerman and Winkler.
13 Michael and Bartoli, "What White Children Need to Know."

opportunity to tell the truth to children. When we talk openly with children about race, we don't burden them. We free them. We allow them to embrace their own identities as well as the identity of each person they encounter. We handicap our children when we operate in racial silence, and we rob them of essential parts of their identities. I suspect that this is especially the case for White or "gray" children like June, Charlie, Porter, Anna, and Renay.

Race Conversations with Children and a Look at Our Own Lives

One of my favorite holiday traditions is to read aloud holiday short stories. One year we gathered Renay, who was ten; Porter, who was seven; Anna, who was six; Lynn, who was five; and June, who was three. I was reading the story "Maggie's Gift" from Katherine Paterson's holiday collection *Angels and Other Strangers*.[14] The story features Mr. McGee, a lonely and cranky older widower, who agrees to take in an eight-year-old girl and her five-year-old brother, who must vacate their children's home on Christmas Eve. As he is on the phone discussing arrangements with Miss Trainor from the children's home, Mr. McGee asks, "By the way, what color are [the children]?"

"White," she says. "Does it matter?"

"Yes," he says. "I have to know what color to get the doll."

I have read the story aloud on many occasions, but this time, this passage struck me, so I paused the reading. In the back of my mind was *Raising White Kids* by Dr. Harvey. I paused the reading to explain to my White grandchildren, "When this story was written, most people believed that White people should have only White baby dolls, and Black people or brown people should have Black or brown dolls." I was secretly amused that I needed to explain this particular distinction between now and then. Renay picked up the narrative: "Yeah, in those days Black people and White

---

14 Paterson, "Maggie's Gift," 40–63.

people weren't allowed to be together. Like if you were White and you wanted to marry someone who was Black, you couldn't." She walked us through all the forbidden racial marriage scenarios she could think of. Then she said, "But Martin Luther King came, and he changed all that."

Porter shouted, "Oh, oh, I know him!" Renay continued, "Martin Luther King said that you can marry whoever you want. The color doesn't matter. It's like chocolate ice cream and vanilla. You can mix them together, and then you have caramel!" This was not the time to demonstrate how bad that analogy was; her loving and lovely sentiment came through.

Anna chimed in, "My baby doll is brown." "I know," I said, "and I remember what you named her." I know because the day she brought the baby doll home from the dollar store, she introduced us. She said, "Peepaw, this is my baby, and she's like you. I named her 'Moana.' I'll call her 'my baby,' but you call her 'Moana.' She's like you. I was gonna get the White one, but it was too much." I pushed a little: "Was the White one the same kind of doll?" "Yeah," she said, "but this one was almost free. The White one was ten dollars." Once again, I chose not to fully engage our first grader in a discussion of why the brown doll was "almost free." Our race-conscious conversations do not have to be inclusive of every possible concern; we can circle back at another time. And if we are paying attention, new opportunities will present themselves.

Children are not the only ones who need these conversations. We all do. In fact, one reason adults shy away from discussing race and find the discussions so difficult is that we are not in touch with our own race stories. In June 2020, I was contacted on social media by a couple. They had met in college. Emily reached out to me to see if I would be willing to talk with her boyfriend, Daniel. She described herself as a White woman who grew up almost exclusively among White people. She is an athlete who sometimes played with or against women of color, but her schools, her church, and her associations were with almost all White people.

Daniel immigrated with his family from Ghana, West Africa, when he was eleven. When I talked to him, he had lived another eleven years in the United States. Back home, race was never an issue because everyone around him was Black and Ghanaian. Neither one of them had the context for understanding race in the United States. They both told me that when incidents like police killings of African Americans reach national attention, they look for resources to understand them. In fact, they had gotten into the habit of watching my 2014 TEDx talk whenever these incidents occur. (Daniel says he has watched the talk twenty to thirty times. Think about why.) But the events of summer 2020 left them both confused and lost. Watching that talk wasn't sufficient, so they took a chance on contacting me. To process their reactions, they had to get in touch with their own racial backgrounds, their own histories of race.

Like Daniel and Emily, we can begin by looking at our own lives. We can also listen to one another's questions. Listening to one another's questions can generate stories, which can spark productive dialogue. And once we begin to see the place of race in our own lives, we can better hear how it impacts the children we love.

Race Questions for Reflection and Discussion

We all have race stories. We can begin to discover and recall our stories by considering these questions. After personal reflection, these questions also provide a valuable starting place for group conversation:

1. On a scale of 1 to 10, how comfortable are you discussing race issues with those racially similar to you? Why?
2. On a scale of 1 to 10, how comfortable are you discussing race issues with those racially different from you? Why?
3. Describe your own history with race. Identify your earliest race-related memories. What are your most profound race-related experiences?

4. What do you know about your family's racial history?
5. What positive race conversations have you had?
6. What difficult race conversations have you had?
7. What race conversations have you had with children?
8. In what settings do you hope to begin further conversations about race?
9. Should race and ethnicity issues be parts of spiritual formation in your church settings? Why or why not?
10. How have you addressed—or how might you address—issues of race and ethnicity (for example, ethnicity in the Bible, historical racism, racially segregated congregations and denominations) in your church settings?

Bibliography

Embrace Race. "Let's Raise a Generation of Children Who Are Thoughtful, Informed, and Brave about Race." Last modified 2021. http://www.embracerace.org.

Gjersoe, Nathalia. "How Young Children Can Develop Racial Biases." Conversation. Last modified March 22, 2018. https://www.iol.co.za/lifestyle/family/parenting/how-young-children-can-develop-racial-biases-13957423.

Hagerman, Margaret A. *White Kids: Growing Up with Privilege in a Racially Divided America*. New York: New York University Press, 2018.

Hagerman, Margaret, and Erin Winkler. "How Kids Learn about Race." Embrace Race. Last modified February 2021. https://www.embracerace.org/resources/how-children-learn-about-race.

Harvey, Jennifer. *Raising White Kids: Bringing Up Children in a Racially Unjust America*. Nashville: Abingdon, 2018.

ICMA. "Glossary of Terms: Race, Equity and Social Justice." Accessed April 10, 2022. https://icma.org/glossary-terms-race-equity-and-social-justice#I.

Kendi, Ibram X. *Antiracist Baby*. New York: Kokila, 2020.

———. *How to Be an Antiracist*. New York: One World, 2019.

Marsh, Jason, Rodolfo Mendoza-Denton, and Jeremy Adam Smith, eds. *Are We Born Racist? New Insights from Neuroscience and Positive Psychology*. Boston: Beacon, 2010.

Memory, Jelani. *A Kids Book about Racism*. Portland, OR: A Kids Book About, 2019.

Michael, Ali, and Eleonora Bartoli. "What White Children Need to Know about Race." National Association of Independent Schools, Summer 2014. https://www.nais.org/magazine/independent-school/summer-2014/what-white-children-need-to-know-about-race/.

Nash, Kindel, Joy Howard, Erin Miller, Gloria Boutte, George Johnson, and Lisa Reid. "Critical Racial Literacy in Homes, Schools, and Communities: Propositions for Early Childhood Contexts." *Contemporary Issues in Early Childhood* 19, no. 3 (September 2018): 256–73. https://doi.org/10.1177/1463949117717293.

Paterson, Katherine. "Maggie's Gift." In *Angels and Other Strangers*, 40–63. New York: Thomas Y. Crowell, 1979.

Peterson, Anthony. "What I Am Learning from My White Grandchildren: Truths about Race." Filmed October 2014 in Antioch, TN. TEDx video, 18:56. https://youtu.be/u5GCetbP7Fg.

Reynolds, Jason, and Ibram X. Kendi. *Stamped: Racism, Antiracism, and You*. New York: Little, Brown, 2020.

Russell, Nicol. "Why & How to Talk to Young Kids about Race." Embrace Race. Accessed November 7, 2021. https://www.embracerace.org/resources/why-how-to-talk-to-young-kids-about-race.

Tisby, Jemar. *The Color of Compromise: The Truth about the American Church's Complicity in Racism*. Grand Rapids, MI: Zondervan, 2019.

Wallis, Jim. *America's Original Sin: Racism, White Privilege, and the Bridge to a New America*. Ada, MI: Brazos, 2016.

Whitney, Jamie, dir. *PAW Patrol*. Season 2, episode 6, "The New Pup." Aired October 18, 2014, on Nick Jr. http://www.nickjr.com/paw-patrol/.

CHAPTER 7

Neighborly Advice

Effective Preaching and
Communication with
Postmodern Families

Kevin Johnson

The scene on the television screen is an aerial model of a neighborhood. We hear the first few notes of music and then see a flashing yellow caution light, reminding us to "slow down." The camera pans slowly over the neighborhood and goes from outside to inside the house. With great anticipation, we settle in to watch as the door opens and out walks Mister Rogers. As he enters, he sings (and we sing along), "It's a beautiful day in the neighborhood; won't you be my neighbor?" We are quietly mesmerized as we feel the warm feelings of childhood. He appears to speak directly to each of us through the television. How does Mister Rogers communicate so effectively? More significantly, how can church leaders learn the communication skills used on a children's television program and apply them to our approach to ministry?

Fred Rogers, affectionately referred to as "Mister Rogers," was a TV host, author, and ordained Presbyterian minister. Rogers suggested that we "listen to the children, learn about them, learn from them. Think of the children first."[1] This is a foundational statement to implementing an approach to preaching and communicating

---

1 Rogers, *World according to Mister Rogers*, 168.

with children and families in today's church society. Connecting children to the life of the church allows us to claim ownership and grow children in the faith. To accomplish this, we must learn how to apply a *Mister Rogers' Neighborhood* approach of communication to today's families by understanding and using Rogers's theological framework—rooted in love for our neighbors—and calling into action diverse intergenerational faith communities while thinking of the children first.

"Why?"

Children ask numerous questions and wonder *why* throughout each day. Church leaders also have many *why* questions that they wonder about. Leaders may wonder why so many families with children are leaving the mainline denominations' worship services. One conclusion is ineffective communication.

The implementation of Rogers's approach to communication allows the church to use a "famous" personality easily recognized by a secular audience. Insights gained from studying Rogers's approach to his television program, his communication techniques, and his reframing of keywords and phrases to enable better understanding provide structure to a new approach to communication.

To respond to the question of *why* families are leaving, the church has tried many ways to connect. We know from experience that the use of impersonal media, stock images, and mass mailings do not reach the unchurched. Those methods are sterile and disconnected. Another hindrance to effective communication is the ineffective use of language. Speaking about duty, obligation, and commitment brings negative responses from the hearers, which creates a disconnect.

"It's You I Like"

Rogers understood that effective communication begins with relationships. Relationships are built by planting seeds that begin the discipleship process. That process includes children. In "A Seminar with Fred Rogers," there was a question-and-answer session between Rogers and the students at Perkins School of Theology. Rogers says, "Long ago I came to feel that relationship is the most important thing in anybody's life, be it relationship with the Lord, or with each other. And so, all of what we do is built on a relationship with the child at home."[2]

Rogers placed priority on relationships, and he used communication to nurture relationships with the people he met. He describes the day that changed his understanding of communication this way:

> One summer, midway through Seminary, I was on a weekend vacation in a little town in New England. I decided on Sunday to go hear a visiting preacher in the little town's chapel. I heard the worst sermon I could have ever imagined. I sat in the pew thinking, "He's going against every rule they're teaching us about preaching. What a waste of time!" That's what I thought until the very end of the sermon when I happened to see the person beside me with tears in her eyes whispering, "He said exactly what I needed to hear." It was then that I knew something very important had happened in that service. The woman beside me had come in need. Somehow the words of that poorly crafted sermon had been translated into a message that spoke to her heart. On the other hand, I had come in judgment, and I heard nothing but the faults.
>
> It was a long time before I realized it, but that sermon's effect on the person beside me turned out to be one of the great lessons of my life. Thanks to that preacher and listener-in-need,

---

2 Howe, "Seminar with Fred Rogers," 1.

I now know that the space between a person doing his or her best to deliver a message of good news and the needy listener is holy ground.[3]

Through the medium of television, Rogers modeled the kind of relationships that provide support, trust, and respect.

Discipleship Creates Ownership

"The church is not a building, the church is not a steeple, the church is not a resting place, the church is a people."[4] These words from the hymn "We Are the Church" remind us that people are the church—people, lovingly called together by God's grace in Jesus Christ, playing, praying, working, worshiping, loving, laughing, struggling, and serving.

To develop better communication, we must first "foster authentic, organic, and consistent relationships with our neighbors."[5] Real relationships create space and natural opportunities to introduce the beginnings of discipleship. Building them is using Jesus as an example to see all the people who live around our churches. It involves nurturing relationships with neighbors, both old and young, who live around our churches, which addresses social and justice issues.

The intentionality of discipleship is not about filling pews, raising budgets, or even keeping the church alive. Rather, disciple making occurs when congregations can shepherd those both in and outside the church into a fuller and more mature understanding of the Christian faith.

Leaders are encouraged to see every task of the church through the lens of disciple making. It is thus that we begin to understand the role of communication differently. This communication

---

3 Rogers, *World according to Mister Rogers*, 126–28.
4 Avery and Marsh, "We Are the Church."
5 SeeAllThePeople, "What Is #SeeAllThePeople?"

creates ownership for both adults and children. Focusing on discipleship can improve a church's culture.

A Mister Rogers Theological Framework

Rogers spent more than thirty years being a neighbor to millions of children. His communication approach connected to the child in each of us. His wife, reflecting on the influence of Fred's mentor, Dr. Margaret McFarland, said, "Margaret once said that Fred was more in touch with his own childhood than anyone she knew."[6] By using Rogers's concepts and a foundation of love, peace, and justice, we can develop a theological framework for effective communication.

Rogers's theology speaks of the gentleness of God. Rogers wrote, "The BIG thing about God is God's faithfulness: not giving up on those whom God has made covenant."[7] God does much more than not give up on us; God accepts and appreciates us as we are. As adults, do we still believe God is that faithful and accepting? Rogers reminds us that most children have not grown out of that belief.

A *Mister Rogers' Neighborhood* theology is rooted in love and being love to others. *Being love* is enacting divine love; it is God's desire that we accept all people just as they are. Rogers put it this way: "Having someone we loved get mad at us did not mean that person had stopped loving us; we had their unconditional love, and that meant we would have their forgiveness, too."[8]

To grow unconditional love and forgiveness, we must help others grow in love, even as we accept them just the way they are. Love is an action, and it requires growth and change internally, which lead to action externally. Rogers explained, "We need to help people to discover the true meaning of love. Love is generally confused with dependence. Those of us who have grown in true

---

6 Today Show, "World according to Mr. Rogers."
7 Long, "Mister Rogers in Heaven."
8 Rogers, *World according to Mister Rogers*, 61.

love know that we can love only in proportion to our capacity for independence."⁹

Caregivers deeply love their children but have discovered they are not effectively equipped to know how to develop the deep connection with them to raise disciples. The understanding of connection is more than love and affection. "Love isn't a state of perfect caring. It is an active noun like struggle. To love someone is to strive to accept that person exactly the way he or she is, right here and now,"¹⁰ explains Rogers. This nurturing of relationship is a vital teaching and modeling component for caregivers.

Rogers did not base his approach on success or achievement. He demonstrated and instilled *shalom* in his viewers. Peace was his gift to us. He reminds viewers to seek peace by slowing down, signaled by a flashing yellow caution light. His affect, songs, and entire demeanor allow viewers to wonder how they might seek and pursue peace. Mister Rogers offers suggestions: empathize with others' feelings; attack the problem, not the person; cooperate as much as possible; and emphasize reconciliation.

According to Rogers's theology, three attitudes help create a state of well-being: self-acceptance, positive hope for the world, and confidence in the future. These elements are discerned by the caregiver and are effective when applied to and modeled in their connections with children. Rogers instills in his viewers that positive state of well-being. "I like you just the way you are," he would remind us, pointing us toward that loving, appreciating God.

The framework then calls one to active love, which produces service and results in acts of justice. The idea of being an inclusive church, one that looks to all people for leadership and ministry and looks at Christian character, includes this framework of active love, service, and justice.

Rogers's theological framework may best be discovered through understanding his ordination:

---

9 Rogers, 89.
10 Rogers cited in Godlewski, "Mr. Rogers Quotes."

When I was ordained, it was for a special ministry, that of serving children and families through television. I consider that what I do through *Mister Rogers' Neighborhood* is my ministry. A ministry doesn't have to be only through a church, or even through an ordination. And I think we all can minister to others in this world by being compassionate and caring. I hope you will feel good enough about yourselves that you will find your own unique ways to do that. You don't ever have to do anything sensational for people to love you. When I say, "It's you I like," I'm talking about that part of you that knows that life is far more than anything you can ever see or hear or touch . . . that deep part of you that allows you to stand for those things without which humankind cannot survive: love that conquers hate, peace that rises triumphant over war, and justice that proves more powerful than greed.[11]

Be Quick to Listen

Good communication involves listening. Becoming an active listener allows us to love our neighbors and be more attentive to others' needs.[12] Attentive love leads to actions of love, which are lived out in the stories of our neighbors.

Loving with action involves listening. Rogers says, "Listening is where love begins: listening to ourselves and then to our neighbor."[13] He adds, "Listening is a very active awareness of the coming together of at least two lives. Listening, as far as I'm concerned, is certainly a prerequisite of love. One of the most essential ways of saying 'I love you' is being a receptive listener."[14]

Being a receptive listener places us in another's shoes. As you prepare, read the Scripture text through the lens of a child at least once. What translations are best heard by a child? What

11 Rogers, *World according to Mister Rogers*, 188–89.
12 Ward, *Speaking from the Heart*, 59.
13 Rogers, *You Are Special*, 115.
14 Rogers, 23.

translations are better heard than read? Remember, effective communication is connecting both verbally and nonverbally.

Are there practices, beliefs, and so on that need better explanation for the child to understand? Take some time to explain Christian symbols and rituals so all can understand. Don't assume everyone can identify them. Solid relationships are formed when you tell your audience that you listen to and love them.

Rogers and Communication

There are three significant areas of focus within Rogers's approach to communication: language, human development, and technology. These areas of focus allow conversations to address the faith-formation needs of children that have been suggested by both caregivers and children.

The book *On Becoming Neighbors* discusses Rogers's ability to create a "heightened parasocial dynamic between himself and his viewer as a result of his keen understanding of embodied communication (e.g., speech tone, sustained eye contact, and relaxed but controlled body movement), opportunities for which television uniquely affords."[15]

On Becoming Neighbors divides space into distinct zones of nonverbal communication depending on how far the speaker stands in relation to the audience. Rogers occupies both personal and social space, according to the author. He does not get close enough to engage in intimate space, nor does he enter a space that preachers typically find themselves in—public space.

The spatial zones in *On Becoming Neighbors* are defined as follows:

1. Intimate space: The most personal zone of communication, where people are zero to one and one-half feet apart.

---

15 Klaren, *On Becoming Neighbors*, 13.

2. Personal space: Conversations among family and friends. People are one and one-half to four feet apart.
3. Social space: Group interactions taking place with people four to twelve feet apart.
4. Public space: The speaker is at least twelve feet away from the audience. This is where most preachers find themselves.

A television set is symbolically tied to social space, as it is found in the home. A computer used for a video call might be considered a contemporary version of a television found in households across this country when Rogers's program began.

Rogers understood the opportunities of using technology, looking directly into the camera and imagining he was talking to one person, heart to heart, in the most personal terms he could muster. Never far from his mind was that deep conviction that *the space between the television set and the viewer is holy ground.*

Language consists of the terms and definitions regularly used in one's setting. Rogers had a unique approach to communication when talking to children and adults in the same room (or in front of the same television, as the case may be). Communication with children that engages only the children is not effective. Rogers states, "Television is an exceedingly personal medium. I do feel that what we see and hear on a screen is part of who we become."[16]

Reflecting on Rogers's messages in his television program, we can learn a lot about how he communicated. New York University professor Jacqueline F. Strayer notes that Rogers used five key elements in communicating: simplicity, focus, precision, tone, and cadence.[17]

Rogers's approach to communication has become known as a "deep and simple" approach. Emerging from this philosophy of going deeper yet using child-friendly language, Rogers initiated a developmental theory now titled simple interactions.

16 *Won't You Be My Neighbor?*
17 Stayer, "Mr. Rogers."

Simple interactions theory reaffirms the importance of human interactions in children's lives. It bases its research on the understanding that the active ingredient in a child's growth is the developmental relationship between the child and another human being. The essence of such relationships is the day-to-day interactions between children and the adults who teach and care for them. Employing the deep and simple approach and using a "simple interactions tool,"[18] caregivers are more appropriately engaged. This helps build a "community of practice" within the church.

In the book *Mister Rogers Talks with Parents*,[19] six necessities of learning are introduced: a sense of self-worth, a sense of trust, curiosity, the capacity to look and listen carefully, the capacity to play, and a time for solitude. The incorporation of these elements will challenge us to communicate with our audience in ways that are deep yet simple.

When communicating, are there certain words that a child needs to know to understand the message? Do you find yourself stuck defining certain words or terms from the text? Do they mean something else in a different space of life? Remember, there are words used in church that we don't use elsewhere in life.

What can we learn from Rogers to communicate more convincingly to an intergenerational audience? Deborah Tannen, a linguistics professor at Georgetown University, says, "Everything that is said must be said in a certain way—in a certain tone of voice, at a certain rate of speed, and with a certain degree of loudness. Whereas often we consciously consider what to say before speaking, we rarely think about how to say it."[20]

Four dimensions that can be analyzed by tone include humor, formality, respectfulness, and enthusiasm. When viewing *Mister Rogers' Neighborhood*, one notices all four elements incorporated into every episode. It is helpful to remember that children hear not

18 Simple Interactions, "Simple Interactions Tool."
19 Rogers and Head, *Mister Rogers Talks with Parents*.
20 Tannen, "Power of Talk."

only words but also voices. When crafting a message to effectively connect to the intergenerational audience, be diligent with the incorporation of all four dimensions.

Many may feel that *Mister Rogers' Neighborhood* was not humorous; however, Rogers did use humor in an appropriate manner. Humor shows your real self and humanness. Remember when Mister Rogers showed his humanness by assembling a tent? When communicating, do you appear to be having fun? Are you expressing enthusiasm? Children identify with the energy and enthusiasm that come through communication.

Merriam-Webster Dictionary defines *cadence* as threefold: "(1) a regular beat or rhythm, (2) the way a person's voice changes by gently rising and falling while he or she is speaking, and (3) an ending part of a piece of music."[21] Rogers is most notably known for the inflection of his voice, but it was his formal education in composing music that found its way into his method of communication. Possessing the ability to incorporate music into communication with an audience allowed Rogers to present his message in a variety of ways. Rogers reminds us to avoid slipping into the "preacher's voice." Being authentic expresses vulnerability and develops trust with the hearers.

When we view *Mister Rogers' Neighborhood*, we are witnessing a conversation between Rogers and the audience, which prompts question-and-answer responses. Technology at that time kept Rogers from getting an aural response, but researchers discovered that children still talked to their television sets. The hearers' responses may be internal, but those responses need recognition.

---

21 *Merriam-Webster*, s.v. "cadence," accessed February 2, 2022, https://www.merriam-webster.com/.

Developmental Understanding and Multiple Intelligence / Multisensory Incorporation

It is most effective for children to experience Bible stories at several stages of their faith journey because their understanding of concepts continues to evolve as they grow. In the early years, share the Bible in story form. As children grow, effective communication allows the meanings of the stories to unfold through conversation and daily living. Children develop in similar ways, according to individual stages of cognitive, social-emotional, physical, and spiritual development; learning styles; and ability levels.

Rogers met regularly with Dr. Margaret McFarland throughout the creation of the television program. Much of her work focused on the meaning of the interactions between caregivers and children. This understanding of human development is vital when communicating to intergenerational audiences. Effective understanding of developmental growth reflects areas of human development, including faith, physical, brain, mental and intellectual, interpersonal, values and ethics, sexuality, family, needs of age, gifts to share, vocation, and expectations of the church.[22]

Thinking and communication involve processing in more than one way. There is weakness in communicating from only our favored ways of thinking. It becomes exclusive to self. When that happens, we are preaching to ourselves, and no one else will hear the message. The result is that we cannot fully connect with a congregation who thinks in different ways from our own.

Through his formal education and weekly meetings with McFarland, Rogers developed an understanding of communication through one's life that is attributed to Howard Gardner's multiple intelligence learning model.[23] The theory of multiple intelligences helps break down barriers between hearers and

---

22 Discipleship Ministries, "Development through the Life Span."
23 Armstrong, *Multiple Intelligences in the Classroom*.

speakers. A good sermon is not just what the preacher says but what the congregation hears, and that depends on how listeners receive, think, understand, and respond. The congregation is a partner in the message. Partnering suggests mutuality between the hearer and the preacher.

This partnership then expands our cognitive repertoire to fully engage congregations more effectively. Implementing the multiple intelligences model will allow for the engagement of the whole person and whole congregation. Barriers to meaning include language, images, anxieties, and defensiveness.

The understanding of how people learn and hear a message differently lies within each person's separate intelligences. There are eight separate learning styles that are depicted on the chart below.[24] Each individual can use all eight, and everyone needs a blend of all of them to be effective.

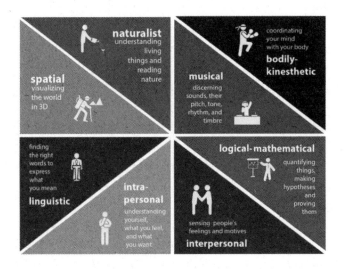

1. Linguistic intelligence (word smart): The use of learning languages—that is, written and spoken. Some people are excellent with the written word but may struggle with oral communication.

24 Marenus, "Gardner's Theory."

2. Intrapersonal intelligence (self-smart): The capacity to understand oneself, including desires and fears, and the capacity to use this understanding effectively in regulating one's life. Characteristics include working alone or praying quietly.
3. Interpersonal intelligence (people smart): The capacity to understand the intentions, motivations, and desires of other people and to work effectively with others.
4. Logical-mathematical intelligence (logic smart): The ability to analyze problems logically, carry out mathematical operations, or investigate issues scientifically.
5. Musical intelligence (music smart): Having skill in performance or composition and an appreciation of musical patterns.
6. Bodily kinesthetic intelligence (body smart): The use of one's whole body or parts of one's body to solve problems. This works well in teaching or reading Scripture and can bring Bible passages to life.
7. Naturalist intelligence (nature smart): The recognition and classification of numerous species—flora and fauna—in one's environment.
8. Spatial intelligence (picture smart): The recognition and manipulation of patterns in wide spaces (pilots) and/or patterns in more confined areas (sculptors, surgeons, chess players, architects). How do you feel hearing a sermon that is delivered behind the pulpit versus somewhere else? How do newcomers experience worship?

Rogers incorporated multisensory teachings and learnings into every episode. Music supports visual learning. Remember the songs that began and ended each episode? Even as he slowly sprinkled fish food over the tank, music was softly playing in the background. The use of visual aids should do just that—aid the message. The use of props (Rogers used puppets), screens, and nonverbal cues will help pinpoint the meaning of the message without challenging the hearer to find deeper meaning with an object lesson.

If we implement this information and understanding, children (and all ages) will benefit from fully hearing the sermon or message we are trying to communicate. The application of these techniques offered by Rogers's approach could include the following:

- creating sermons that engage adult ways of thinking
- allowing space for different ways of biblical interpretation
- bringing equality for the entire community of God—a community where children are treated with equality
- giving witness that God is concerned for the entirety of our lives, including childhood and adolescence
- fostering a community of wonder that will lead to understanding who God is and who God made us to be

Learn to Speak "Freddish"

A final resource that encourages more effective communication is the 1977 pamphlet produced by Rogers and *Mister Rogers' Neighborhood*'s television script writers. This pamphlet stemmed from the tactic that came to be known as "Freddish" language. The pamphlet offers suggestions for effectively communicating with children.[25]

Tell Me a Story

Rogers used television to communicate his message to an audience. Today, videoconferencing allows communication to look very different. We have the capability to meet with others without geographic constraints. The possibilities for more effective communication when both sides can speak in real time are tremendous.

To best create this meaningful dialogue, it is recommended to use the power of story. Stories provide opportunities to invite children into the message. Stories create accessibility while allowing

---

25 King, "Mister Rogers."

for the interpretation of the message from unique perspectives. Stories unite the teller and the listener in a shared experience. Stories can change both thoughts and relationships. Stories provoke wonder. Stories invite participatory hearers, not casual observers. Use open-ended questions that allow children to build on what they have heard and wonder alongside the family.

Even more powerful is the opportunity to invite others to share their stories. This creates a culture of discipleship, as people begin to share their faith with others. This may occur during worship or around familial conversation.

Rogers reminds communicators to address the struggles of life. Regardless of age, we all struggle. Topics such as divorce or death shouldn't be avoided. Elementary-age children desire a response to social justice. They possess a "go-and-do" attitude and want to see change. How does your communication give real-life applications, invoke a response (internal or external), and provoke a "go-and-do" attitude for the entire family?

Gifts to Empower

Finally, it is important for children to feel empowered to make their own choices in faith development. This empowerment allows their relationships with God to be for themselves—not for the sake of caregivers or the church.

If the church empowers children, their commitment to the institution may be lifelong. The theological frameworks of parents (shaped by their own childhoods) must also be taken into consideration. This will challenge ministry leaders in equipping and acknowledging discipleship for families. Leaders must understand that adults bring their memories of religious institutions—positive and negative—to their understandings of discipleship and effective parenting.

Effective communication must create a culture of listening and encouragement. This includes modeling how to learn from every person—especially the children. We cannot make a lasting impression on children and families by stepping over the adults. Healthy learning occurs by example. Communication should last well beyond the initial hearing of the message. We should equip adults with the *why* questions we all expect will come on the car ride home after church. This modeling of faith formation in worship should occur *with* children to create ownership.

Mister Rogers' Neighborhood looked exactly the way Rogers wanted it to. The program resonated with children and adults. Every episode was the product of a carefully crafted process that included an understanding of effective communication, human development, and the use of technology. Employing Rogers's approach to communication enables church leaders to understand that effective preaching and communication should also be the result of a careful, academically informed process.

When Jesus told his followers to be like children, he was pointing toward the vulnerability and openness of a child. Rogers resonated, "The child is in me still . . . and sometimes not so still."[26] Amy Hollingsworth, author of *The Simple Faith of Mister Rogers*, summarizes Rogers's theological principles and values as subtle but consistent threads to be witnessed by his television audience: "Fred Rogers visited so quietly with the children of America that nobody dreamed he was a Presbyterian minister. He used puppets instead of a pulpit and instilled the basic principles of the Christian faith. He made those values real for his audience."[27]

Effective communication embraces a "think of the children first" approach. It includes familiarity with the Bible and the ability to share faith stories. Effective communicators relate meaningfully to the people around them and participate in ministries of compassion and justice. Thanks to Mister Rogers and his neighborhood, this is truly good neighborly advice.

---

26 Rogers, *World according to Mister Rogers*, 47.
27 From the publisher's summary for Hollingsworth, *Simple Faith of Mister Rogers*.

Bibliography

Armstrong, Thomas. *Multiple Intelligences in the Classroom*. Alexandria, VA: Association for Supervision and Curriculum Development, 2000.

Avery, Richard K., and Donald S. Marsh. "We Are the Church." In *The United Methodist Hymnal*, 558. Carol Stream, IL: Hope, 1972.

Discipleship Ministries. "Development through the Life Span." August 17, 2009. https://www.umcdiscipleship.org/resources/development-through-the-life-span.

Godlewski, Nina. "Mr. Rogers Quotes: Wisdom from the Children's Television Host on His Birthday." *Newsweek*, March 20, 2018. https://www.newsweek.com/fred-rogers-birthday-quotes-wont-you-be-my-neighbor-movie-854013.

Hollingsworth, Amy. *The Simple Faith of Mister Rogers: Spiritual Insights from the World's Most Beloved Neighbor*. Nashville: Integrity, 2005.

Howe, Leroy. "A Seminar with Fred Rogers." *Perkins Journal*, Fall 1977, 1.

King, Maxwell. "Mister Rogers Had a Simple Set of Rules for Talking to Children." *Atlantic*, June 8, 2018. https://www.theatlantic.com/family/archive/2018/06/mr-rogers-neighborhood-talking-to-kids/562352/.

Klaren, Alexandra. *On Becoming Neighbors: The Communication Ethics of Fred Rogers*. Pittsburgh: University of Pittsburgh Press, 2019.

Long, Michael. "Is Mister Rogers in Heaven? Fred Rogers and the Faithfulness of God." *Huffington Post*. Updated May 18, 2015. https://www.huffpost.com/entry/is-mister-rogers-in-heaven_b_6880448.

Marenus, Michelle. "Gardner's Theory of Multiple Intelligences." Simply Psychology, June 9, 2020. https://www.simplypsychology.org/multiple-intelligences.html.

Neville, Morgan, dir. *Won't You Be My Neighbor?* Documentary. Universal Pictures, 2018.

Paulson, John, dir. *Mister Rogers: It's You I Like; A Star-Studded Tribute to America's Favorite Neighbor*. DVD. PBS Productions, 2018.

Rogers, Fred. *The World according to Mister Rogers: Important Things to Remember*. New York: Hachette, 2003.

———. *You Are Special: Words of Wisdom for All Ages from a Beloved Neighbor*. New York: Penguin, 1994.

Rogers, Fred, and Barry Head. *Mister Rogers Talks with Parents*. Pittsburgh: Family Communications, 1983.

SeeAllThePeople. "What Is #SeeAllThePeople?" Accessed February 2, 2022. https://www.seeallthepeople.org/the-movement.

Stayer, Jacqueline. "Mr. Rogers: Five Essential Truths of His Communication." Institute for Public Relations, August 7, 2018. https://instituteforpr.org/mr-rogers-five-essential-truths-of-his-communication.

Tannen, Deborah. "The Power of Talk: Who Gets Heard and Why." *Harvard Business Review*, September–October 1995. https://hbr.org/1995/09/the-power-of-talk-who-gets-heard-and-why.

The Today Show. "The World according to Mr. Rogers." October 10, 2003. https://www.today.com/popculture/world-according-mister-rogers-1C9014197.

Wagner Brothers Productions. *Mister Rogers & Me*. DVD. PBS Distribution, 2011.

Ward, Richard F. *Speaking from the Heart: Preaching with Passion*. Eugene, OR: Wipf & Stock, 2001.

Other Resources on Fred Rogers

Behr, Gregg, and Ryan Rydzewski. *When You Wonder, You're Learning: Mister Rogers' Enduring Lessons for Raising Creative, Curious, Caring Kids*. New York: Hachette, 2021.

Belcher-Hamilton, Lisa. "The Gospel according to Fred: A Visit with Mr. Rogers." *Christian Century*, April 13, 1994, 382–84.

Beverly Chafin, Theresa. "Pretending an Opera Together: Fred Rogers, Collaborative Creativity, and Television Opera for Preschoolers." PhD diss., University of Georgia, Athens, 2016. https://getd.libs.uga.edu/pdfs/chafin_theresa_b_201608_phd.pdf.

Collins, Mark, and Margaret Mary Kimmel. *Mister Rogers' Neighborhood. Children, Television, and Fred Rogers*. Pittsburgh: University of Pittsburgh Press, 1996.

Edwards, Gavin. *Kindness and Wonder: Why Mister Rogers Matters Now More Than Ever*. New York: HarperCollins, 2019.

King, Maxwell. *The Good Neighbor: The Life and Work of Fred Rogers*. New York: Abrams, 2018.

Lietz, Jeana. *Journey to the Neighborhood: An Analysis of Fred Rogers and His Lessons for Educational Leaders*. Chicago: Loyola University Chicago, 2014.

Long, Michael G. *Peaceful Neighbor: Discovering the Countercultural Mister Rogers*. Louisville, KY: Westminster John Knox, 2015.

Madigan, Tim. *I'm Proud of You: My Friendship with Fred Rogers*. New York: Gotham Books, 2006.

Mason, Mark. "Six Effective Webinar Engagement Strategies That Wow Crowds." Flow. Accessed November 2, 2022. https://www.flowapp.com/webinar-engagement-strategies/#Webinar_Engagement_Strategies_That_Really_Work_with_Crowds.

Poole, Harrison Grant. "Repurposing Principles and Successful Pedagogical Techniques from Mister Rogers' Neighborhood for the Early Childhood Music Classroom." *General Music Today* 31, no. 2 (January 2018). https://journals.sagepub.com/doi/10.1177/1048371317705162.

Rogers, Fred. *Dear Mister Rogers, Does It Ever Rain in Your Neighborhood? Letters to Mister Rogers*. New York: Penguin, 1996.

———. *Life's Journeys according to Mister Rogers*. New York: Hachette, 2005.

———. *Many Ways to Say I Love You: Wisdom for Parents and Children from Mister Rogers*. New York: Hachette, 2006.

———. *The Mister Rogers Parenting Book: Helping to Understand Your Young Child*. Philadelphia: Running Press, 2002.

———. *Talking with Young Children about Death*. Pamphlet. Pittsburgh: Family Communications, 1979.

Rogers, Fred, Hedda Sharapan, Grace Ketterman, and Sue Bredekamp. *The Hurt That They Feel*. Birmingham, AL: New Hope, 2004.

Rubin, Judith. *Lessons from Mister Rogers Neighborhood*. DVD. Pittsburgh: Expressive Media, 2014.

Simple Interactions. "Simple Interactions Tool." Fred Rogers Center, Latrobe, PA. Accessed December 4, 2022. https://www.simpleinteractions.org/.

Tuttle, Shea. *Exactly as You Are: The Life and Faith of Mister Rogers*. Grand Rapids, MI: Eerdmans, 2019.

Whitmer, Margaret, and Joseph J. Kennedy IV, prods. *Fred Rogers: America's Favorite Neighbor*. DVD. Family Communications and WQED Multimedia, 2003.

Zoba, Wendy Murray. "Won't You Be My Neighbor: At the Center of Mister Rogers' Cheery Songs and Smiles Lies a God-Ordained Mission to Children?" *Christianity Today* 44, no. 3 (March 6, 2000): 38–44.

SECTION 3

Communal Spirituality in Church Life

Growing in Ministry with All Generations Together

What might it mean for your church leaders to engage in deeper conversations on the ways that children's spirituality is enhanced within a network of intergenerational, communal church life?

This section begins with a chapter titled "Discerning Congregational Change through a Nonanxious Intergenerational Model." The author, J. P. Conway, writes from his own experience as a pastor and professor, which puts him in a perfect position to address how church pastors and other ministry leaders might engage congregations in discerning change through a nonanxious intergenerational model. Conway simply yet effectively tells of his own congregation's systematic journey through such a conversation. He addresses congregational systems and processes of change, and building on the work of scholars in the field of family systems, Conway provides a model for healthy growth to take place. This may be a useful chapter for you to pass along to your senior pastor and/or church governing committee to provide an on-ramp for a healthy intergenerational dialogue to begin.

In Chapter Nine, Karin Middleton gifts the readers with a wealth of research. Her chapter, "Why Spiritual Nurture of Young Children Matters," gives a rationale as to how and why spiritual development during the earliest years of a child's life flourishes when adults intentionally invest in it and is best cultivated in multigenerational faith communities. As well, Middleton addresses a multidimensional view of children and writes of the benefits of understanding the unique distinctions between adults and children that allow both—adults as well as children—to lead and receive from one another as *pilgrims* and *colearners* together on the journey of faith. This chapter also lends itself well to study and conversation within a church staff and/or governing body.

The final chapter in this section, "(*Un*)Divided Worship: Children Leading and Belonging in the Worshiping Community," was coauthored by Trevecca Okholm, coeditor of this book, and Edwin (Ed) Willmington, who brings his unique perspective to the conversation of children and worship as the director of the Brehm Center for Worship, Theology, and the Arts at Fuller Theological Seminary. For Willmington and Okholm, the jumping-in points are their own layered experiences with children's engagement in the worshiping environment. This is a topic of passion and research for them both. The chapter is filled with personal stories as well as research studies, such as the works of Kara Powell and the Fuller Youth Institute.

All three of the chapters in this section can become perfect dialogue starters within church teams, engaging the discussion on the place and potential of children in the community of faith as well as the role of generationally inclusive worship in a child's spiritual development.

CHAPTER 8

Discerning Congregational Change through a Nonanxious Intergenerational Model

Joseph P. Conway

Change often creates anxiety. Much of the time, the more meaningful the change, the more heightened the anxiety. Since religious faith intrinsically invokes the human search for meaning, change in church settings may cause significant anxiety. In my teaching role at a Christian university, I often process with students concerning their church background and practices. Regularly, they share memories of church as a place of fear and anxiety. As I gently probe, they normally report stories of discord over congregational change. In their emerging adult eyes, they can somewhat understand the change conversations of years prior. However, as children or adolescents, they were unaware of the crucial issues at play, often because well-intentioned adults excluded them from the process. While one can be excluded from a process or conversation, one can rarely be excluded from anxiety. In fact, the "not knowing" can make it much worse. One friend recounted his childhood pain at seeing his church family, the near entirety of his emotional support system, argue incessantly over something called *premillennialism* before the church divided and split. This left a gaping hole in his childhood, even though it was years before he could spell *premillennialism*, much less understand it.

I serve as the minister for an urban congregation of 160 people in a free church tradition, Churches of Christ. Most adults in our congregation work in education, health care, or technology. Children and teens represent 35 percent of our total congregation, and over the last decade, we've committed to an intergenerational model of ministry and congregational life. Our default setting is to resist age segregation and include all generations together in worship, classes, events, and service. Our age-segregated classes are the exception, not the rule. In 2019, we began a year of discernment as we contemplated an expanded theology of female leadership in worship and ministry, moving along the continuum from complementarianism toward egalitarianism. As we entered a season of considering change, we committed to continue our intergenerational posture as well as cultivate a nonanxious environment. Admittedly, we wondered how the inclusion of children and teenagers would affect the process. Still, the leadership team believed it crucial to continue the embrace of our intergenerational model while paying attention to anxiety within our congregation.

From countless personal experiences and the anecdotes of others, I've seen the way anxiety hurts faith retention. Anxious church environments often lead to toxic religious atmospheres, which can weaken faith retention among young adults. We had concerns about arriving at a "right" stance on the issue but leaving a harmful wake of anxiety. We sought to lead a healthy, biblical conversation around the issue while also maintaining a healthy, biblical atmosphere and process.

Several authors significantly shaped our understanding of the congregational system, processes of change, and both collective and personal anxiety. First, building on the work of Murray Bowen, Jewish psychologist and consultant Edwin Friedman applies family systems theory to congregational life in his classic work *Generation to Generation: Family Process in Church and Synagogue*. Friedman "deemphasizes the notion that our conflicts and anxieties are due primarily to the makeup of our personalities, and suggests, instead, that our individual problems have more to do with our relational networks, the makeup of others' personalities, where we stand within the relational systems, and how we function within that position."[1] Congregational change does not depend on isolated individuals coming to separate personal conclusions and then dispassionately voicing their positions. Both desire for and resistance to change take shape in a system full of enthusiasm and anxiety that reacts and responds to others. To avoid being swept up in the system and losing volition, Friedman accentuates the need for differentiation to stay healthy within a system: "Differentiation means the capacity of a family member to define his or her own life's goals and values apart from surrounding togetherness pressures, to say 'I' when others are demanding 'you' and 'we.'"[2]

In our discernment process, *differentiation* became a buzzword for our leadership team. Among ourselves in our frequent gatherings, we practiced calm agreement and disagreement without undue pressure or abandonment. Friedman shows how a well-differentiated person who remains present in the system without being anxious (a nonanxious presence) helps reduce the spread of anxiety and relieve that which remains. Alongside our study and knowledge of theology and the Bible, we found being a nonanxious presence to be the most important part of the process. As Friedman says, "The capacity of members of the clergy to contain their own anxiety regarding congregational matters, both those not related to them, as well as those where they become the identified focus, may be the most significant capability in their arsenal."[3]

Second, we spent time processing Peter Scazzero's "The Emotionally Healthy Church: A Strategy for Discipleship That Actually Changes Lives." Scazzero ponders the neglect of emotional health

---

1 Friedman, *Generation to Generation*, 13.
2 Friedman, 27.
3 Friedman, 208.

within Christian thinking on discipleship. It's not uncommon for churches to have pious, committed Christians with significant Bible knowledge who, sadly, act emotionally immature most of their lives. Scazzero's work reminded our leadership team that our spirituality must include emotional maturity. In Scazzero's matter-of-fact words, "Emotional health and spiritual maturity are inseparable. It is not possible to be spiritually mature while remaining emotionally immature."[4] Anxiety can lead to temper tantrums framed as righteous indignation or harsh controlling techniques described as shepherding, yet Scazzero reminds us to declare those responses spiritual immaturity.

We knew that our announcement of possible change would create anxiety in terms of both too much change and not enough change. Increasingly, we became convinced that a healthy, unified outcome would depend more on our ability to be emotionally healthy than our ability to offer clever arguments or even explanatory insights into Scripture. When we communicated with other church leaders who had recently undergone changes, we continually heard how often seemingly unrelated issues rise to the surface. Change and anxiety will reveal whatever is unhealthy in a system. This can be seen as negative, but of course, it can also be seen as positive. If a community can see revealed areas of unhealthiness, it can embrace the opportunity to become healthier. Therefore, the church can actually become a discipleship tool to increase the emotional health of participants. Scazzero says it this way: "While I believe in the important place of professionally trained Christian counselors to bring expertise to the church, I believe the church of Jesus Christ is to be the primary vehicle for our growth in spiritual and emotional maturity."[5] During and afterward, several people reported that our process caused them to see unhealthy patterns in their relationships with their parents, spouses, children, and fellow church members. These surprise revelations caused them to

---

4 Scazzero, *Emotionally Healthy Church*, 10.
5 Scazzero, 18.

reflect and pursue personal emotional health in ways that made them grow as disciples of Jesus.

Third, dovetailing with Friedman and Scazzero, our leadership team read *Managing Leadership Anxiety: Yours and Theirs* by Steve Cuss. He encourages question asking and reflection in the face of anxiety. In his words, "Anxiety is a signal, not a root cause. It is a siren that a storm might be coming; it is not the storm itself. Getting to the root cause is key to transformation and systemic health."[6] Throughout our process, we kept leaning into causal questions: Why does this make us anxious? The answers helped us know what to discuss and how to discuss it. Moreover, understanding helps create compassion, which creates empathy, which prevents reactivity. We saw the contagion of anxiety in both others and ourselves when reflection did not occur. Thinking of systems, Cuss reminds us, "Systems become anxious when members of a system adopt and escalate one another's anxiety and reactivity."[7] Perhaps the most helpful part of Cuss's work came from his focus on process. For several years, we had focused on the content of the potential change. Put differently, we dove into biblical and theological positions around gender roles in church. All this proved necessary, and yet so often, the content did not drive the conversation like we thought it would. Cuss predicts just that: "Leading a productive, non-anxious conversation about a difficult or sensitive topic is essential to process-level change. Remember, people pay attention to content but react to process, so you'll have to be prepared for an anxious response and your ability to be non-anxious will be key."[8]

This proved true in our situation, as we fielded many more process and outcome questions than biblical and theological questions. Lastly, Cuss's thoughts on de-escalation proved helpful, especially in relation to our intergenerational process. Cuss writes, "One of the simplest ways to de-escalate anxiety is to develop a

---

6 Cuss, *Managing Leadership Anxiety*, 18.
7 Cuss, 101.
8 Cuss, 107.

knack for playfulness."[9] We found that having children and teens in the room often enabled playfulness in terms of both exercises and illustrations. On top of that, simply having children and teens in the room softened the conversation in noticeable ways.

Last, seemingly unrelated to this process, I read Sissy Goff's *Raising Worry-Free Girls: Helping Your Daughter Feel Braver, Stronger, and Smarter in an Anxious World*. As I read it, I saw insight into both girls and boys, children and adults. Goff situates fear, worry, and anxiety on an escalating continuum.[10] If we can ask the right questions and seek wise practices around fear, we can work to minimize worry and anxiety. This radically shaped our process because fear loomed everywhere, raising concerns such as the following:

- What if the church makes changes, and I have to leave?
- What if the church doesn't make changes, and I have to leave?
- What if we go against the Bible?
- What if we cave to modern culture?
- What if the silencing of women causes the next generation to leave the faith altogether?

We tried to engage, assess, and probe fears throughout to minimize escalation into anxiety. The following concept from Goff really impacted me as well: "Anxiety always involves an overestimation of the problem and an underestimation of [one]self."[11] It is essential to adequately frame problems; not every problem is the end of the world. A flat tire is bad but not the same as a car crash. We knew it would be essential to honestly and accurately frame the consequences of changing or not changing. Moreover, we knew that the ability to find a solution was not just about the issue itself but about our capacity as disciples of Jesus to channel the Spirit and embrace our worth and power in Christ. Goff

---

9 Cuss, 143.
10 Goff, *Raising Worry-Free Girls*, 31.
11 Goff, 31.

focuses on helping children solve their own problems: "If we solve our kids' problems for them, they don't develop the ability to problem-solve, which I believe is one of the primary deterrents of anxiety."[12] More than just kids, giving adults space to help craft solutions enhances their confidence and diminishes their anxiety. Back to kids, I picture the myriad issues on the horizon for them to spiritually discern long after they've grown up and left our city. Their inclusion in the process offers more than just their insight and growth in the present. It offers a way for them to develop the confidence to discern future challenges around faith without being overwhelmed by anxiety. I am convinced their inclusion in processes of discerning change will increase their faith retention.

Four Process Goals

The elders and I had four goals. First, we wanted to lead the congregation through a biblical, theological, and historical study of sex and gender and how each of these shapes roles in families and churches. Second, we wanted people to feel good about our process in terms of transparency and hospitality. Third, we wanted young and old to learn to listen to and understand different perspectives without demonizing others as well as how to process anxiety without resorting to fear. Fourth, bluntly, we wanted to avoid a church split.

To cultivate a nonanxious, intergenerational environment for congregational discernment, we took the deliberate step of applying family systems theory. We embraced our interconnectivity and interdependence. Resisting hyperindividualism, we faced the truth that we affect one another. Specifically in terms of anxiety, we recognized that both anxiety and calm have contagious effects. In other words, a father's anxiety about congregational change shapes his relationships with his wife, children, and fellow church members. It's the proverbial iceberg beneath complaints about the

12 Goff, 57.

color of the foyer carpet or church budget funds spent on donuts. At some point, we all find ourselves on the receiving end of someone else's anxious behavior. If unaware or immature, we absorb this anxiety and pass it on. However, we don't have to. We are not just a system but individuals with boundaries in a system. We can be around anxiety without absorbing it. Family systems language uses the term *differentiation* to describe remaining a healthy self amid a system. By leaning into this understanding, we can see and understand the anxiety in ourselves and others without passing it on or making it our own. Of course, this is easier said than done. How would we enact this? We chose four steps.

Four Steps to Leading Change

First, we trained leaders in family systems theory. My initial exposure to this had come from reading Friedman in graduate school. I shared these concepts with our leadership team. Then I gave them copies of the works by Scazzero and Cuss. In our weekly meetings, we sought to practice emotional health. We named the anxieties in our own lives and talked about the ways our families and families of origin shaped our personalities, leadership styles, and approaches to change. We confessed when differentiation became challenging for us to maintain. All in all, our leadership team pursued family systems theory, understanding, and language. At a weekend leadership retreat early in the process, we prayed for each person in our church by name and their concerns. This took around four hours. Later that day, we sketched out our process. Then we ended the day with a time of relinquishment. We wrote all our hopes and dreams as well as fears and concerns for our church down on a notecard, and then, during a time of prayer, we tore them up. We named it all and gave up the right to control it. We could all sense a tangible reduction in anxiety.

Second, we maintained intergenerational classes on the area of potential change as well as the topic of anxiety. Middle- and high-school students were included in our classes on biblical interpretation and theology of sex and gender, where they had the opportunity to ask questions and comment. The students had front-row seats to adults agreeing and disagreeing with one another. They saw adults challenge one another directly and then hug and laugh afterward. Four particular classes stand out.

In one class, we studied anxiety. Specifically, we relied on Jesus's words in Matthew 6 and the story of Jesus walking on water. We acknowledged that these stories have often been used in a blame-and-shame posture, which sadly has a tendency to cause anxiety to spiral. In contrast to this, we sought to read these passages through the lens of Jesus's compassion. We talked about worry as the body's natural response to unique and uncertain events. We looked at anxiety as an alarm clock. Instead of responding with "I need to have more faith and not worry," we asked, "How does my faith speak to my worry?" We proclaimed a Jesus that is with us in our anxiety with gentle presence, not scolding scorn. Moreover, we admitted our areas of ignorance. We admitted that we're not experts on mental health, that research continues to come out, and that sometimes, prescription drugs can be helpful. We went around the room, and both young and old named the things that cause them worry. We talked about trust and worry as a continuum and shared what has helped us move toward trust and away from worry. We saw children and teens discover faith as a means for anxiety alleviation rather than for increasing anxiety.

In another class, we illustrated how anxiety moves in systems. One person held a ball of yarn, and as I told the following story, they passed the yarn around. A father has a hard day at work, so he comes home grumpy, telling the kids to pick up the yard. The older sibling receives this anxiety and passes it on to the younger sibling by telling them it's all their fault. The younger sibling absorbs the anxiety and complains that they're having spaghetti again. The mother, who cooked dinner that night, receives the anxiety and passes it on to an underfunctioning employee in an email later that night. That employee absorbs the anxiety and passes it on to their family, and so on, and so on. After using a nonchurch example, we talked bluntly about how potential change in our church functions in a like manner. Underlying anxiety about potential changes often manifests as frustration—for example, "When is someone going to change those lightbulbs in the classroom?" or "Why are the kids running after worship?" At this point, we discussed differentiation, being around anxious people without becoming anxious. We discussed how a nonanxious presence can stop the cycle. Moreover, we acknowledged that anxiety can never be eradicated, but that when we can see it and name it, it holds less power. This provoked a spirited, helpful conversation.

In a different class, we talked about major and minor beliefs. Specifically, we talked about Jesus's words in Matthew 23:23, where the Pharisees neglected the weightier matters of justice, mercy, and faithfulness. To illustrate this, we brought in a Jenga tower, which had three different colors for low, middle, and high beliefs. We talked about foundational beliefs that, if removed, threaten the whole tower. As with the Jenga blocks, foundational beliefs cannot be removed without consequence. This spawned a conversation about essential and nonessential beliefs and practices as well as those in the middle. This helped all ages see the weighted nuance in beliefs about the nature of Jesus, music style in worship, the sacraments, and how to alleviate poverty. The realization that our proposed change was not on the foundational bottom layer for most, despite its importance, alleviated anxiety for many in the room.

In yet another class, we talked about understanding the culture at work in the Bible. We spaced out adults, teens, and children on a timeline from the Old Testament era to the New Testament era to the modern day. We read a selection of scriptures alongside a description of what was going on at that time. In this way, all ages could see the cultural context and the redemptive nature of biblical teaching in its time. While maintaining Jesus as the apex of God's revelation, we demonstrated why some teaching seems curious to us now because of its original context. Admittedly, this class proved challenging, as we sought to uphold the social location of Scripture alongside its authority. Not everyone felt good about this class, for a variety of reasons, and yet it produced healthy dialogue.

For our third step, I preached directly on emotional health and anxiety in ways that fostered intergenerational dialogue. As a reminder, we include all ages in worship, so all sermons reach an intergenerational audience. I led a six-week series that relied heavily on the previously mentioned books by Sissy Goff and Peter Scazzero. I taught a lot about how our families of origin and backgrounds shape our reception to change. We embraced the holistic depictions of human flourishing in the Bible, such as when Jesus calls us to love God with our heart, soul, mind, and strength. More than just a few sermons, we sought to elevate emotional intelligence, bringing it into our everyday conversations instead of casting it out to the margins as a threat to true spirituality and mature intellectualism. The pandemic shaped the reception of these sermons. Primarily, families listened to these messages at home in their living rooms over our podcast feed. Because of this, I offered questions and opportunities to pause the recording and dialogue. The height of this was a sermon on passing on the faith to the next generation. I let the church know a week in advance that I'd be asking parents to list three things on notecards that they hoped their children would continue to believe and practice. They had to limit it to three. Moreover, members without children at home were encouraged to write a letter to a child or teenager at church with whom they had a relationship. I heard a lot of positive feedback about this approach. However, the intensity and intimacy of this caused one family to kindly and firmly beg for the end of virtual church. This has been our experience with authentic and vulnerable intergenerational conversations. They are meaningful but challenging, often revealing what has taken root as well as what hasn't.

Fourth, the leadership team divided into pairs, and their families met with every single-family unit. These gatherings played a pivotal role and loomed large in our process. We asked them three questions: How are you doing? How is life in our church going for you? What do you believe about this potential change? These conversations mainly happened over meals. Often, the kids would stay for a bit before scattering to play. Still, this enabled our leadership to interact with every single child and adult in the church. Many teens stayed in for the entire conversation. The word *discernment* became a buzzword in our church, as we called these gatherings "discernment." You could overhear people, even kids, say, "We've got discernment tonight." By doing this, we sought to demonstrate how every voice matters in the church regardless of age or background. We cemented the embrace of family process. Moreover, we promoted the truth that meaningful, healthy change should happen thoughtfully, sensitively, and often slowly. On several occasions, teenagers sat in on all the conversations. I'll never forget a seventeen-year-old's response after a particularly vulnerable two-hour conversation: "So that is what this is like."

Twenty-two months after beginning what we thought would be a yearlong experience, we reached the culmination of this intergenerational, nonanxious discernment of change. Certainly, the COVID-19 pandemic complicated the process and the analysis of the results. The overwhelming majority of the congregation agreed with the changes. Ten percent of our congregation left. Certainly, this caused pain on both sides, yet for most, this process served as a catalyst for spiritual growth, even if the individual or family chose to leave. Repeatedly, individuals told me this process encouraged them to be more reflective and intentional about their roles in their family systems and our church system.

The inclusion of children and teens not only helped our process but helped prepare them for future considerations of change and ensuing anxiety. Looking back, I can't imagine doing it without them. Overall, we believe we successfully modeled the following truths: Spiritual health includes emotional health. Churches can have hard, respectful conversations. Every voice, regardless of one's age, not only matters but contributes to the process. God will not protect us from all anxiety, but amid anxiety, Jesus propels us toward hope. That hope in Jesus has roots, strong roots, in God's love. And as 1 John 4:18 says, "Love drives out fear."

Bibliography

Cuss, Steve. *Managing Leadership Anxiety: Yours and Theirs*. Nashville: Thomas Nelson, 2019.

Friedman, Edwin. *Generation to Generation: Family Process in Church and Synagogue*. New York: Guilford, 1985.

Goff, Sissy. *Raising Worry-Free Girls: Helping Your Daughter Feel Braver, Stronger, and Smarter in an Anxious World*. Bloomington, IN: Bethany House, 2019.

Scazzero, Peter. *The Emotionally Healthy Church: A Strategy for Discipleship That Actually Changes Lives*. Grand Rapids, MI: Zondervan, 2003.

CHAPTER 9

Why Spiritual Nurture of Young Children Matters

Karin Middleton

Several years ago, I asked some of my church colleagues in children's ministry if they would be interested in reading an overview of what I was learning through my graduate research at Fuller Seminary. They responded with a resounding "Yes!" Likewise, in the international mission agency with which I work, I regularly hear from colleagues with young children that they are looking for paradigms and resources to better equip them to steward their children's faith. To this end, I offer the following highlights from our field's research, including key paradigms and best practices for thinking about young children's spiritual formation.

Spiritual development begins during the earliest years of a child's life and flourishes when adults intentionally invest in it. While parents hold primary responsibility for their child's faith formation, it is best cultivated in multigenerational faith communities—as it has been since biblical times and which will be explained further in the following pages. Additionally, this chapter includes examples from scholar-practitioners on the significance of welcoming children into faith communities, wisdom on when and how to facilitate a process of children discovering God, and insights on creating intentional worship environments. What follows reviews both literature and best practices across various

Christian traditions in support of parents, church leaders, and anyone investing in the spiritual lives of young children.

Why Very Young Children?

Researchers and practitioners alike affirm very young children's spiritual vibrancy. Founded in 1986 with the vision of "a world where the religious life of the child was honored," the National Association of the Catechesis of the Good Shepherd states, "God and the child have a unique relationship with one another particularly before the age of six."[1] A pioneer in children's spiritual formation, Sophia Cavalletti notes that "in the religious sphere, it is a fact that children know things no one has told them."[2] Edward Robinson observed children younger than five have "significant religious (or spiritual) experiences," but due to their inability to explain them, adults may easily dismiss or ignore these early spiritual experiences.[3] Likewise, James Estep advises adults to never underestimate children's faith capacity.[4] The *Catechism of the Catholic Church* calls parents to "associate them from their tenderest years with the life of the Church"[5] and educate children in the faith beginning in the "child's earliest years."[6] Moreover, Justin L. Barrett's scientific research reveals that "children are prone to believe in supernatural beings . . . during the first four years of life due to ordinary cognitive development in ordinary human environments."[7] These findings are exemplified in a story of a young girl asking her three-day-old brother, "Tell me about

---

1 "History" and "Home" pages, Catechesis of the Good Shepherd, accessed March 2022, http://www.cgsusa.org.
2 Cavalletti, *Religious Potential*, 42.
3 Edward Robinson referenced in Westerhoff, "Church's Contemporary Challenge," 363.
4 Estep Jr., "Christian Nurture of Children," 74.
5 Catholic Church, "Duties of Family Members," 2225.
6 Catholic Church, *Catechism*, 2226.
7 Barrett, *Born Believers*, 3.

God—I've almost forgotten."⁸ Pause for a moment and consider how the young child intuitively knows the practical reality of Psalm 139:13: "For it was you who formed my inward parts; you knit me together in my mother's womb" (NRSV).

Young children merit spiritual nurture because they are made in God's image (Gen. 1:27). The Catholic Church declares that "parents must regard their children as *children of God* and respect them as *human persons*."⁹ Third-century theologian Cyprian of Lyons readily acknowledged children's full humanity[10] and used the wonderfully honoring term *newly born persons*[11] when referring to very young children in his writings. As children of God, children have a "right to respect and to be helped as they mature" rather than judged inappropriately by criteria designed to assess adults' abilities and aptitudes.[12]

Spirituality distinguishes humans from all other created beings. Researchers describe the "intrinsic nature of the human spirit"[13] and find young children instinctively know and develop an "intuitive belief system"[14] as "spiritual beings."[15] Yet it is difficult for adults to grasp the depth of young children's spiritual experiences, as they are not able to verbally articulate them due to limited vocabularies and abilities to present them in ways adults understand. In 1902, the Harvard-trained psychologist and philosopher William James astutely termed this difficulty *ineffability* because these experiences resist being described.[16] The limitation of expression does *not* imply the absence of spiritual experiences and understanding. Quite the contrary—the "spiritual nature of

---

8   T. Wyatt Watkins recounting an incident recorded in Palmer, "Unfettered Wonder," 132.
9   Catholic Church, *Catechism*, 2222; italics in the original.
10 Bunge, "Biblical and Theological Perspectives," 7.
11 Allen, *Nurturing Children's Spirituality*, 69.
12 Catechesis of the Good Shepherd website, accessed January 31, 2022, http://www.cgsusa.org.
13 Loder, *Logic of the Spirit*, 109.
14 King, "Nature and Functions," 19.
15 King, 7.
16 William James in King, "Nature and Functions," 48.

a person" is "at least as important as the physical, cognitive, emotional and social dimensions"[17] that are more tangibly tended. We may, then, be confident that very young children are hardwired for spirituality.

A Multidimensional View of Children

Recognizing that children are spiritual may not be enough. Understanding the unique distinctions between adults and children allows us to both lead them and receive from them. Marcia Bunge aptly presents three sets of juxtaposed truths about children to aid adults in accurately viewing and relating to them. First, children have strengths and gifts to offer, yet they are vulnerable.[18] Rather than viewing children as "weaker" members of the body of Christ (1 Cor. 12:22), we would be wise to recognize that all people benefit when we receive the gifts and unique strengths children offer, even—or especially—when derived from their vulnerability. For example, a four-year-old may be more likely to invite a homeless person into her home than her older sibling. Adults benefit from the example of her compassion, yet the child needs protection from unknown possible risks.

Second, while children possess spiritual capacity, they still require significant and nuanced guidance.[19] Adults with multidimensional views of children avoid theologies that focus singularly on total depravity or children as innocents without original sin. Terms that emphasize mutual journeying through life, such as *pilgrims*[20] and *colearners*,[21] may help navigate these multifaceted relationships. Third, like adults, although children are still morally developing, they may offer spiritual wisdom.[22] The story of

---

17 May et al., *Children Matter*, 83–84.
18 Bunge, "Biblical and Theological Perspectives," 6.
19 Bunge, "Biblical Theological Perspectives," 6.
20 May et al., *Children Matter*, 35.
21 Berryman, *Godly Play*.
22 Bunge, "Biblical Theological Perspectives," 6.

young Samuel demonstrates these dimensions dynamically. As a boy, Samuel was chosen by God to deliver his message to Eli. However, Eli first needed to coach Samuel on how to listen to God (1 Sam. 3:4–18). Here we see that keeping children's strengths and vulnerabilities in mind prepares adults to both learn from children and facilitate their spiritual growth. Such a multidimensional view of children equips adults to welcome children into the church and family with healthy mutuality.

It is worth noting that children have responsibilities too. According to the fourth commandment, children are to honor and obey their parents unless doing so causes them to sin, act unjustly, or neglect loving Jesus as Lord.[23] Respect for parents "has its roots in the fear of God."[24] Children can learn to honor God by tangibly honoring their parents. In addition to children's responsibilities, families benefit from parents viewing parenting as a service rather than a status or privilege to be lorded over children.[25] In this way, all members of the community honor and respect one another in love.

Our Responsibility in Faith Formation

Scripture clearly and repeatedly entrusts adults—parents specifically—to pass faith on to their children.[26] In Deuteronomy 6, Moses teaches the community to observe the law "so that you and your children and your children's children may fear the LORD your God all the days of your life" (Deut. 6:2 NRSV). Moses continues instructing the community, "Recite [the commandments] to your children and talk about them when you are at home and when you are away, when you lie down and when you rise" (Deut. 6:7 NRSV). Discipleship cannot be confined to dedicated times or places; rather, the community embodies and transmits faith at all times

---

23 Bunge, 18–21.
24 Catholic Church, *Catechism*, 2217.
25 Mercer, *Welcoming Children*, 135.
26 For example, Deut. 4:9; 6:4–9; 11:19; Prov. 22:6; Eph. 6:4.

and in all circumstances. Considered "the domestic church," the family establishes "the place where children receive the first proclamation of faith . . . a community of grace and prayer, a school of human virtues and of Christian charity."[27] In short, communities of faith—particularly parents—are accountable for stewarding children's faith formation.

While parents are primarily responsible for forming faith in their children, the church maintains the responsibility to equip and support them. While knowing these responsibilities, "historically believers have struggled with how best to apply these truths."[28] Often, church leaders focus on ministry with adults while relying heavily on minimally trained volunteers to nurture children's faith. (This may be due in part to the focus of seminary education on preparing pastors for ministry exclusively to adults.[29]) The following historically orthodox statements may guide faith communities in thinking about children:

1. God loves children and desires for them to know him.
2. Children are negatively impacted by sin.
3. God has made provisions for addressing the impact of sin.
4. Children are capable of genuine spiritual walks with God.
5. In children, God sees qualities of faith that should characterize adults who would be part of his Kingdom.
6. Parents should be equipped and supported in their critical roles as children's primary instructors and models of the Christian faith.
7. The church as a whole has a responsibility to help with the spiritual nurture and instruction of children.
8. We need to include children in beneficial ways in the life and practice of the church as they grow.

---

27 Catholic Church, *Catechism*, 1666.
28 Harwood and Lawson, *Infants and Children*, 5.
29 Mercer, *Welcoming Children*, 218.

9. Children are to grow to own their faith, not simply rest on the faith of their parents.[30]

By reflecting on the practical implications of these statements, parents and faith communities may more thoughtfully nurture children in their care.

Despite knowing the biblical mandate and research findings and access to ministry resources, the responsibility for developing children's spirituality remains largely unrealized.[31] This may stem from the systemic outsourcing of this responsibility. Parents frequently abdicate this responsibility to the church for many reasons, such as feeling ill-equipped because they lacked adequate spiritual nurture as a child.[32] As previously noted, parents hold primary responsibility for their children's faith formation, yet they need the church to support and equip them in this effort, as witnessed across diverse Christian traditions. David C. Cook observes, "When it comes to entities that God has created specifically to make disciples and accomplish His mission, there is the church ... the family ... and ... nothing else."[33] Similarly, a Catholic children's faith former, Cavalletti, expresses this partnership by stating, "The catechist's work is not complete without the parents' contribution, but the reverse is also true. We are dealing with two different ways, which are complementary and not alternatives."[34] Therefore, parents and the church form a God-designed partnership to carry out this biblical mandate of passing on faith.

---

30 Harwood and Lawson, "Comparing Five Theological Views," 45–46.
31 Allen, *Nurturing Children's Spirituality*, 344.
32 This is the most common reason I hear when talking with parents from many denominations in the US and several countries in Europe.
33 Joiner, *Think Orange*, 79.
34 Cavalletti, *Religious Potential*, 156.

Welcoming Children

Jesus taught that to welcome children in his name is to welcome him (Matt. 18:5). Yet in many communities, children only find welcome in the church if they do not act like children.[35] However, the extent to which the church welcomes children defines the scope of influence the church may have upon them that will either "encourage or hinder [children] in coming to Jesus."[36] Pope Francis commented that "it is a beautiful homily when a child cries in church,"[37] countering the value that babies should be quiet in order to be present. Further, to welcome children directly builds relational equity, as spirituality is transferred through relationships with "bi-directional interaction."[38] And bidirectional relationships allow for mutual contributions, as noted earlier. When churches welcome children with unmasked needs, emotions, and shortcomings, adults may find themselves likewise acceptable without being "all cleaned up."[39]

Churches may provide welcome by offering age-appropriate experiences. During Luther's Reformation, children received reading instruction so that they could more fully participate in the liturgy. After World War II, programs such as Young Life, InterVarsity, and Youth for Christ[40] as well as the Sunday school movement[41] emerged to address age-specific needs. With the cultural shift away from churches offering a worship hour followed by a Sunday school hour for both adults and children, many churches retained worship for adults and instruction for children. Cultural and developmental reasons in addition to church growth strategies

---

35 Mercer, *Welcoming Children*, 31.
36 May et al., *Children Matter*, xi.
37 Mares, "Pope Francis."
38 King, "Nature and Functions," 47.
39 Mercer, *Welcoming Children*, 256.
40 Allen and Ross, *Intergenerational Christian Formation*, 36–37.
41 Mears (1890–1963) pioneered published curriculum for persons of all ages to be utilized in addition to whole congregation worship services in response to waning biblical literacy. See Roe, *Dream Big*.

and individualism have all contributed to the shift toward separating generations in worship.[42]

Should churches then eliminate separate, age-appropriate experiences in order to welcome children? Sonja Stewart and Jerome Berryman offer a restorative paradigm for intentional age-specific church experiences in which the purpose of "apart" ministry is equipping children for "together" worship.[43] Yet it should not replace it. This leads the church to a both/and approach to nurturing faith through age-appropriate experiences and intergenerational formation[44] opportunities that genuinely welcome children.

Multigenerational Relationships

Historically, faith communities included all generations, which is congruent with the way God initiates relationship with all people.[45] Fifth-century Celtic Christians exemplified nurturing children's intimacy with God by fully integrating faith and children into community life. Celtic children brought hope and joy and were welcomed with anticipation at birth. Unlike other cultures throughout history, Celtic Christians did not value children for their financial benefits (such as additional labor) or see them as financial burdens. The community rejoiced in their personhood, learning from their awe and wonder while providing them with ongoing spiritual nurture.[46] Children functioned as indispensable members of Celtic communities. It appears the Celts intuitively understood the following research discoveries concerning intergenerational faith communities.

Faith formation is deeper, sticks longer, and stimulates more frequent prayer when churches worship, serve, socialize, and learn

---

42 Allen and Ross, *Intergenerational Christian Formation*, 36–45.
43 Stewart and Berryman, *Young Children and Worship*, 13.
44 Allen and Ross, *Intergenerational Christian Formation*, 69.
45 Allen and Ross, 77–84.
46 Crabtree, "Forbid Not the Little Ones," 78–91.

together.⁴⁷ Learning together may be accomplished through parallel learning or in small groups outside of the Sunday teaching time. Moreover, intergenerational activities significantly benefit both children and adults. When included in the faith community, "children in turn contribute to the *growth in holiness* of their parents."⁴⁸ Critically, "while faith itself is a gift of God, the *understanding* of that faith is learned within the faith community."⁴⁹ Approaching ministry to, for, and with children from this vantage point, church communities benefit from offering both age-specific and multigenerational faith experiences.

Notably, children model childlike faith through their "openness to being altered by God's presence and their response of love for God and others."⁵⁰ Although children readily demonstrate unguarded responses to God, adults need time and interaction with children in order to learn from them. For example, after gazing at a large crucifix for some time, an ordinarily very active four-year-old calmly whispered, "Did it hurt him?" Hearing his piercing question forever changed the way his preschool teacher experienced Jesus's sacrifice. Her faith grew deeper because she paused to spend fifteen minutes with a child in a moment of wonder. Additionally, this togetherness provides a deep sense of belonging.⁵¹ Essentially, we may learn from Celtic tradition and Irenaeus of Lyons respectively that children first belong to the faith community, then believe with the faith community, and finally grow in knowledge concerning their faith.⁵² Therefore, when and how to expose children to faith becomes our next critical consideration.

---

47 Allen and Ross, *Intergenerational Christian Formation*, 47.
48 Catholic Church, *Catechism*, 2227; italics in the original.
49 Morgenthaler, *Right from the Start*, 104; italics in the original.
50 Beste, "Second Graders' Spirituality," 296.
51 Allen and Ross, *Intergenerational Christian Formation*, 48.
52 Mosher, "Irenaeus' Stages of Faith," 107.

Sequence of Discovery

From their earliest days, children naturally wonder about the world around them, particularly things in nature. When directed toward God, wonder blossoms into worship.[53] Cavalletti notes that "there exists a relationship between the child and God that is more deeply rooted than in the intellect alone."[54] Therefore, before children are ready to logically grapple with biblical narratives, young children need experiences with Jesus. Babies and young children are not as passive as previously thought,[55] simply passing time before being able to receive knowledge through overtly stated lessons. On the contrary, they regularly construct concepts based on their experiences. For example, a child learns to conceptually identify a wide variety of objects as "chairs" through experience over time. When applied to the spiritual landscape, this process is known as grasping "essentiality"[56] through big-picture concepts, such as *God is good*, *God loves me*, and *God is real and present in my life*. Additionally, young children are not averse to these and other theologically formative ideas or experiences. Rather, they bring meaning[57] as adults facilitate children's encounters with God.[58] Barrett encourages adults "not to sell children short by assuming that just because a concept seems difficult for adults, it must be difficult for children."[59] Often, young children do not fully comprehend the world around them and thus are not disturbed by the mysteries of God in the same way as adults.

Out of step with children's contentment with theological openness, adults may be tempted to introduce factual comprehension and "correct" moral application of the Bible too early. Cavalletti insists "that faith as encounter with the living God must precede

---

53 Fuller, *Opening Your Child's Spiritual Windows*, 51.
54 Cavalletti, *Religious Potential*, 31.
55 King, "Nature and Functions," 15.
56 Cavalletti, *Religious Potential*, 47.
57 King, "Nature and Functions," 46–47.
58 King, 38.
59 Barrett, "Childlike Faith," 71.

any presentation of Christian moral principles."[60] Once a child has an encounter with Jesus, it is natural to desire to know more about God and respond to God's love through actions pleasing to him (moral behavior). Cavalletti warns, "If we put too great or too early an emphasis on man's response, our attention will be centered on man rather than on God and then strain will prevail in our relationship with God."[61] When such early fixation on human response is avoided, the foundation of faith may be fixed on what Jesus has done for us. In this way, Scripture may remain a dynamic text when we do not emphasize fact-comprehension *about* God that has been discovered by someone else, as will be elaborated upon shortly. To this point, in 1906, Horace Bushnell cautioned adults not to make faith "a drudgery" because it is a "real living faith."[62] He noted that "untimely intrusions of religion will only make it odious—the child cannot be crammed with doctrine."[63] In short, research indicates that very young children benefit from first encountering God relationally before learning about God intellectually.

Facilitating the Discovery of God

How might adults facilitate encounters between young children and God? Cavalletti's Catechesis of the Good Shepherd[64] and Sonja Stewart and Jerome Berryman's adaptations for liturgical Protestant congregations Young Children and Worship[65] and Godly Play[66] provide an approach lauded throughout literature on children's spiritual formation. Catechesis of the Good Shepherd introduces young children to the Good Shepherd through Psalm 23 and the use of wooden figures. After twenty years of practical research, Cavalletti found children resonate with the Good Shepherd more

60 Cavalletti, *Religious Potential*, 6–7.
61 Cavalletti, 87.
62 Bushnell, *Christian Nurture*, 374.
63 Bushnell, 377–78.
64 See the Catechesis of the Good Shepherd website.
65 Stewart and Berryman, *Young Children and Worship*.
66 Berryman, *Godly Play*.

than any other representation of God. Chronological introduction, beginning with Genesis, proves irrelevant to the young child, as they are still developing the concept of time. Furthermore, introducing God as Father runs the risk of conflating human figures in the child's life with God.[67]

Building on Cavalletti, Berryman, and Stewart's pioneering work, other researcher-practitioners, such as Catherine Stonehouse and Scottie May, describe this same process of facilitating encounters with God as "reflective engagement,"[68] while Lacy Finn Borgo describes it as "spiritual conversation with a child," noting that "play can incorporate wonder and mystery as well as create the conditions for union."[69] Similarly, taking cues from Ignatius's *Spiritual Exercises*, Jared Patrick Boyd offers a guide for leading school-age children in experiences with Jesus in his book *Imaginative Prayer*.[70] In each of these renditions, the adult presents open-ended Scripture passages to facilitate the discovery of God and promote transcendent experiences.[71] Jesus taught using parables frequently without explanation. When facilitators allow children to discover God through open-ended presentations of parables and narratives, they foster children's natural strength of opening meaning in contrast to adults' proclivity to close meaning.[72] Cavalletti cautions facilitators against filling in narrative details that the biblical text intentionally left vague, as it could suppress wonder.[73] (Do not worry, particular theological nuances will be refined as the child matures.) This approach promotes experiencing God before acquiring knowledge about God. As adults, "our natural inclination is to make meaning *for* the child," yet Borgo asserts that "this is decidedly unhelpful,"[74] as adults cannot know

67 Cavalletti, *Religious Potential*, 73.
68 Stonehouse and May, *Listening to Children*, 78.
69 Borgo, *Spiritual Conversations*, 78.
70 Boyd, *Imaginative Prayer*.
71 Ratcliff, "Spirit of the Past," 32.
72 Berryman, *Godly Play*, 95.
73 Cavalletti, *Religious Potential*, 65.
74 Borgo, *Spiritual Conversations*, 67.

all the Holy Spirit's movements. Despite the adult's initial lack of theological control, facilitating the discovery of God by opening meaning allows children to intimately encounter God rather than merely learn about God.

Creating an Intentional Environment

In addition to welcoming and facilitating a child's discovery of God, several other factors impact children's spiritual foundations significantly. Time spent in prayer is foundational to facilitating encounters with Jesus. Young children are naturally contemplative[75] and simply enjoy God. This sense of wonder and delight manifests in prayers of thanksgiving and praise. Specifically, "the prayer of children up to the age of seven or eight is almost exclusively prayer of thanksgiving and praise."[76] Introducing prayers of petition and moral lessons too early may shift a child's focus from God to human concerns and thus may limit the young child's ability to experience Jesus.[77] In time, prayers will include petitions as well as traditional written prayers. Yet for young children, prayer is equally about listening to the Holy Spirit and speaking praise and thankfulness. Children's ministers uphold this priority when remembering that activities, such as reenactments and drawings, should be responses to times of discovery rather than the objective of time spent together.

The form of engagement with children also matters. Above, we considered the substance of facilitating encounters with Jesus before promoting content and moral application. Yet *how* we communicate is equally important.[78] Human interactions shape children more than media and biology.[79] And young children do

---

75 Cavalletti, *Religious Potential*, 156.
76 Cavalletti, 123.
77 Cavalletti, 123.
78 Berryman, *Godly Play*, 78; Stonehouse and May, *Listening to Children*, 84.
79 Diamond and Amso, "Contributions of Neuroscience to Our Understanding of Cognitive Development," 30.

not allow content to override nonverbal cues as easily as adults. Therefore, prioritizing time for children to pray conveys that relationship *with* God takes priority over talking *about* God. Moreover, the physical space in which we worship communicates how intentional (or not) we are about creating a sacred place to meet with God. Our timeliness and consistency (or lack thereof) model for young children how they ought to prioritize worship. Finally, our unspoken attitudes toward God are obvious to children. Pope Francis reminds parents "that their personal example at home will help their child to grow in faith,"[80] while Barrett asserts that children "need to see parents and other members of their religious community acting like they believe"[81] as models for relationship with God.

Conclusion

God created children with a heightened openness to his presence, affording a time-sensitive opportunity for parents and the church to form them. Children under the age of six are naturally contemplative, as demonstrated in their proclivity to wonder; when directed toward God, wonder becomes worship. In contrast to adults, who prefer to close meaning, children easily rest in opening meaning, which allows them to delight in the mysteries of God.

While parents are primary faith formers, God designed the church to partner with and equip parents to cultivate children's faith. A multidimensional view of children prepares adults to both guide and learn from children, thereby laying the foundations for church participation. When welcomed into faith communities, children and adults mutually benefit from one another's examples and contributions, as children model childlike faith as only they can. Yet separate, age-appropriate activities designed to prepare children for meaningful, multigenerational worship experiences

---

80 Mares, "Pope Francis."
81 Barrett, "Childlike Faith," 71.

empower and honor children. Parents and facilitators serve children well by introducing God as the Good Shepherd and presenting parables without explanation to allow children the opportunity to discover God for themselves. Adults demonstrate the significance of prayer, the priority of worship, and faith through their own relationships with God.

God gives families and faith communities a wonderful gift in the spiritual vibrancy and openness of the youngest members of the body of Christ. Seizing the opportunity of very young children's spiritual capacity, parents and the church are called to spiritually nurture children from their earliest days so they may encounter the living God and set them on a trajectory of lifelong faith.

Bibliography

Allen, Holly Catterton, ed. *Nurturing Children's Spirituality: Christian Perspectives and Best Practices*. Eugene, OR: Cascade Books, 2008.

Allen, Holly Catterton, and Christine Lawton Ross. *Intergenerational Christian Formation: Bringing the Whole Church Together in Ministry, Community and Worship*. Downers Grove, IL: InterVarsity, 2012.

Barrett, Justin. *Born Believers: The Science of Children's Religious Belief*. New York: Free Press, 2012.

———. "Childlike Faith: What Developmental Science Tell Us about Children's Religious Beliefs." Interview by Holly Catterton Allen. *Christianity Today*, June 2012, 71.

Berryman, Jerome. *Godly Play: An Imaginative Approach to Religious Education*. Minneapolis: Augsburg, 1991.

Beste, Jennifer. "Second Graders' Spirituality in the Context of the Sacrament of Reconciliation." In *Understanding Children's Spirituality: Theology, Research, and Practice*, edited by Kevin E. Lawson, 283–306. Eugene, OR: Cascade Books, 2012.

Borgo, Lacy Finn. *Spiritual Conversations with Children: Listening to God Together*. Downers Grove, IL: InterVarsity, 2020.

Boyd, Jared Patrick. *Imaginative Prayer: A Yearlong Guide for Your Child's Spiritual Formation*. Downers Grove, IL: InterVarsity, 2017.

Bunge, Marcia. "Biblical and Theological Perspectives on Children, Parents, and 'Best Practices' for Faith Formation: Resources for

Child, Youth, and Family Ministry Today." *Dialog: A Journal of Theology* 47, no. 4 (Winter, 2008): 348–60.

———. "Biblical Theological Perspectives and Best Practices for Faith Formation." In *Understanding Children's Spirituality: Theology, Research, and Practice*, edited by Kevin E. Lawson, 3–25. Eugene, OR: Cascade Books, 2012.

———, ed. *The Child in Christian Thought*. Grand Rapids, MI: Eerdmans, 2001.

Bushnell, Horace. *Christian Nurture*. New York: Charles Scribner's Sons, 1906.

Catholic Church. *Catechism of the Catholic Church*. 2nd ed. Vatican: Libreria Editrice Vaticana, 2016.

———. "Duties of Family Members." In *Catechism*, 2225.

Cavalletti, Sofia. *The Religious Potential of the Child: Experiencing Scripture and Liturgy with Young Children*. Chicago: Archdiocese of Chicago, Liturgy Training, 1992.

Crabtree, Mara L. "Forbid Not the Little Ones: The Spirituality of Children in the Celtic Christian Tradition." *Sage Journal* 4, no. 2 (2007). https://doi.org/10.1177/073989130700400204.

Diamond, Adele, and Dima Amso, "Contributions of Neuroscience to Our Understanding of Cognitive Development." In Junn and Boyatzis, *Annual Editions*, 30–34.

Estep, James R. "The Christian Nurture of Children in the Second and Third Centuries." In Allen, *Nurturing Children's Spirituality*, 61–77.

Fuller, Cheri. *Opening Your Child's Spiritual Windows: Ideas to Nurture Your Child's Relationship with God*. Grand Rapids, MI: Zondervan, 2001.

Harwood, Adam, and Kevin E. Lawson. "Comparing Five Theological Views and Ministry Practices." In Larson and Keeley, *Bridging Theory and Practice in Children's Spirituality*, 45–46.

———, eds. *Infants and Children in the Church: Five Views on Theology and Ministry*. Nashville: B&H Academic, 2017.

Joiner, Reggie. *Think Orange*. Colorado Springs: David C. Cook, 2009.

Junn, Ellen, and Chris Boyatzis. *Annual Editions: Child Growth and Development 12/13*. 19th ed. New York: McGraw-Hill Education, 2011.

King, Pamela Ebstyne. "The Nature and Functions of Religious and Spiritual Development in Childhood and Adolescence." PhD diss., Fuller Theological Seminary, Pasadena, CA, 2015.

Larson, Mimi L., and Robert J. Keeley. *Bridging Theory and Practice in Children's Spirituality: New Directions for Education, Ministry, and Discipleship*. Grand Rapids, MI: Zondervan Reflective, 2020.

Loder, James. *Logic of the Spirit: Human Development in Theological Perspective*. San Francisco: Jossey-Bass, 1998.

Mares, Courtney. "Pope Francis: It Is Beautiful When Babies Cry at Mass." *Catholic News Agency*, January 12, 2020. https://www.catholicnewsagency.com/news/43256/pope-francis-it-is-beautiful-when-babies-cry-at-mass.

May, Scottie, Beth Posterski, Catherine Stonehouse, and Linda Cannell. *Children Matter: Celebrating Their Place in the Church, Family, and Community*. Grand Rapids, MI: Eerdmans, 2005.

Mercer, Joyce Ann. *Welcoming Children: A Practical Theology of Childhood*. St. Louis: Chalice, 2005.

Morgenthaler, Shirley K. *Right from the Start: A Parent's Guide to the Young Child's Faith Development*. St. Louis: Concordia, 2001.

Mosher, Jennifer Haddad. "Irenaeus' Stages of Faith." In *Understanding Children's Spirituality: Theology, Research, and Practice*, edited by Kevin E. Lawson, 106–18. Eugene, OR: Cascade Books, 2012.

Palmer, Parker. "Unfettered Wonder." In Allen, *Nurturing Children's Spirituality*, 132.

Ratcliff, Donald. "'The Spirit of the Past': A Century of Children's Spirituality Research." In Allen, *Nurturing Children's Spirituality*, 21–42.

Roe, Earl O., ed. *Dream Big: The Henrietta Mears Story*. Ventura, CA: Regal Books, 1990.

Stewart, Sonja M., and Jerome W Berryman. *Young Children and Worship*. Louisville, KY: Westminster John Knox, 1989.

Stonehouse, Catherine, and Scottie May. *Listening to Children on the Spiritual Journey: Guidance for Those Who Teach and Nurture*. Grand Rapids, MI: Baker Academic, 2010.

Westerhoff, John, II. "The Church's Contemporary Challenge: Assisting Adults to Mature Spiritually *with* Their Children." In Allen, *Nurturing Children's Spirituality*, 363.

CHAPTER 10

(*Un*)Divided Worship
Children Leading and Belonging in the Worshiping Community

Edwin (Ed) M. Willmington and Trevecca Okholm

"Kids' Worship"

When planning to visit a church with some family members, I (Ed) checked out the church website and saw a banner stating that "Kids' Worship" would be offered during one time period in the morning. Being a person interested in worship, my attention was piqued. Arriving at the church, I went through the required sign-up protocol and received my approved visitor badge, which allowed me to visit "Kids' Worship." I was excited to attend, since it was an unusual opportunity for me. I was ushered into a room set up with a low, small stage in the front; a big screen to one side of the platform; and colorful benches for seating. Music played on the sound system while parents dropped off children. When it was time to begin, one of the adult leaders went to the platform and shouted, "Are you ready for worship?" All the kids yelled, "Yeah!" and instantly, a music video lit up the screen and speakers pumped out music. A small group of kids identified this as their cue to run up onto the stage and begin to dance. There was no leader, and almost no one was singing. The music also seemed to be a cue for at least half of the kids to completely ignore what was going on. Some continued to run around the room, playing tag as they crawled under the open benches, and one or two walked over to a corner to stand and do nothing. This pattern went on for three back-to-back songs, complete with lyrics like "Boingo, boingo, boingo, bop!" As I observed, my heart sank, and I thought, "This is what they call 'Kids' Worship?'" I wondered about ducking for cover to hide from a potential heavenly lightning strike! After taking a breath, I had a more horrific thought: "What I'm seeing is a formative model that parents and kids are associating with worship." Though I had greatly anticipated this time of "Kids' Worship," it became a frightening specter of both the present and future practice of worship in that church.

Once I detoxed a bit from the experience, I pondered what the trajectory might be for those children a decade or so ahead: How would they be included in church life? Would they even still be there? In fact, significant numbers of people do leave the church and/or even their faith once they reach age eighteen and move into adulthood.[1] Depending on what the research questions are, how they're asked, and how the numbers are dissected, the percentages of those who leave the church in their young adult years are shockingly high.[2,3] While some return later in life, and there are statistics showing several factors contribute to the percentages,[4] I wondered if this might be an indication that our isolationist approach to worship life has contributed to those percentages. I also wondered if a new paradigm for worship ministry might be a catalyst for filling in some of the gaps of isolation that have been created in the church. Do any of those factors relate to the ways in which many churches have done "Kids' Worship" over the past few decades?

For some time, Fuller Youth Institute (FYI) has researched the growing gap between youth and the larger church. In a podcast, FYI

---

1 See research on youth walking away from church—for example, Smith and Denton, *Soul Searching*.
2 Earls, "Most Teenagers."
3 Yoder, "Why Youth Leave."
4 Kinnaman, *You Lost Me*.

leader and author of *Sticky Faith*[5] Kara Powell delineated different factors related to students leaving the church. In the podcast, she quoted David Briggs in stating that even though there are more people becoming professional youth leaders, "we have this growing canyon between a congregation and a youth ministry."[6] Other *Sticky Faith* research states, "Of all the youth group participation variables that we've seen, being involved in intergenerational worship and relationship was one of the variables most highly correlated to young people's faith. . . . The gap between the overall congregation and youth ministry is growing, which ends up being toxic to young people's faith."

A more recent FYI study titled *Growing Young* dissected the philosophical structures of churches that are *not* aging but instead remaining well balanced in generational attendance or becoming younger. One of the aspects of the *Growing Young* study is that the number one identified challenge in reaching young people was not the culture, not the parents, not the young people themselves but issues within their own congregation. In fact, 37 percent of those surveyed identified systems and structures within the church as the main obstacles to reaching youth.[7]

One positive attribute of churches that are growing young is a high level of involvement of students across all areas of church ministry, not just within their youth group. They recommended that churches "ditch Teen Sunday!"—the once-a-year Sunday when the youth are allowed in the "big church" to usher, sing their songs, pray, provide testimonies, and read Scripture. They are then kindly invited to take their loud music and go back to their rooms and come out when invited—typically to report on summer camp or short-term mission trips. I read *Growing Young* certain it would propose a common formula for how worship life is structured in churches that are growing young. To my surprise, there was no common formula.

5 Powell and Clark, *Sticky Faith*.
6 Briggs, "No. 1 Reason."
7 Powell, Mulder, and Griffin, *Growing Young*.

Knowing the authors of the book, I decided it would be worth buying a lunch to pursue that topic a little deeper. As it turns out, there was only one common thread in the studied churches when it came to worship: the youth were regularly involved in the larger worship life of the growing young churches. They were invited to pray, sing, read Scripture, give announcements, and usher. They were welcome to join the wider age range of people in the worship life of the church. There is an inverse correlation between the welcoming atmosphere of a church and the statistics of those who leave as they move into adulthood, enabling churches to grow younger.

I began to wonder the following:

- Do some of these same principles extend down from teenagers to grade-school-age children?
- How do pastoral and worship leadership involve themselves in bridging the canyons of isolation?
- If churches that are growing young are inviting the youth to be present, is it possible that some of those same welcoming principles apply to younger ages as well?

The Place and Potential of Children in the Community of Faith

Many churches, pastors, and parents have overlooked what children are able to comprehend and contribute. As professors of Christian formation Scottie May, Beth Posterski, Catherine Stonehouse, and Linda Pannell explain in their pivotal book on the place of children in the worshiping community,[8] the participation of children in the worshiping community has the potential to benefit and bless all generations. One of the points they make is that in the church, we need to begin thinking of *worship* as a verb rather than as a noun: "When we focus on the verbs of worship, it helps

8 May et al., *Children Matter*.

us discern the abilities of children to participate in acts of worship: give thanks, call on him, make him known, sing to him, glory in him, rejoice, remember, bring offerings, praise. How many of these are children capable of doing and at what age? Even little ones—two-and three-year-olds can sing, praise, and give thanks. They also can show reverence on their own."[9]

By looking at *worship* as a verb, an active stage where we are all rehearsing and being formed together into the body of Christ, we are better able to create spaces of purpose and belonging. Ross Parsley, in his book *Messy Church: A Multigenerational Mission for God's Family*, compares worship to the family meal, referring to it as "the family worship table" for which "the dream is to create a [worship] environment where people come with anticipation and expectation of what God will say and do as we gather to enjoy the bounty of God's table and fellowship with one another and with the Holy Spirit."[10] Ross goes on to say,

> Many of our churches have decided to stop having family dinners. We've relegated young people to the kids' table because it's easier that way. All the kids eating at the table with the grownups is messy, and it's just too much work. It creates awkward moments. . . . Grandma and Grandpa can only take so much noise, you know. Parents are busy with preparations and hosting. Teenagers feel more comfortable with their own kind anyway, and frankly, that relieves most parents and grandparents for a couple of hours on a Sunday morning. . . . Many churches approach ministry to people through the lens of an educational system instead of through the analogy of the family. . . . Instead of the organic sharing of an experience, we have opted to niche market the church experience to each unique demographic. . . . A meal is a multisensory encounter with many complementary tastes, smells, textures, and dialogues. The family meal is

---

9 May et al., 219.
10 Parsley, *Messy Church*, 65.

interactive, communal, and provides the perfect illustration of God's family of believers.[11]

In her book *The Religious Potential of the Child*,[12] Sofia Cavalletti has an amazing chapter titled "God and the Child" in which she relays stories of children's abilities to understand and display their faith—in some cases shining a light on the shallow faith of adults. As I have observed on many occasions, this ability to understand their faith carries over to children's abilities to lead others too. I (Trevecca) have been in professional ministry with children for nearly forty years, and the ability of most children to respond to God with spiritual depth never ceases to amaze me! For example, Mateo is a surfer dude, a Southern California kid with boundless energy and wit—yet in our generationally inclusive worship, he gently anoints the heads of our prayer team with oil and prays a blessing over them in quiet reverence. Several of our church's kids, even as young as three years old, love when they are asked to give this blessing to adults in our worship service each week. Mateo also holds up holy hands as he sings, and his three-year-old sister loves dancing in the aisles during the music. One of my favorite examples of Mateo's spiritual initiative and leadership is a video his mom shared of him leading his family in Eucharist at home. He was only five at the time, but he took his invitation to his family to join him in Eucharist very seriously. When it came to words of institution,[13] I was amazed that Mateo repeated the words of our pastor almost verbatim. He didn't learn this in Sunday school or at home, he learned by observing our pastor repeating these words each week during our worship service. I could continue with countless other examples of the effects of young children participating fully in worship.

---

11 Parsley, 67.
12 Cavalletti, *Religious Potential*.
13 The "words of institution" are traditionally referred to and quoted from 1 Cor. 11 during Eucharist or Communion.

When we find ways for children to both participate and lead us in our corporate worship, they are capable. When children are placed in situations like the "Kids' Worship" Ed observed, they will often treat it as an opportunity for play and craziness with their peers; however, when we present them with opportunities to enter into holy spaces and show them that we value their participation, they almost always bless us with their ability to respond in worship.

The practice of corporate worship offers an unsurpassed sense of belonging with and to the larger community of faith. Our observations also note that the larger and more "successful" a church becomes, the more children are at risk of becoming siloed or isolated.[14] Larger churches are able to provide separate spaces for children where they can be self-sufficient and cared for, but the walls of isolation are tall and wide when it comes to "belonging" or welcoming children into the larger church-family community.

"Suffer" the Little Children?

Most children's ministry leaders have heard and even quoted the perhaps indignantly spoken words of Jesus in Mark 10:14: "Suffer the little children to come unto me" (KJV). However, our modern-day use of the word *suffer* as related to children is more often understood as pain or struggle than as the concept of giving permission. Thus, we often isolate the little children and forbid them to enter the worship space for fear that "they will be a bother and cause chaos." In fact, the opposite is true: Jesus commands the disciples to welcome children into his presence. When it comes to corporate worship gatherings in local churches, many congregations have isolated children rather than "suffering" or "allowing" them to be a part of the congregational gathering. When isolation occurs, the children suffer in the painful sense, and the whole faith community, including the big people, suffers as well.

14 May, Stemp, and Burns, "Children's Place."

In her pivotal book *Parenting in the Pew*, Robbie Castleman writes,

> I have heard more than a few parents confess, "I used to get more out of church before I had kids." But the bigger issue is, what does God get out of worship.... In the psalms we read or sing, "Bless the Lord, O my soul." However, our chief concern is usually "Bless my soul, O Lord!"... Children can infringe on our worship experience. I know more than a few parents who have resented the distractions ushered into the pew by the presence of their children. Many just give up. However, children do not have to interfere with *God's* experience of worship. Worship is first a blessing to God, and he values the presence and praise of children (Matthew 18:14; Mark 10:14; Luke 18:16).[15]

There is a growing conviction that worship has become "the Great Assumption" of the church. Church leaders and others assume that because a group of people gathers in a certain space and time, sings, prays, and learns from a sermon, worship has then occurred. This may be true, but it may not be too. In a survey of approximately twenty church websites, I (Ed) further substantiated some of my assumptions. Almost every church has a dropdown menu titled "ministries." I decided to click on those "ministries" menus, looking for "worship," and discovered that the majority had no menu item called "worship." Some had "music," which seemed to mostly provide information about what musical opportunities were available in the church. Others had some reference to worship connected to Sunday services in other menus, again seeming to support my thought that worship was assumed but not treated as a bona fide, legitimate church ministry.

For earlier centuries in the church, the worship gathering served as the primary setting for spiritual activity and faith formation. Corporate worship (i.e., all ages in the community worshiping

---

15 Castleman, *Parenting in the Pew*, 24.

together) has been a focused communal act where Scripture has been read and explained, spiritual practices have been developed, formational rituals and liturgy have been observed, all the activities of life can be lifted toward God, and various responses to God's work in us can be expressed. Worship is the revelation of God to his people and the upward offering of response to God—a dialogue between the Creator and God's creation. As such, worship is the power and discernment grid through which all ministries should pass. In worship, we gather to bring everything we have to God and are, in return, sent into the world to shine his light around us. Worship is central, not to be treated as trivial or assumed. Horizontally focused ministries, while good and necessary, often have taken a higher rank over the worship life of any given church. This is little surprise in our consumer-driven culture. Church growth philosophies have sometimes dictated how a church should become "successful," which has at times prescribed that the gathering of people is attraction based rather than worship focused. The question should be asked, "Whatever happened to God-sensitive worship?"[16]

Beyond the church leaders, congregants are also part of the worship assumption and are not always sure of their purpose for being in a corporate worship service. A George Barna poll showed that "attendance at worship services is, by their admission, generally the only time they think about worshiping God, eight out of ten church goers do not feel they have entered into the presence of God, or experienced a connection with Him, during a worship service—in the past year—only one out of every four churched believers says that when they worship God, they expect Him to be the primary beneficiary of their worship."[17] (Most people say *they* expect to get the most from the experience.) It seems that people have no idea that when they gather for corporate worship, they

---

16 For an excellent guided study of "God-focused worship," see Castleman, *Story Shaped Worship*.
17 Barna, *Revolution*.

are to act, not passively receive. Is it any wonder that I saw what I saw in "Kids' Worship"?

The Role of Worship in Faith Formation and Child Spirituality

Because music is my professional career, I cannot help reflecting on how music has changed in our worshiping communities. These changes have impacted the historical setting of worship mentioned above and, in turn, impacted the formational power of our corporate worship for adults as well as children. Music has been viewed as an important expression of faith throughout both the Old and the New Testament eras. From the Old Testament Levites who served multiple roles in temple worship to the apostle Paul's instructions to use "psalms, hymns, and spiritual songs" to "teach and admonish" one another in faith, music had a role in faith formation. Martin Luther gave a high priority to music as a method to both teach the faithful and evangelize those in need of faith. Teachers in Luther's schools were required to possess musical skills in order to use music as a tool for teaching children. In 1763, Charles Wesley published *Hymns for Children*, which served a direct formational purpose alongside the catechism he would teach to children. Isaac Watts authored a collection of twenty-seven songs, scriptures, and prayers: *Dr. Watts's Hymns and Moral Songs for the Use of Children*. While the singing of traditional hymns has certainly waned in recent times, the efforts of Keith and Kristyn Getty[18] and others have promoted singing traditional hymns with children as a means of transmitting faith. In my own experience, I have joined others to create artistic resources to use with children to express theological convictions, such as the Five Solas Project.[19] There are also resources being developed that involve children and families to provide worship leadership for churches based on spiritual

---

18 For examples, see their website: http://www.GettyMusic.com.
19 Visit the Jubal House website for information about the Five Solas Project. See "So, What Are These Sola Things?"

formation themes.[20] Singing and praying our theology pays great dividends not only in the present but for a lifetime of growing faith in God. As the role of music changed in our worship over the past century or so, we lost a vital means for faith formation both for adults and for children.

Prioritizing God-sensitive or God-focused worship and the role of worship in faith formation will naturally lead to some decisions that affect ministry activities. In an undivided, integrated model of worship, leaders of worship will reach out to collaborate with children's ministry directors and vice versa. They will engage in some common study of worship, discuss how they will join in developing structures for training, and create sequential, prioritized places of "belonging" in the worship lives of children within the entire church ministry. Together, they can ask God to give them a vision for true "Kids' Worship" that is God focused rather than self-focused.

The Value of Family Worship

In developing a strategy, a fundamental starting place will be outside of the physical church walls, in the home—family worship. According to data from the *National Study of Youth and Religion*, "82 percent of children raised by parents who talked about faith at home, attached great importance to their beliefs and were active in their congregations, were themselves religiously active as young adults."[21] In that study, you can just hear the echoes of Deuteronomy 6:6–7: "These commandments that I give you today are to be on your hearts. Impress them on your children. Talk about them when you sit at home and when you walk along the road, when you lie down and when you get up."

After blinking at the statistics of how much time is consumed running children from school to soccer, ballet, and similar

---

20 Yoder, "Why Youth Leave."
21 Briggs, "No. 1 Reason."

activities—not to mention the amount of time spent on electronic devices—we should aggressively encourage families to place margins on some of these practices. As good as all those activities are for mental, emotional, physical, and social development, rather than being passive, we in church ministry have an opportunity to assist families to assess their present priorities in the light of long-term formation.[22] We know we're dreaming, but we both wonder if families understand that the likelihood of their child becoming a professional soccer player is remote, but developing into a lifelong worshiper is possible for all children. Should we not then prioritize some time for family worship? In his book *A Neglected Grace*, Jason Helopoulos provides a list of practical benefits of family worship, one of which is that it "equips our children for corporate worship."[23] As families read and listen to the Word of God, hear and offer prayers, and sing songs, these same elements in corporate worship will take on new meanings. Liturgical elements become normalized as expressions of faith rather than one-off, unfamiliar sets of actions occurring once a week. Modern hymn writers Keith and Kristyn Getty model a "read, sing, pray"[24] format with their family, and Ivy Beckwith prescribes "story, ritual, and relationship."[25] These forms can also crack open the doors to the leadership of children in the worshiping community. There isn't one activity in those formats that a seven-to-ten-year-old (and, in some cases, even quite a bit younger) can't do—and often more proficiently than adults. This is the ultimate "passing the faith along." The value of normalizing worship in the lives of children cannot be overestimated.

Now having grandchildren, when I hear my daughter or her husband announce that it is family worship time, one child runs to get a Bible, and the other runs to bring a storybook. Then while squeezed between grandparents or sitting on a lap, they

---

22 Joiner, *Think Orange*.
23 Helopoulos, *Neglected Grace*, 47.
24 Getty and Getty, *Sing!*
25 Beckwith, *Formational Children's Ministry*.

read, pray, and sing—even praying for me! Amazing! During Advent, they walk to the Advent calendar hanging on the pantry doorknob, pull a scripture from a pocket dated for that day on the calendar, read the scripture, pray, and sing a song of prayer for the return of Jesus. Discipline? Yes! Requires a vision? Yes! Result? Priceless!

Children Worshiping with Other Children

Second, let's raise the bar in providing opportunities for children to worship with other children. When serving in a church, my job description always had a statement of oversight and involvement with the worship and arts lives of children in the church. As we have stated, we have lost the connection between worship leadership and children in most churches, and we have suffered—in the painful sense—in some distinct ways. Think about it: if we're going to bridge the canyon of worship isolation, one connection in that bridge will be providing a place for kids to worship with other kids, even lead other kids—a practice that can continue at all ages throughout the entire worshiping community. When we give children important responsibilities, they very often surprise us! I (Trevecca) have found this to be true over and over again in my decades of children's ministry.

There are marvelous places to begin when reimagining your places and spaces for children in worship with other children. The whole of *worship and wonder* approaches to faith formation[26] is based on worship and a form of liturgical rhythm. James H. Ritchie fills the pages of his delightful and encouraging little book on the practice of worship and the presence of children with stories of the children he has interviewed on their experiences of worship: "'Worship is holy,' asserted Michael [age eleven], 'kind of because it gets you close to God. It brings you more into God's life instead of your average "you" life. I mean, you're not like on the streets of

---

26 Okholm, "Invitation to Worship," 65–75.

LA where people are shooting guns at other people. That's not holy. But when you're in church, silent, you're praying to God. You're asking God to give you mercy. It's just holy.'"[27]

Providing such holy spaces for children to worship will likely involve some shifting of typical children's ministry philosophy and practice. Some restructuring might involve reallocating a portion of the church school ministry from "worship" to what is truly worship at an age-appropriate level. This will consist of more than singing "kids' songs" with a video, reading a Bible story, and completing a craft. Children's teachers often resort to some interesting activities that are hard to call worship. This is a call for the leader of worship and children's director to invite some focused study on worship, create some vision, and recruit some specific people who will join their skills with the vision to provide leadership.[28]

Children and Adults: Leading Worship Together

Lastly, the culminating step is to discover regular and creative ways to welcome children into corporate (a.k.a. adult) worship and create space for them to discover their place of belonging in the midst of generations worshiping together. Our observation is that typically, when children are invited into the adult worship space, it is to sing a song, wave to any family members present, be cute, and then be marched off. The parents on those Sundays often actually sit close to the front, wave back to their kids, have phones in hand for pictures and videos, and then leave when the kids leave. What formational model are we molding when we do that? Kids can't help but be cute or funny, especially when they believe it is expected, but they are capable of so much more.

---

27 Ritchie, *Always in Rehearsal*, 26–27.
28 See the bibliography at the end of this chapter for resources on leading a focused study on worship with your ministry team.

Holly Catterton Allen and Christine Lawton Ross's book *Intergenerational Christian Formation* includes a wonderful chapter on intergenerational worship,[29] offering a strong case for "broadening the scope" of worship along with practical models. Yes, it takes some significant planning ahead, but it is the path to true undivided worship! Eight-year-olds can read or recite Scripture, ten-year-olds can pray, and nine-year-olds can provide liturgical dance expressions. Even six-year-olds—like in the story of Mateo earlier in this chapter—can anoint adults in ministry! And yes, they can even sing while they're there too, much like the *Growing Young* study affirms—not only is welcoming children into the worship space important; allowing them to provide forms of leadership should be validated as well. Children who are welcomed and valued become familiar with the space of worship. They have experienced personal and corporate ministry before God in that space, and they quickly learn that they "belong."

We have a significant gap in many churches between the children and the larger church family. We often wonder, With these models of family worship, true worship experiences of kids with kids, and kids being welcomed as participants and leaders into multigenerational worship, will people be so inclined to leave the church at age eighteen? Or will they bridge the islands of isolation, the silos the church has created, and find being part of a worshiping community to be an important part of their lives beyond age eighteen?

In his book *Worship Matters*, Bob Kauflin talks about his "twenty-year rule." Kauflin speculates that when someone is born into the church where he is responsible for the worship life, they will be under his worshiping care for twenty years before they leave for life in other places. So when they leave—and we add our own interpretation here—from their worship life in the church, will they know about the Triune God? Will they know about confession? Will

---

29 Allen and Ross, *Intergenerational Christian Formation*, 189.

they know about postures of worship? Will they recognize "holy," as in the stories of children in Ritchie's research?[30] Will they anticipate the return of Christ? Or as Kauflin says, "Would they think worship is about music, and not much more?"[31]

Bibliography

Allen, Holly Catterton, and Christine Lawton Ross. *Intergenerational Christian Formation: Bringing the Whole Church Together in Ministry, Community and Worship*. Downers Grove, IL: InterVarsity Academic, 2012.

Barna, George. *Revolution: Finding Vibrant Faith beyond the Walls of the Sanctuary*. Carol Stream, IL: Tyndale House, 2005.

Beckwith, Ivy. *Formational Children's Ministry: Using Story, Ritual, and Relationship*. Grand Rapids, MI: Baker, 2010.

Berryman, Jerome. *Becoming like a Child: The Curiosity of Maturity beyond the Norm*. New York: Church Publishing, 2017.

———. *Children and the Theologians: Clearing the Way for Grace*. Harrisburg, PA: Morehouse, 2009.

Bolsinger, Tod. *It Takes a Church to Raise a Christian: How the Community of God Transforms Lives*. Grand Rapids, MI: Brazos, 2004.

Briggs, David. "The No. 1 Reason Teens Keep the Faith as Young Adults." *Huffington Post*, December 29, 2014. https://www.huffpost.com/entry/the-no-1-reason-teens-kee_b_6067838.

Castleman, Robbie. *Parenting in the Pew: Guiding Your Children into the Joy of Worship*. Downers Grove, IL: InterVarsity, 2013.

———. *Story Shaped Worship: Following Patterns from the Bible and History*. Downers Grove, IL: InterVarsity, 2013.

Cavalletti, Sofia. *The Religious Potential of the Child: Experiencing Scripture and Liturgy with Young Children*. Chicago: Liturgy Training, 2019.

Earls, Aaron. "Most Teenagers Drop Out of Church When They Become Young Adults." Lifeway Research, January 15, 2019. https://lifewayresearch.com/2019/01/15/most-teenagers-drop-out-of-church-as-young-adults/.

---

30 Ritchie, *Always in Rehearsal*.
31 Kauflin, *Worship Matters*, 119.

Edie, Fred. *Book, Bath, Table, and Time: Christian Worship as Source and Resource for Youth Ministry*. Cleveland: Pilgrim, 2007.

Getty, Keith, and Kristyn Getty. *Sing! How Worship Transforms Your Life, Family, and Church*. Nashville: B&H, 2017.

Helopoulos, Jason. *A Neglected Grace: Family Worship in the Christian Home*. Fearn, UK: Christian Focus, 2013.

Joiner, Reggie. *Think Orange: Imagine the Impact When Church and Family Collide*. Colorado Springs: Cook, 2009.

Jubal House. "So, What Are These Sola Things?" Accessed November 4, 2022. http://www.jubalhouse.com/five-solas-project/.

Kauflin, Bob. *Worship Matters: Leading Others to Encounter the Greatness of God*. Wheaton, IL: Crossway, 2008.

Kinnaman, David. *You Lost Me: Why Young Christians Are Leaving Church . . . and Rethinking Faith*. Grand Rapids, MI: Baker, 2016.

Larson, Mimi, and Robert Keeley, eds. *Bridging Theory and Practice in Children's Spirituality: New Directions for Education, Ministry, and Discipleship*. Downers Grove, IL: InterVarsity, 2020.

May, Scottie, Beth Posterski, Catherine Stonehouse, and Linda Cannell. *Children Matter: Celebrating Their Place in the Church, Family, and Community*. Grand Rapids, MI: Eerdmans, 2005.

May, Scottie, Katie Stemp, and Grant Burns. "Children's Place in the New Forms of Church: An Exploratory Survey of These Forms' Ministry with Children and Families." *Christian Education: Journal Research on Educational Ministry* 8, no. 2 (November 2011): 278–305.

Mercer, Joyce. *Welcoming Children: A Practical Theology of Childhood*. Nashville: Chalice, 2005.

Okholm, Trevecca. "An Invitation to Worship and Wonder: An Overview of Contemplative Models of Spiritual Formation." In *Story, Formation & Culture: Current Approaches to Children's Spirituality & Ministry*, edited by Benjamin D. Espinoza, James Riley Estep Jr., and Shirley Morgenthaler, 65–75. Eugene, OR: Wipf & Stock, 2018.

Parsley, Ross. *Messy Church: A Multigenerational Mission for God's Family*. Colorado Springs: Cook, 2012.

Powell, Kara E., and Chap Clark. *Sticky Faith: Everyday Ideas to Build Lasting Faith into Your Kids*. Grand Rapids, MI: Zondervan, 2011.

Powell, Kara E., Jake Mulder, and Brad Griffin. *Growing Young: Six Essential Strategies to Help Young People Discover and Love Your Church*. Grand Rapids, MI: Baker, 2016.

Ritchie, James. *Always in Rehearsal: The Practice of Worship and the Presence of Children*. Nashville: Discipleship Resources, 2005.

Smith, Christian, and Melinda Lundquist Denton. *Soul Searching: The Religious and Spiritual Lives of American Teenagers*. New York: Oxford University Press, 2005.

Yoder, Marc. "Why Youth Leave the Church: 10 Surprising Reasons." Church Leaders, May 19, 2021. https://churchleaders.com/children/childrens-ministry-articles/166129-marc-solas-10-surprising-reasons-our-kids-leave-church.html.

SECTION 4

Coming Alongside Children in Challenging Contexts

When people consider children's ministries, they often first think of Bible stories, creative activities, imaginative play, and spiritual friendships. Childhood is meant to be a time of innocence, growth, and exploration. For many children, however, childhood is also a time of navigating significant grief, loss, and trauma. No demographic is immune to the effects of the brokenness of the world, and a child in a loving home, well-resourced community, and intentional church may experience trauma or tragedy in much the same way as a child in a more difficult setting. In this section, three researcher-practitioners seek to equip children's ministry leaders with the resources to attend to children who have experienced trauma, advocate for their safety and healing, and walk with them through grief and suffering.

Recognizing that children may carry hidden areas of suffering, striving to make ministry areas safe from potential harm to children, and seeking thoughtful, life-giving ways to come alongside children in difficult situations are important steps for all ministry leaders to prepare themselves to attend to children navigating trauma or loss. In any given week, a child we minister to regularly may experience a sudden trauma, or a new child may enter our ministry context carrying grief or woundedness. By familiarizing themselves with basic resources in advance, children's ministry leaders can respond thoughtfully and further prepare themselves to meet the contextualized needs of the specific child in their ministry setting.

In Chapter Eleven, "The God of the Child: Trauma and Spirituality," Esther Zimmerman explores how trauma may shape a child's understanding or experience of God. Even young children work to make sense of their difficult life experiences in light of what they know about God's character. What does it mean to know God's love after a natural disaster, abuse, illness, or the death of a loved one? Does God allow or will the suffering of children? While the words that children use to express these concerns differ from the ways adults express concerns of theodicy, they are nonetheless working through the same questions. Parents, ministry leaders, and caring adults in the faith community can seek to better understand how this might look in the life of a child and how to come alongside them as they work through grief and trauma.

In Chapter Twelve, "Theology and Abuse: Vulnerability in the Midst of Religious Institutions," Stacey Wilson of Melbourne, Australia, who studies and speaks on child abuse in institutional settings, explores cultural risk factors related to child abuse and its effect on children's spiritual development. While Wilson's particular research context is unfamiliar to most readers, the stories point to universal principles from which ministry leaders in every context might learn. In fact, reading these lessons in a cross-cultural context may help some readers more fully consider the possibilities of abuse within their own context as they intentionally examine their own ministry for similar risk factors. Readers around the world will benefit from examining how power structures and certain theological and doctrinal beliefs might lead to a higher propensity for child abuse as they seek to create safe spaces for children within their own ministry contexts. In addition to adopting and enforcing standard safety regulations, ministry leaders can thoughtfully consider how their community contexts and theological teachings may contribute to or compound childhood abuse traumas.

Finally, Lacy Finn Borgo shares "Accompanying Children and Teens through Loss," largely informed by her work in spiritual direction with children living in a transitional housing context. While some forms of loss or trauma are inflicted on children by perpetrators, other children experience loss through illness, death, natural disasters, or other unfortunate and unpredictable circumstances. In either case, children and teens seek to make spiritual sense of their suffering, and Borgo offers practical insight to help adults in their faith communities walk alongside them as they navigate pain, questions, and wonderings in light of God's character and God's Word.

Often, it is in times of trauma and suffering that children test their spiritual beliefs and experiences against the realities of life. By creating places where children are kept safe from abuse and being willing to acknowledge and patiently walk alongside children experiencing grief, loss, and suffering, Christian communities can share God's love in powerful, practical ways. For many ministry leaders, this means acknowledging and attending to their own places of grief and loss in light of God's love so they can then share a true and robust hope that both acknowledges the reality of brokenness in the world and gives witness to the hope offered in the love of Christ.

As you begin this weighty section of the book, may you know the love of our Creator God, the hope of Christ, and the peace of the Holy Spirit that surpasses understanding. May you have wisdom to discern the next steps, courage to take them, and strong support from your community as you minister to God's beloved children.

CHAPTER 11

The God of the Child
Trauma and Spirituality[1]

Esther L. Zimmerman

Four decades ago, Ana-Maria Rizzuto[2] challenged ministry leaders to pay attention to the "God of the child," writing, "No child arrives at the 'house of God' without his pet God under his arm."[3] Many children in our communities come to church with a view of God that has been forged in the context of trauma. What kind of God do these children bring with them, and how might we join them more authentically on their journey toward the God of the Bible?

Adverse Childhood Experiences

Research within the health sector in the last twenty-five years has examined the pervasive and long-lasting effects of Adverse Childhood Experiences (ACEs) on children's development.[4] From 1995 to 1997, the Center for Disease Control and Kaiser Permanente conducted a groundbreaking study of over seventeen thousand adults

---

1 Sections of this chapter are taken from the author's published dissertation.
2 Ana-Maria Rizzuto was a psychoanalyst who focused on religious experience. Her book *Birth of the Living God* distinguishes between a child's cognitive understanding of God, which she calls "God-concept," and a child's affective experience of God, which she calls "God-image." She suggests that a person may hold a formal belief in God that is at odds with their unverbalized but deeply held feelings about God.
3 Rizzuto, *Birth of the Living God*, 8.
4 Hughes et al., "Effect of Multiple Adverse Childhood Experiences," 356–66.

that investigated the relationship between ACEs and health.[5] Researchers surveyed participants on ACEs of neglect, abuse, and household dysfunction in ten specific categories: family violence, mental illness, or substance abuse; divorce or incarceration of parents; emotional or physical neglect; and physical, emotional, or sexual abuse as children.

Based on the number of experiences reported, participants were assigned an ACE score. Researchers then compared participants' ACE scores with their health histories. Numerous subsequent studies continue to confirm and expand on the conclusions of the original study.[6]

These studies have repeatedly found the following:

1. ACEs are much more common than is generally recognized. Half of respondents had at least one ACE, a quarter had multiple ACEs, and one in sixteen had four or more ACEs. The study also debunked the myth that ACEs are confined to families living in poverty or urban areas.[7]
2. ACEs significantly impact a child's development with long-term negative consequences. In short, children with higher ACE scores are more likely to develop life-threatening emotional and physical health conditions. They are also more likely to struggle at school and exhibit self-destructive behaviors.[8]

These ACEs study findings highlight that many children in our churches and communities are wrestling with difficult circumstances and that these experiences are significantly impacting their development.[9]

---

5 Felitti et al., "Relationship of Childhood Abuse," 17–18.
6 Hughes et al., "Effect of Multiple Adverse Childhood Experiences"; Shern, Blanch, and Steverman, "Toxic Stress."
7 Souers and Hall, *Fostering Resilient Learners*.
8 Shern, Blanch, and Steverman, "Toxic Stress."
9 Frawley-Odea, "Childhood Abuse and Neglect."

ACEs and Development

ACEs physically impact a child's developing brain. In healthy childhoods, children experience mild to moderate stress in the context of supportive relationships. These normal childhood experiences of stress activate appropriate brain responses to environmental threats. However, when children experience intense or prolonged stress, particularly without adequate support, their response systems are overstimulated, resulting in toxic levels of stress.[10]

Early childhood exposure to toxic stress has lifetime consequences. Physically, the effects of toxic stress are seen through higher risks in almost every health category. Neurologically, toxic stress "weakens the architecture" of the developing brain.[11] In practice, toxic stress trains the young child to become a "survivalist." Because the child's early experience of life has demonstrated the need to "fight" or "flee" at a moment's notice, the child's brain learns to respond based on emotion and instinct rather than logic and reasoning. Karyn Purvis and others note that "when the primitive brain is on duty, more advanced areas of the brain ... get shut down."[12] ACEs also create memories that continue to shape a child's view of the world, as "the brain continually prepares itself for the future based on what happened before."[13]

Adverse Childhood Experiences and Spiritual Development

Children's experiences of trauma also impact their spiritual development. Writing of children in Liberia who experienced the trauma of civil war, Phyllis Kilbourn observes that "trauma

---

10 For more on the impact of stress, see Shern, Blanch, and Steverman, "Toxic Stress."
11 Harvard University's Center on the Developing Child, "Brain Architecture."
12 Purvis, Cross, and Sunshine, *Connected Child*, 50.
13 Siegel and Bryson, *Whole-Brain Child*.

robs children of precious childhood treasures, treasures that were meant to lay the spiritual foundations for their lives."[14] When a child's worldview is developed in the crucible of ACEs, the child's view of themselves, view of God, and relationship with God are affected.[15] However, a review of the literature suggests that not all children respond to trauma in the same way. ACEs may result in spiritual disconnection, spiritual damage, and/or spiritual questioning and spiritual sensitivity in children.

Spiritual Disconnection

Some children who have experienced trauma may experience *spiritual disconnection*—a sense that God is irrelevant to their world. Young children form their fundamental beliefs about God, themselves, and their world as they interact with their world.[16] As a result, children are constantly at work making meaning from their lives and circumstances and weaving a narrative to live by.

Ideally, a child's world reflects the nature and character of the Christian God. As children experience the loving care of a family, they come to understand the loving care of God. As children experience worship in a community of faith, they are pointed to the God who deserves the worship of all people. As children experience the security of a just community, they are pointed to a God who is just and provides safety. However, when children's worlds reflect little of God's character and human dignity, their spiritual narratives may be shaped negatively.[17] Children evaluate new information in light of existing information and their own logical processes.[18] This process of evaluation may produce conflicts for a child whose prior experience does not seem to align with Christian

---

14 Kilbourn, "Trauma and Loss," 34.
15 Maltby and Hall, "Trauma, Attachment, and Spirituality."
16 Brueggemann, "Vulnerable Children"; Bridger, *Children Finding Faith*; Cupit, *Perspectives on Children*; Nye, *Children's Spirituality*; MacCullough. *Undivided*.
17 Crompton, *Children, Spirituality, Religion and Social Work*.
18 Harris, *Trusting What You're Told*.

teaching. Glenn Cupit cautions that "whatever children hear about God's 'otherness,' his perfection, purity, beauty and worthiness for worship, will be partly gauged against the way such characteristics are expressed in the environments in which children live."[19] Kathryn Copsey, writing in the context of disadvantaged children in London's housing schemes, also reflects on the spiritual disconnection disadvantaged children may feel: "[God's world] has obviously nothing to do with Jamie's world. He knows his world. His world is not beautiful. No one has ever shown him anything in his world that could engender a sense of awe and wonder.... He finds it impossible to take on board the ideas of God as a creator or of a world that is to be valued and treated with respect."[20]

Spiritual Damage

Children's early experiences of neglect and trauma may also cause spiritual damage. Erik Erikson identified the first and primary task of infants and young children as developing healthy trust.[21] This trust comes naturally to an infant, who is completely dependent on the care of others, but whether that trust can be preserved depends on the response of caregivers to the infant's needs.[22] When caregivers ignore the needs of the child (neglect) or respond to the child with harm (abuse), the child's innate trust is damaged and replaced with mistrust.[23] As a result, a child who experiences early abuse or neglect may struggle to trust anyone—including God.[24] Erikson himself viewed the development of healthy trust as foundational to healthy religious development.

Spiritual damage to children may be exacerbated by religious teaching that does not account for a child's experience of life.

19 Cupit, *Perspectives on Children*, 88.
20 Copsey, *From the Ground Up*, 80.
21 Erikson, "Eight Ages of Man," 247–74.
22 Surr, "Links between Early Attachment Experiences," 129–41.
23 Erikson, "Eight Ages of Man."
24 Bryant-Davis et al., "Religiosity, Spirituality, and Trauma," 306–14.

Karen-Marie Yust writes, "Keisha's spiritual questions stemmed from her ambivalent view of herself and her previous exposure to conservative religious teachings. She imagined a God of retribution, quick to anger and eager to punish. While she wanted to avoid punishment, she also believed that she deserved to suffer because of what she had done."[25]

Some ministry leaders inadvertently reinforce children's damaged perceptions of God through their own attitudes and behaviors. A counselor recounts the story of a pastor's wife who asserted that "people don't change or heal not because they were injured as children but because their hearts are not open to God."[26] For this ministry leader, mistrust and questions were natural results not of childhood trauma but of intentional rebellion against God.

Spiritual Questioning

Traumatic experiences may also prompt children to wrestle with spiritual questions. James Garbarino suggested that trauma challenges meaningfulness and that young children feel conflict most keenly, as they are still in the process of forming their worldviews.[27] Trauma cannot be easily assimilated into a child's existing views but requires the child to alter their foundational frames of meaning.[28] The effort to produce meaning from difficult circumstances may prompt deep spiritual questions from the child.[29] In fact, the spiritual questions children ask during a time of crisis are very similar to the questions adults ask: Who am I? Where is God? Who can I trust?[30] The primary difference is the language that is used to ask and answer them.[31]

25 Yust, "(Non) Cosmetic Ministry," 129.
26 Van Deusen and Courtois, "Spirituality, Religion," 29–54.
27 Garbarino and Bedard, "Spiritual Challenges," 467.
28 Garbarino and Bedard; Van Deusen and Courtois, "Spirituality, Religion."
29 Yust, "(Non) Cosmetic Ministry"; Nye, *Children's Spirituality*; Wagener and Malony, "Spiritual and Religious Pathology."
30 Nye, *Children's Spirituality*.
31 Handzo, "Talking about Faith," 173–83.

Children do not all respond in the same way to those questions.[32] Crisis is, by nature, a short-term state, and children will resolve it with or without the help of adults.[33] However, when core issues of meaning are not resolved satisfactorily, children continue to struggle. A qualitative study among at-risk African American adolescent girls found that many struggled with depression and were unable to find coherent meaning in their difficult circumstances. The authors speculated that healthy meaning making following trauma requires both a coherent worldview and the support of a healthy social group.[34]

When children's difficult spiritual questions are not resolved, some children reject their belief in God completely.[35] However, other children may continue to outwardly profess belief in a powerful and loving God while internalizing a very different lived experience of God. This disconnect between outer religious belief and inner spirituality is devastating to healthy spiritual growth.[36]

Spiritual Sensitivity

Children's spirituality researcher Rebecca Nye observes that "the more difficult children's life circumstances are, the more spiritual sensitivity and spiritual hunger they may have."[37] While trauma threatens a child's spiritual development by raising issues of meaningfulness, coherence, and trust, it may also prompt some children to seek comfort in a relationship with God. Robert Coles (1990) was challenged by the deep spiritual questions and reflections shared by children living in the favelas of Brazil.[38] Similarly, researchers in India found that adolescents who reported higher

32 Way, "Practitioner's View of Children," 144–57.
33 Sahler, "Understanding and Caring," 56–65.
34 Sales, Merrill, and Fivush, "Does Making Meaning Make It Better?," 97–110.
35 Garbarino and Bedard, "Spiritual Challenges."
36 Rizzuto, *Birth of the Living God*; Maltby and Hall, "Trauma, Attachment, and Spirituality."
37 Nye, *Children's Spirituality*, 91.
38 Coles, *Spiritual Life of Children*.

numbers of ACEs also reported an increased desire to connect with God or another higher power.[39] In his longitudinal study of Lutheran children, Kalevi Tamminen found that children who reported spiritual experiences were most likely to have felt God's presence during times of crises or loneliness.[40] South African researchers interviewed children who were growing up without families in institutions, foster homes, or child-headed households. They found that every child they interviewed spoke about a faith in a higher being who knows, loves, and guides them personally.[41] Working with adolescents in the North American foster system, researchers reported that 95 percent of respondents found meaning through their relationship with God—even while continuing to engage in destructive behaviors.[42] These studies suggest that the impact of ACEs on children's spiritual development is not automatically negative.

Spiritual Development and Hope for Children

ACEs such as neglect, abuse, and household dysfunction influence the spiritual development of children. Longitudinal ACEs studies have repeatedly concluded that ACEs combine to produce negative outcomes for children—physically, socially, and emotionally.[43] However, healthy spirituality in children may help mitigate the negative impact of ACEs in other areas of their development.

Studies among adults suggest that belief in a personal God helps individuals cope better with difficult life events.[44] Studies with children in difficult circumstances also suggest that faith

---

39 Santoro et al., "Adverse Childhood Experiences," 185–94.
40 Tamminen, "Religious Experiences in Childhood," 61.
41 Roby and Maistry, "Spirituality of Vulnerable Children," 11.
42 Jackson et al., "Exploring Spirituality among Youth," 107–17.
43 Larkin, Felitti, and Anda, "Social Work and Adverse Childhood Experiences," 1–16.
44 Pargament, *Psychology of Religion*; Gall et al., "Spirituality and the Current Adjustment"; Walker et al., "Changes in Personal Religion/Spirituality."

increases children's abilities to cope with ACEs.[45] Healthy spiritual development may increase children's resilience by providing a coherent narrative and connecting them with God and others.

Healthy Spirituality Offers a Coherent Narrative

Healthy spirituality creates a coherent narrative that can answer a child's significant questions and offer perspective on their difficult circumstances.[46] Difficult circumstances seem to prompt children to ask spiritual questions and search for meaning. However, faith in the God of the Bible and his story can help a child discover meaning in their own story.[47] This faith in God may provide a picture of a greater reality that puts individual suffering into perspective.[48]

Healthy Spirituality Offers Connections with God and Others

Children grow in resilience because they experience deeper connectedness with God.[49] However, healthy spirituality also helps children experience deeper connectedness with others.[50] The positive effects of healthy spirituality were investigated by Ghanaian researchers among children living at an orphanage.[51] They found that spirituality contributed to the well-being of orphaned children by helping them develop better coping skills, maintain hopeful outlooks on life, feel better about themselves, and connect them to a wider support network.

---

45 Coles, *Spiritual Life of Children*.
46 Coles; McSherry and Smith, "How Do Children Express Their Spiritual Needs?"; Bryant-Davis et al., "Religiosity, Spirituality, and Trauma."
47 Gall et al., "Spirituality and the Current Adjustment," 101–17.
48 Welch, "How Do We View Suffering?," 283–310.
49 Coles, *Spiritual Life of Children*, 137–51.
50 Santoro et al., "Adverse Childhood Experiences," 294–306.
51 Salifu Yendork and Somhlaba, "I Am Happy Because," S32–S39.

Implications for Ministry with Children from Hard Places

A review of available research suggests that ACEs are common and that they will influence children's spiritual development just as they influence other areas of children's development. As a result, joining children from hard places on the spiritual journey may require a more patient and nuanced approach to ministry.

Specialists working with Tearfund offer a scathing critique of traditional Christian education for children at risk. They write, "[The traditional model of Christian education in families] assumes childhood spent in loving, Christian families. The challenge for Christians working with abused, neglected, impoverished, war-affected or orphaned children is to find ways of conveying to them that God loves them despite the apparent evidence to the contrary."[52]

Ministry leaders will most effectively join children from hard places on their spiritual journeys when they become people of safety, share the big story of God, and allow children to respond authentically.

Become People of Safety

Children with ACEs need to experience their ministry leaders as trustworthy people who can be relied on. Since children's perceptions of God are influenced—at least in part—by their perceptions of important adults, it is vital that parents and ministry leaders reflect the consistent, loving, and truthful character of God as they interact with children.[53] However, adults also need to understand that developing trust will take time for children whose life experiences have developed "deeply encoded fear responses."[54]

---

52 Ennew and Stephenson, *Questioning the Basis of Our Work*, 69.
53 Bridger, *Children Finding Faith*; Cupit, *Perspectives on Children*.
54 Purvis, Cross, and Sunshine, *Connected Child*, 52.

Share the Big Story of God

Children's early experiences of trauma may result in distorted views of themselves, others, and God. As a result, spiritual healing must eventually confront these spiritual lies with spiritual truth.[55] Often, children's ministry presents children with truth in simplistic and propositional forms. However, this approach to truth is inadequate to address the deep spiritual lies held by children whose life experiences have been hellish.

There is beauty and great power in the fullness of God's story.[56] It is a story of human beings with inherent worth and value as God's children, of how sin has ravaged every part of God's creation, and of God, who has entered into the story and is at work to redeem, restore, re-create, and reclaim all that was lost and broken. However, children easily miss the power of God's story when it is presented as a collection of unrelated, largely irrelevant, and individual stories.[57]

Sharing the whole story enables children to see themselves and their stories within God's story. The Bible has much to say about injustice, abuse, deprivation, and violence. It explores the full range of human emotions: love, joy, peace, and kindness as well as anger, depression, bitterness, and hurt. Ministry leaders must explore the Bible more widely and deeply with children who are hurting. Counselors have suggested that "gaining a spiritual and emotional connection with such stories might help clients of various ages to make meaning out of their own experience of suffering, if processed in an age-appropriate way."[58] Children who understand God's story can recognize God's voice speaking in their own stories. Edward Welch suggests that children who have suffered need to hear God say the following: "Put your suffering into speech. You have been sinned against. I am with you and

---

55 Crawford, "From Spiritual Harm," 161–78.
56 Goheen, "Urgency of Reading," 469–83.
57 Stonehouse and May, *Listening to Children*, 81–92.
58 Walker et al., "Addressing Religious and Spiritual Issues," 178.

love you. Know that I am God. There is a purpose in suffering."[59] In the context of the larger story of God, these are not simplistic platitudes but profound truths about the God of the scriptures in a child's story.

Allow Children to Respond Authentically

The house of God must be a place where children and young people are invited to come as they are, with their honest questions and struggles and without fear of condemnation.[60] Allowing children to respond authentically does not mean that Christians abandon objective truth. Giving freedom to question means that they are willing to engage a child's subjective experience and help them make meaning as they come to understand and experience the God of the scriptures.[61]

Ministry leaders may feel threatened by the deep questions and doubts that children may express. However, the way they respond to these questions has profound implications for how children resolve spiritual conflict. If Christians respond to questions dismissively or defensively, the conversation is shut down, and children are left to create their own meaning.[62] Recalling his own experience as a child at risk, Dan Lovaglia writes of his mentors, "There was never a question that was off-limits. I could be real and raise messy faith issues with them, knowing they would listen and give me thoughtful responses."[63] Children who have experienced pain are looking not necessarily for theological answers but for the validation of themselves and their questions.[64] David

---

59 Welch, "How Do We View Suffering?," 295.
60 Crompton, *Children, Spirituality, Religion and Social Work*; Yust, "(Non) Cosmetic Ministry."
61 Yust; Newton, *Heart-Deep Teaching*.
62 Lester, *Pastoral Care with Children*; Crompton, *Children, Spirituality, Religion and Social Work*.
63 Lovaglia, *Relational Children's Ministry*, 131.
64 Lester, *Pastoral Care with Children*.

Csinos and Ivy Beckwith write, "When we treat a child's questions with respect, we are treating the child with respect."[65]

For some children, a genuine response to Scripture may look like noncompliance on the surface. Nye cautions ministry leaders to consider, "What happens if you are the child who connects intimately to the angry dark reality of the Flood while the rest blithely see Noah's story as a message about God's kindness to animals and knack for beautiful rainbows?"[66] For such a child, pressure to join in a celebratory game will get in the way of a personal and meaningful response to truth. Ministry leaders must be willing to enter the story with children and consider how it looks and feels from their perspective.[67] It is only in entering the story with the child and walking in it together that the child can truly come to see and experience the presence of God in the midst of it.

Cultivate Patience on the Journey

In many North American evangelical churches, the goal of ministry with children has been early conversion. However, spiritual development in any child is a process rather than an event.[68] This perspective is especially important in ministry with children who have experienced trauma. Children form their worldviews slowly over time and through a variety of experiences. Developmental trauma impacts the way that children see themselves, others, and God, and reforming their worldviews will also take time.

Often, spiritual development may appear to be "two steps forward and three steps backward." Patience is essential as children and young people wrestle with their spiritual identities. Yust observes, "As in any dynamic process, the conceptual connections

---

65 Csinos and Beckwith, *Children's Ministry*, 95.
66 Nye, *Children's Spirituality*, 93.
67 Crompton, *Children, Spirituality, Religion and Social Work*; Copsey, *From the Ground Up*; Berryman, *Spiritual Guidance of Children*; Strachan, "Children, Mission."
68 Stonehouse, *Joining Children*.

with which a traumatized young woman is experimenting are marked in pencil, subject to erasure as their effectiveness is evaluated and alternative approaches are tried. Since faithfulness is a lifelong transformational practice, it is not appropriate to expect adolescents to do their spiritual work in indelible ink."[69]

It is vital that ministry leaders working with children from hard places are aware of the spiritual effects of trauma on children and that they are willing to practice patience as they walk with children.[70]

Conclusion

Significant numbers of children in our churches and communities have multiple ACEs. These early experiences of trauma are likely to influence their spiritual development, offering unique opportunities and challenges for ministry leaders. Ministry leaders who desire to join children from hard places on their spiritual journeys must be willing to be people of safety, share the big story of God, and allow children to respond authentically. They must also learn to practice patience as they walk with children from hard places.

Bibliography

Berryman, Jerome W. *The Spiritual Guidance of Children: Montessori, Godly Play, and the Future*. New York: Morehouse, 2013.

Bridger, Francis. *Children Finding Faith: Exploring a Child's Response to God*. Bletchley, UK: Scripture Union, 2000.

Brueggemann, Walter. "Vulnerable Children, Divine Passion and Human Obligation." In *The Child in the Bible*, edited by M. Bunge, 399–422. Grand Rapids, MI: Eerdmans, 2008.

Bryant-Davis, Thema, M. U. Ellis, E. Burke-Maynard, N. Moon, P. A. Counts, and G. Anderson. "Religiosity, Spirituality, and Trauma Recovery in the Lives of Children and Adolescents." *Professional Psychology:*

---

69 Yust, "(Non) Cosmetic Ministry," 130.
70 Maltby and Hall, "Trauma, Attachment, and Spirituality."

Research and Practice 43, no. 4 (2012): 306–14. https://doi.org/10.1037/a0029282.

Coles, Robert. *The Spiritual Life of Children*. New York: Atlantic Monthly, 1990.

Copsey, Kathryn. *From the Ground Up: Understanding the Spiritual World of the Child*. Oxford: Bible Reading Fellowship, 2005.

Crawford, Christa F. "From Spiritual Harm to Spiritual Healing." In *Healing for Hurting Hearts: A Handbook for Counseling Children and Youth in Crisis*, edited by P. Kilbourne, 161–78. Fort Washington, PA: CLC, 2013.

Crompton, Margaret. *Children, Spirituality, Religion and Social Work*. Aldershot, UK: Ashgate, 1998.

Csinos, David, and Ivy Beckwith. *Children's Ministry in the Way of Jesus*. Downers Grove, IL: InterVarsity, 2013.

Cupit, C. Glenn. *Perspectives on Children and Spirituality*. Bletchley, UK: Scripture Union Australia, 2005.

Ennew, Judith, and Paul Stephenson. *Questioning the Basis of Our Work: Christianity, Children's Rights and Development*. Teddington, UK: Tearfund, 2006.

Erikson, Erik H. "Eight Ages of Man." In *Childhood and Society*, 247–74. New York: W. W. Norton, 1993. First published 1950.

Felitti, Vincent J., R. F. Anda, D. Nordenberg, D. F. Williamson, A. M. Spitz, V. Edwards, and J. S. Marks. "Relationship of Childhood Abuse and Household Dysfunction to Many of the Leading Causes of Death in Adults." *American Journal of Preventive Medicine* 14, no. 4 (2009): 245–58. https://doi.org/10.1016/s0749-3797(98)00017-8.

Frawley-Odea, Mary Gail. "Childhood Abuse and Neglect Take Their Toll." *National Catholic Reporter* 52, no. 15 (2016): 1.

Gall, Terry Lynn, Viola Basque, Marizete Damasceno-Scott, and Gerard Vardy. "Spirituality and the Current Adjustment of Adult Survivors of Childhood Sexual Abuse." *Journal for the Scientific Study of Religion* 46, no. 1 (2007): 101–17.

Garbarino, James, and C. Bedard. "Spiritual Challenges to Children Facing Violent Trauma." *Childhood* 3, no. 4 (1996): 467. https://doi.org/10.1177/0907568296003004004.

Goheen, Michael W. "The Urgency of Reading the Bible as One Story." *Theology Today* 64, no. 4 (2008): 469–83. https://doi.org/10.1177/004057360806400405.

Handzo, George F. "Talking about Faith with Children." In Lester, *When Children Suffer*, 173–83.

Harris, Paul L. *Trusting What You're Told: How Children Learn from Others*. Cambridge, MA: Harvard University Press, 2012.
Harvard University's Center on the Developing Child. "Brain Architecture." 2019. https://developingchild.harvard.edu/science/key-concepts/brain-architecture/.
Hughes, Karen, Mark A. Bellis, Katherine A. Hardcastle, Dinesh Sethi, Alexander Butchart, Christopher Mikton, Lisa Jones, and Michael P. Dunne. "The Effect of Multiple Adverse Childhood Experiences on Health: A Systematic Review and Meta-analysis." *Lancet Public Health* 2, no. 8 (2017): 356–66. https://doi.org/10.1016/s2468-2667(17)30118-4.
Jackson, Lovie J., C. R. White, L. O'Brien, P. DiLorenzo, E. Cathcart, M. Wolf, D. Bruskas, P. J. Pecora, V. Nix-Early, and J. Cabrera. "Exploring Spirituality among Youth in Foster Care: Findings from the Casey Field Office Mental Health Study." *Child and Family Social Work* 15 (2010): 107–17.
Kilbourn, Phyllis. "Trauma and Loss." In *Healing for Hurting Hearts: A Handbook for Counseling Children and Youth in Crisis*, 33–44. Fort Washington, PA: CLC, 2013.
Larkin, Heather, V. J. Felitti, and R. F. Anda. "Social Work and Adverse Childhood Experiences Research: Implications for Practice and Health Policy." *Social Work in Public Health* 29, no. 1 (2014): 1–16. https://doi.org/10.1080/19371918.2011.619433.
Lester, Andrew D. *Pastoral Care with Children in Crisis*. Louisville, KY: Westminster John Knox, 1985.
———, ed. *When Children Suffer: A Sourcebook for Ministry with Children in Crisis*. Philadelphia: Westminster, 1987.
Lovaglia, Dan. *Relational Children's Ministry: Turning Kid-Influencers into Lifelong Disciple Makers*. Grand Rapids, MI: Zondervan, 2016.
Loveall, Rebecca, K. Flanagan, C. Morrison, and M. Sorenson. "Contextualized Social Justice: Entering into Culture to Bring Life to Worthy Children." In *Exploring and Engaging Spirituality for Today's Children: A Holistic Approach*, edited by L. Tolbert, 294–306. Eugene, OR: Wipf & Stock, 2014.
MacCullough, Martha. *Undivided: Developing a Worldview Approach to Biblical Integration*. Colorado Springs: Purposeful Design, 2016.
Maltby, Lauren E., and T. W. Hall. "Trauma, Attachment, and Spirituality: A Case Study." *Journal of Psychology and Theology* 40, no. 4 (2012): 302–12. https://doi.org/10.1177/009164711204000405.
McSherry, Wilfred, and J. Smith. "How Do Children Express Their Spiritual Needs?" *Pediatric Nursing* 19, no. 3 (2007): 17–20.

Mitchell, M. B., C. F. Silver, and C. J. Ross. "My Hero, My Friend: Exploring Honduran Youths' Lived Experience of the God-Individual Relationship." *International Journal of Children's Spirituality* 17, no. 2 (2012): 137–51.

Newton, Gary C. *Heart-Deep Teaching: Engaging Students for Transformed Lives.* Nashville: B&H Academic, 2012.

Nye, Rebecca. *Children's Spirituality: What It Is and Why It Matters.* London: Church House, 2009.

Pargament, Kenneth I. *The Psychology of Religion and Coping.* New York: Guilford, 1997.

Purvis, Karyn B., D. R. Cross, and W. L. Sunshine. *The Connected Child: Bring Hope and Healing to Your Adoptive Family.* New York: McGraw-Hill, 2007.

Rizzuto, Ana-Maria. *The Birth of the Living God: A Psychoanalytic Study.* Chicago: University of Chicago, 1979.

Roby, J., and M. Maistry. "The Spirituality of Vulnerable Children in South Africa: Implications for Social Development and Welfare." *Journal of Social Development in Africa* 25, no. 2 (2010).

Sahler, Olle Jane Z. "Understanding and Caring for the Child in Crisis." In Lester, *When Children Suffer*, 56–65.

Sales, Jessica M., N. A. Merrill, and R. Fivush. "Does Making Meaning Make It Better? Narrative Meaning Making and Well-Being in At-Risk African-American Adolescent Females." *Memory* 21, no. 1 (2013): 97–110. https://doi.org/10.1080/09658211.2012.706614.

Santoro, Anthony F., S. Suchday, A. Benkhoukha, N. Ramanayake, and S. Kapur. "Adverse Childhood Experiences and Religiosity/Spirituality in Emerging Adolescents in India." *Psychology of Religion and Spirituality* 8, no. 3 (2016): 185–94. https://doi.org/10.1037/rel0000038.

Shern, David L., A. K. Blanch, and S. M. Steverman. "Toxic Stress, Behavioral Health, and the Next Major Era in Public Health." *American Journal of Orthopsychiatry* 86, no. 2 (2016): 109–23. https://doi.org/10.1037/ort0000120.

Siegel, Daniel J., and T. P. Bryson. *The Whole-Brain Child: 12 Revolutionary Strategies to Nurture Your Child's Developing Mind.* New York: Random House, 2012.

Souers, Kristin, with Pete Hall. *Fostering Resilient Learners: Strategies for Creating a Trauma-Sensitive Classroom.* Alexandria, VA: ASCD, 2016.

Stonehouse, Catherine. *Joining Children on the Spiritual Journey: Nurturing a Life of Faith.* Grand Rapids, MI: Baker, 1998.

Stonehouse, C., and S. May. *Listening to Children on the Spiritual Journey: Guidance for Those Who Teach and Nurture*. Grand Rapids, MI: Baker, 2010.

Strachan, Wendy. "Children, Mission and the Bible: A Global Perspective." In *Bible in Mission*, edited by Pauline Hoggarth, Fergus MacDonald, Bill Mitchell, and Knud Jorgensen, 81–92. Oxford: Regnum Books International, 2013.

Surr, John. "Links between Early Attachment Experiences and Manifestations of Spirituality." *International Journal of Children's Spirituality* 16, no. 2 (2011): 129–41. https://doi.org/10.1080/1364436X.2011.580725.

Tamminen, Kalevi. "Religious Experiences in Childhood and Adolescence: A Viewpoint of Religious Development between the Ages of 7 and 20." *International Journal for the Psychology of Religion* 4, no. 2 (1994): 65–85.

Van Deusen, Stephanie, and C. A. Courtois. "Spirituality, Religion, and Complex Developmental Trauma." In *Spiritually Oriented Psychotherapy for Trauma*, edited by Jamie Aten, 29–54. Washington, DC: American Psychological Association, 2015. https://doi.org/10.1037/14500-003.

Wagener, L. M., and H. N. Malony. "Spiritual and Religious Pathology in Childhood and Adolescence." In *The Handbook of Spiritual Development in Childhood and Adolescence*, edited by Eugene C. Roehlkepartain, Pamela Ebstyne King, Linda Wagener, and Peter L. Benson, 137–49. Thousand Oaks, CA: SAGE, 2006.

Walker, D. F., H. W. Reid, T. O'Neill, and L. Brown. "Changes in Personal Religion/Spirituality during and after Childhood Abuse: A Review and Synthesis." *Psychological Trauma: Theory, Research, Practice, and Policy* 1, no. 2 (2009): 130–45.

Walker, Donald F., J. B. Reese, J. P. Hughes, and M. J. Troskie. "Addressing Religious and Spiritual Issues in Trauma-Focused Cognitive Behavior Therapy for Children and Adolescents." *Professional Psychology: Research and Practice* 41, no. 2 (2010): 174.

Way, P. "A Practitioner's View of Children Making Spiritual Meanings in Bereavement." *Journal of Social Work in End-of-Life & Palliative Care* 9, nos. 2–3 (2013): 144–57. https://doi.org/10.1080/15524256.2013.794032.

Welch, E. "How Do We View Suffering?" In *Healing Children of War: A Handbook for Ministry to Children Who Have Suffered Deep Traumas*, edited by Phyllis Kilbourne, 283–310. Federal Way, WA: World Vision Resources, 1995.

Salifu Yendork, Joana, and N. Z. Somhlaba. "'I Am Happy Because of God': Religion and Spirituality for Well-Being in Ghanaian Orphanage-Placed Children." *Psychology of Religion and Spirituality* 9, no. 1 (2017): S32–S39. https://doi.org/10.1037/rel0000094.

YMCA of the USA, Dartmouth Medical School, and Institute for American Values. *Hardwired to Connect: The New Scientific Case for Authoritative Communities. A Report to the Nation from the Commission on Children at Risk*. New York: Institute for American Values, 2003.

Yust, Karen-Marie. "(Non) Cosmetic Ministry: Reclaiming Hope among Abused Adolescents." In *Children, Youth, and Spirituality in a Troubling World*, edited by Mary Elizabeth Moore and Almeda Wright, 123–36. St. Louis: Chalice, 2008.

CHAPTER 12

Theology and Abuse
Vulnerability in the Midst of Religious Institutions

Stacey Wilson

> No one believed what we said. They'd just say to you, "Don't lie. The Church doesn't do things like that." Well, I tell you they did.
> —Royal Commission into Institutional Responses to Child Sexual Abuse (RCIRCSA)

We were gathered with a group of pastors from the Uniting Church of Australia on the land of the Burramattagal clan of the Darug people, around mats woven by the people of the Pacific Islands; the rising scent of eucalyptus trees surrounded us as the day rapidly warmed toward the predicted afternoon thunderstorms. I have mixed feelings about this particular part of my country. It is the land of my father's family, themselves economic migrants from Scotland. It holds the stories and songs of the world's oldest continuous civilization, but it is also the place where tall ships brought the violence of colonization that spread through this land like a cancer.

Powerful men declared this place *terra nullius*—nobody's land—dismissing the people and culture present.[1] Yet as I sit here,

---

1 National Library of Australia Collection, "James Cook's Secret Instructions."

being welcomed by the descendants of those people, I am again struck by the wounded history of this land. In this truly stunning setting, it is easy to forget that this nation, like so many others, was built upon the practices of genocide, forced migration, and stolen children—the work of great empires whose actions were all too often justified and enacted by Christian religious institutions.[2]

Preparing to speak publicly on abuse within religious institutions that first time, I was overwhelmed by uncertainty. This topic, as difficult as it is, is of vital importance to the church as a whole. I felt a heavy sense of responsibility to hold the stories of victims and survivors[3] in a way that was respectful and honored the strength it had taken to share them. I was also aware of the impact that undertaking this work had on me personally—my anger, grief, and inevitable self-preserving desensitization; the desire to shock people into action; the urge to walk away; the need to share these stories while questioning the best way to do so; the temptation to reframe the discussion as a more palatable intellectual exercise. After two long years immersed in a research project that has profoundly changed me, I found myself physically sitting in the midst of this complex history with church leaders, victims, survivors, friends, and colleagues, realizing I was about to challenge some of their sincerely held beliefs. Yet again asking myself, What did I hope to achieve?

Children's Spirituality

It is common to use the lens of developmental theory to explore the way a child's conscious understanding of their relationship with God changes over time. We do so with the hope of nurturing this development by providing opportunities for children to experience and engage with their own spirituality within a supportive

---

2 Pope Alexander VI, "Demarcation Bull."
3 The phrase "victims and survivors" will be used throughout this paper because RCIRCSA participants self-identify as either victims or survivors, and I seek to honor that choice.

community of faith. The Children's Spirituality and Intergenerational Ministry movements have highlighted the validity of a child's capacity to participate deeply in relationship with the Triune God. These movements encourage practitioners to consider the specific needs of children within their communities and the unique contributions children make as full members of the body of Christ. The work undertaken in this field is wide-ranging. Yet as David Csinos, in his examination of the role of culture in research into children's spirituality and theology, observes, "A significant amount of research into children's spirituality and theology involves a quest to learn about what children think—their theological and spiritual ideas surrounding all sorts of topics—at the expense of learning about how children make theological meaning in the first place."[4] Csinos's challenge focuses on the impact of broader national culture on the collective meaning making and theological thinking of children. His work demonstrates that the culture surrounding faith communities has a powerful impact not only on what children believe but also on the way children create theological meaning and on the sources they trust in constructing these belief systems.[5] However, when considering the spiritual lives and development of children, we cannot ignore the horrific juxtaposition of two truths: the church, which has a deep and continued commitment to the care and well-being of children, has also been an environment that puts children in harm's way. This chapter will examine the culture that exists within church congregations and religious institutions and explore cultural risk factors identified by those who have experienced abuse as children within religious institutions. It will inquire also into the ways that a range of theological commitments unintentionally contribute to that risk of abuse.

---

4 Csinos, "From the Ground Up," 60.
5 Csinos, 54.

Abuse within Religious Institutions

The recent history of the church has been not only marked but also shaped by the abuse of children within its institutions. Across the world, victims and survivors have borne witness to the horrific abuse they suffered within church-run residential care homes, schools, and mother and baby homes as well as congregational settings.[6] Numerous public inquiries have been completed over the last twenty-five years across the world examining the experiences of children in the midst of the church's missional and ecclesial practices. These inquiries have consistently revealed the systematic abuse of some of the most vulnerable members of our society. They also reveal that physical, emotional, and spiritual violence are inextricably woven into both the pedagogy and the theology of religious institutions, which in turn gives rise to a brutal form of missiology played out on the bodies of children and women. Added to this abuse is a deliberate and pervasive action taken to protect the reputation and status of the religious institutions involved, shielding the perpetrators from criminal investigations or other consequences and thus facilitating further abuse.

The church has willingly participated in and profited from the systematic removal and detainment of Indigenous[7] and impoverished children[8], involuntary child migration,[9] and the forced removal of babies from unwed mothers.[10] Despite extensive

---

6 Committee on the Rights of the Child, *Concluding Observations*; RCIRCSA, *Religious Institutions*, bks. 1–3; Commission to Inquire into Child Abuse, *Final Report*; Office of the Attorney General, *Report I*; Independent Inquiry Child Sexual Abuse, *Safeguarding in the Church*.
7 Human Rights and Equal Opportunity Commission, *Bringing Them Home*; Truth and Reconciliation Commission of Canada, *Honouring the Truth*; Secretary of the Interior Deb Haaland, *Memorandum*.
8 Senate Community Affairs References Committee, *Forgotten Australians*.
9 Senate Standing Committee on Community Affairs, *Lost Innocents*; United States Office of Indian Affairs, *Fifty Seventh Annual Report*; One Hundred Tenth Congress, *Legacy*.
10 Senate Community Affairs References Committee, *Forgotten Australians*.

global attention, abuse that occurs within religious institutions remains largely unexamined using a theological or institutional cultural lens.[11]

It is tempting to believe that something so contrary to the spirit of Christianity—namely, the abuse of children—might be nothing more than a terrible aberration perpetrated by a few "bad apples" and the product of a particular social context that thankfully no longer exists. However, this attitude has repeatedly resulted in little more than superficial procedural changes unaccompanied by any deep work of changing the culture that has enabled abuse to continue.[12] Dr. Marie Keenan, an Irish psychologist and researcher, in her expert testimony to the Australian Royal Commission, stated, "If the sexual abuse crisis . . . has served to surface the issues of gender, power, the theology of priesthood, and organizational culture, it can also be said that the organizational Church has failed thus far to begin to address these important structural, theological, and organizational issues."[13] This chapter invites the reader to walk alongside those who have sacrificed much to share their stories and to honor their courage by willingly and humbly examining the difficult truths about the embodiment of theological and doctrinal culture that leads to such devastating failures.

---

11 The author completed digital searches for the words *abuse*, *sex*, and *sexuality* in the works marked in the bibliography with an asterisk. One work returned a positive result where 21 percent of Catholic youth reported that "clerical abuse scandals have made me question my faith" (Kinnaman, *You Lost Me*, 23). There was no further reference made to this finding. Similarly, a journal key word frequency study of the *International Journal of Children's Spirituality*, undertaken by John Chi-Kin Lee, identified the top sixteen key words used over the ten-year period from 2009 to 2019; *abuse*, *sex*, and *sexuality* did not feature. While not comprehensive, this sample of significant works suggests a paucity of work completed in this field on the children of abuse within religious institutions. See Chi-Kin Lee, "Children's Spirituality."
12 Kaufman and Erooga with Stewart et al., *Risk Profiles*, 84.
13 RCIRCSA, *Religious Institutions*, bk. 2, 637.

Australian Royal Commission into Institutional Responses to Child Sexual Abuse

In November 2012, Prime Minister Julia Gillard launched the Australian Royal Commission into Institutional Responses to Child Sexual Abuse (RCIRCSA), whose final report was handed down in 2017. The RCIRCSA received over sixteen thousand submissions, heard over eight thousand personal testimonies, and reviewed over one thousand written accounts from victims, survivors, and their families.[14] The majority of these testimonies—59 percent—referenced abuse that had taken place in institutions managed by religious organizations, and a further 14 percent referenced abuse that had taken place during religious activities.[15] Of the 4,000 institutions identified, 1,691 were religious institutions.[16] Most perpetrators were male and held roles as religious leaders and/or teachers.[17] Sixty-four percent of victims and survivors were male.[18] On average, it takes victims and survivors twenty-four years to disclose abuse.[19]

At the time of writing, the RCIRCSA was one of only two national inquiries that had been completed globally.[20] The Australian RCIRCSA report alone offers a unique comparison between religious and secular institutions. As such, this report was chosen for analysis.

---

14 RCIRCSA, *Executive Summary*, 1.
15 RCIRCSA, *Religious Institutions*, bk. 1, 11.
16 RCIRCSA, *Executive Summary*, 5; RCIRCSA, *Religious Institutions*, bk. 1, 11.
17 RCIRCSA, *Executive Summary*, 10.
18 RCIRCSA, 8.
19 RCIRCSA, 23.
20 The Irish government handed down the findings of the Commission to Inquire into Child Abuse, *Final Report*, in 2009. The Australian Commission reviewed the findings of inquiries from the following regions: the United States, Canada, the Republic of Ireland, the United Kingdom (England, Wales, Scotland, Northern Ireland), Europe (Belgium, the Netherlands, Germany, Italy, France, Spain), South America, Africa, and Asia. RCIRCSA, *Religious Institutions*, bk. 1, 162.

Study Context

In 2019, I received funding to conduct a review of the testimony collected in the RCIRCSA's final report. Using a modified grounded theory methodology and a risk management framework, volume 16 was coded for theological and doctrinal beliefs and practices that victims and survivors identified as increasing the risk of abuse occurring, inhibiting disclosure, and promoting poor institutional responses. This study also acknowledged that for victims and survivors, there is power in having their stories heard, believed, and acted on. As one survivor, "Eugenie," stated in their testimony to the Commission, "By telling my account to the Royal Commission I am another voice not lost in the wilderness of the non-believed."[21]

Findings

The testimonies offered by victims and survivors pull the reader into a world of profound suffering where violence, fear, shame, and powerlessness dominate the narrative. Most of the abuse described occurred in situations that afforded the perpetrators high levels of environmental and social control, such as schools or residential care homes where children were physically, socially, and emotionally isolated and often fully dependent.[22]

The RCIRCSA found that holding "spiritual or moral authority over a child" and occupying positions of prestige result in "the perpetrator being afforded a higher level of trust and credibility" and that these were two of the key risk factors for abuse unique to religious institutions:[23] "People in religious ministry are conferred with a unique status and spiritual authority which means they can exert considerable power over children. Research that we commissioned into the role of organizational culture in child sexual abuse noted that 'the more power adults possess over children

---

21 RCIRCSA, bk. 1, 110.
22 RCIRCSA, bk. 1, 20.
23 RCIRCSA, *Executive Summary*, 10.

and young people in institutions, the better positioned they are to sexually abuse them.'"[24] There is clear and extensive evidence that abuse has a profound impact on the spiritual development of the child. These effects are carried into adult life and result in increased negative outcomes for the individuals affected.[25] Victims and survivors describe the effect on their spirituality using the language of "loss," "violence," and "anger" and describe their faith as being "stolen" from them:

> I felt lost in the only world I knew. It is very hard to explain the depth of this despair given my background. I was essentially questioning my very existence.[26]

> I was so angry. . . . I had nothing. I lost God. I lost my belief. I lost my innocence. I lost my spirit.[27]

> My beliefs were shattered by the actions of his representatives, and I have never forgiven those violations and the abandonment I felt. The hypocrisy of his so-called representatives caused me to lose faith in the God I held so dear, and in humanity.[28]

This language is echoed in the wider research in phrases like "soul murder" and "spiritual death."[29] Victims and survivors, even as children, appear to have understood the profound impact of this loss. Many have revealed that they did not disclose their abuse, in part, to shield their parents from similar harm to their spiritual identity:

---

24 RCIRCSA, *Religious Institutions*, bk. 1, 355.
25 RCIRCSA, *Executive Summary*, 16.
26 RCIRCSA, *Religious Institutions*, bk. 1, 487.
27 RCIRCSA, bk. 1, 487.
28 RCIRCSA, bk. 1, 487.
29 Cornwell, *Dark Box*, 169.

> I never told anybody at the time because it would've broken my mother's heart, I think. She was a strict Catholic and the priest was, you know, up on a pedestal to be admired, and they couldn't do anything wrong in her eyes.... I've never told her.[30]

> I did not tell my parents about the abuse at the time.... I didn't want to shake my parents' faith and I didn't want to devastate them.[31]

This instinct is exploited by perpetrators:

> He actually said to not to tell them (parents) about the time he and I were spending together because it would hurt them [sic].[32]

The devastation of abuse affected not only victims and survivors but also families, church congregations, and whole communities:

> My parents were utterly shattered, shattered, by the revelations of abuse to their three sons. Their faith and their trust in the church was destroyed.... Our faith has now been lost.[33]

> Child sexual abuse doesn't just tear individuals and families apart. In my experience, its claws reach into the community as well, whether they know it or not.[34]

It is not possible in this chapter to fully examine the complex and interconnected factors that contribute to an increased risk of abuse within religious institutions. However, it is important

---

30 RCIRCSA, *Religious Institutions*, bk. 1, 325.
31 RCIRCSA, bk. 1, 490.
32 RCIRCSA, bk. 1, 320.
33 RCIRCSA, bk. 1, 490.
34 RCIRCSA, bk. 2, 513.

to note that contrary to popular opinion, RCIRCSA found that there were risk factors unique to religious institutions that were not present in the secular institutions they examined.[35] The connection between religion and experiences of abuse creates what has been described as a "toxic transference," resulting in a form of "spiritual death."[36] One survivor described his experiences as an "enduring spiritual cancer" that had destroyed his relationship with God:

> "I assume I'm like a silent majority of Church survivors—unable to work within Church structure as it stands... the buildings, the personnel, the rituals that became inextricably juxtaposed with sex, sexuality and misuse of power."[37]

Theology and the Child

As I examined the RCIRCSA report, I was often shocked by the complex theology woven throughout the testimonies of victims and survivors. Perhaps less surprising were the ways certain doctrinal belief systems were defended in the face of overwhelming evidence of the risks they posed to children. Herein lies the tension of this collective trauma event.[38] Strongly held beliefs regarding issues of faith are difficult to challenge without undermining the spiritual identities of individuals and religious communities. There are those whose vocation and income are dependent on the system under examination, and any questioning of such poses a threat. The process of critiquing and deconstructing shared meaning is painful.

Recently, I had a conversation with the minister who led our faith community during my childhood. He was devastated when I

---

35 RCIRCSA, bk. 1, 387.
36 RCIRCSA, bk. 1, 488.
37 RCIRCSA, bk. 1, 479.
38 For further exploration of the concept of collective trauma, see Hirschberger, "Collective Trauma."

told him that my childhood faith had been shaped by a deep sense of fear and shame. His nuanced understanding of theology had been beyond my comprehension and left me with an image of an all-powerful, judgmental God who scared me. I did not experience abuse within this community; indeed, it was a place where I felt loved and cared for. Yet the image of God I formed and the God-child relationship I experienced were built on a foundation of anxiety and a deep sense of unworthiness. Jerome Berryman warns of the impact of "overheard theology."[39] A child in a congregational setting inevitably encounters complex theology and needs support to process this experience.

The vast majority of people holding positions of religious leadership have never and will never intentionally cause harm to the children in their care; however, such commitment does not ensure that children are unharmed.

My research revealed that certain theological and doctrinal belief systems and practices can contribute to the development of institutional structures and cultures in a way that increases the risks to children and that attracts exploitation by perpetrators. Broadly, these relate to certain ideas about creation, priesthood, sin, and redemption. In naming these, I do not intend to here offer a theological interrogation or critique of these complex and multifaceted doctrines. Rather, I seek only to convey what has been reported by victims and survivors.

What follows here explores the vulnerable elements of the doctrines of the created order, of original sin, and of penal substitutionary atonement as they have been experienced and interpreted by children within the ministry and mission of the church. These have been selected because of their significance in the RCIRCSA findings and because of the impact they were shown to have on the spiritual formation of children and on institutional responses to abuse.

---

39 Berryman, *Talking Theodicy with Children*, 1–13.

The Child in the Midst of Our Doctrine of Creation

The idea that within creation, there exists a particular order of superiority, a hierarchy of beings, has its origins in the philosophy of Plato's *scala natura*, the ladder of life.[40] The work of theologians such as Augustine of Hippo and Thomas Aquinas, giants of Western Christianity, was strongly influenced by this idea, and it has in turn shaped the doctrines and structures of some religious institutions.[41] Dr. Thomas P. Doyle, OP, Dominican priest, canon lawyer, and survivor advocate, in his expert testimony to the RCIRCSA, states the following: "The official teaching of the Catholic Church holds that the hierarchical model was willed by God. . . . The teaching and tradition that the hierarchical governmental system is of Divine Origin is essential for the support of the power of the hierarchical leaders."[42] In some faith traditions, this belief is justified and legitimized by further grounding this vision of created being in divine ontology itself, promoting, with varying degrees of care and sophistication, the idea of a hierarchy of relations in the Trinity itself. It is important to note, however, that even faith traditions that do not espouse such a vision, whether explicitly or implicitly, frequently embody a hierarchical worldview in their practices.

It is also important here to recognize the difference between leadership and a hierarchical worldview, although leadership structures often provide a good indication of the cultural hierarchies at play. For the purpose of this chapter, a *hierarchy* is defined as a belief that an innate and unquestionable superiority exists in one person over another. The RCIRCSA identified hierarchies of leadership, gender, race, and sexuality as impacting the risk of abuse.[43] For example, the exclusion of women from leadership

---

40 Lovejoy, *Great Chain of Being*.
41 Shand, *Central Works of Philosophy*.
42 RCIRCSA, *Religious Institutions*, bk. 2, 645.
43 RCIRCSA, bk. 1, 29, 43–45, 46–47, 152–54.

and governance roles was identified as a significant risk factor for the abuse of children.[44] The RCIRCSA focused, in detail, on one particularly powerful hierarchy within religious institutions—namely, clericalism.

Clericalism

Clericalism is a doctrinal belief system that maintains that religious leaders are morally superior to everyone else, a position that bolsters such leaders' moral authority: "Survivors who grew up in the Catholic and Anglican faiths told us that as children they were taught that 'priests, Brothers and nuns were closer to God,' that priests were 'up there like with God,' were 'next to God,' had 'a direct link to God,' 'were gods,' or were 'the representation of God.' Survivors told us that they had been taught as children that priests were 'the next step down from God . . . all-powerful and special,' and 'incapable of sin.'"[45] The RCIRCSA found that clericalism is usually present in faith traditions that have a rigidly hierarchical worldview[46] and hold a patriarchal image of God.[47] It is important to note that while many of the faith traditions examined by the RCIRCSA hold articulated doctrines of clericalism, others embodied this belief system despite stating otherwise.

Clericalism often manifests as an authoritarian style of ministerial leadership and the belief that the holiness and grace bestowed on the church are shared with and mediated through the religious leader.[48] The use of titles of leadership—such as Father, Pastor, Brother/Sister, Bishop, Elder, and Major—and the wearing of robes or uniforms are also characteristics of clericalism.[49] Another feature of clericalism is role-based status and authority

44 RCIRCSA, bk. 1, 29.
45 RCIRCSA, bk. 1, 454.
46 RCIRCSA, bk. 2, 614.
47 RCIRCSA, bk. 2, 617.
48 RCIRCSA, bk. 2, 614.
49 RCIRCSA, bk. 2, 615.

that can be expressed through control of and access to the church's sacraments, which are the signs of God's grace, and with that, the capacity to withhold them.[50]

Impacts of Clericalism on the Risk of Child Abuse

The RCIRCSA's final report states, "It appears to us that clericalism sits at the center, where it is interconnected with, and in some instances is the root or foundation of, the other contributing factors."[51] The clearest risk factor presented in the data was the belief that the abuse of children does not occur within religious organizations and that religious leaders do not abuse children: "Many parents were unable to believe (religious leaders) could be capable of sexually abusing a child. In this environment, perpetrators who were people in religious ministry often had unfettered access to children."[52] The RCIRCSA found that "parents and children (were) over-trusting clergy and not questioning them when they should."[53] This belief also fueled a culture where disclosure was dismissed as untrue. As one survivor recalls, "I also felt it was pointless to tell anyone because it would have been his word against mine and I thought that because he was such a 'Godly figure,' he would automatically be believed over me."[54] Clericalism also motivates religious institutions to prioritize the protection of the status and reputation of the church and religious leaders over the welfare of the child. This contributes to a culture of victim blaming and disclosure punishment that continues even after the abuse itself has ended.[55]

---

50 RCIRCSA, bk. 2, 614, 615.
51 RCIRCSA, bk. 2, 616.
52 RCIRCSA, bk. 1, 23.
53 RCIRCSA, bk. 1, 736.
54 RCIRCSA, bk. 1, 520.
55 RCIRCSA, bk. 1, 639.

The impact of clericalism on the spirituality of children is significant. Embedding a child in a culture of clericalism enabled perpetrators to link abuse with the God-child relationship: "I felt uncomfortable. Really uncomfortable with it, but God was involved... and so I was becoming really confused with the whole thing."[56] Religious language and positional authority were used to convince the child that the abuse was sanctioned by God, such as in the following examples:

"We're doing God's work."[57]

"It was okay, because if it was wrong, God wouldn't let it happen."[58]

"If [she] loved God, it would be okay to (description of abuse) because he was God's representative."[59]

Abuse was also framed as part of the sanctification process:

"Pain and suffering was a way to get closer to God."[60]

"The clergy are actually divine in the sense that they are chosen by God, they are the embodiment of God.... Maybe God had chosen me for something special."[61]

Victims and survivors report that often, they did not fully understand the nature of what was occurring, thus linking the abuse with their spiritual identities, with their relationships with God, and with the church. The long-term and profound impact on the

---

56 RCIRCSA, bk. 1, 451.
57 RCIRCSA, bk. 1, 529.
58 RCIRCSA, bk. 1, 454.
59 RCIRCSA, bk. 1, 454.
60 RCIRCSA, bk. 1, 521.
61 RCIRCSA, bk. 1, 464.

spiritual formation of victims and survivors cannot be understated: "I don't have any faith. The church and everything it stands for is a demon to me. I believe in God, but I don't believe in the way that man has portrayed God. I believe it has been built on lies. What happened to me when I was a child has been ingrained into me."[62]

The Child in the Midst of Our Doctrines of Sin

In Western Christianity, *hamartiology*—the field of theology that focuses on the study of sin—has been shaped by a deeply embedded but often unconsciously held doctrine: Augustine's doctrine of original sin. In its most basic form, this doctrine states that all human beings are sinful from birth and, as such, subject to divine judgment. After the reformations in the sixteenth century, proponents of the theologies of Martin Luther and John Calvin further developed this Augustinian doctrine, employing the language of "the bondage of the will" and "total depravity" to describe the human state from birth. Such ways of thinking about sin have profoundly impacted the way children and, in particular, their behavior are interpreted.

One task of the qualitative evaluation I completed was to compile a list of ways that victims and survivors reported being described within religious institutions. The list includes descriptions like "filthy little beast," "dirty little bugger," "ungrateful little bastard,"[63] "evil,"[64] "a lying, blaspheming little bastard,"[65] "scum of the earth," "slut," "filthy pig,"[66] "devil,"[67] "filthy little brat,"[68] "filthy

---

62 RCIRCSA, bk. 1, 488.
63 RCIRCSA, bk. 3, 52.
64 RCIRCSA, bk. 1, 473.
65 RCIRCSA, bk. 1, 495.
66 RCIRCSA, bk. 1, 401.
67 RCIRCSA, bk. 1, 471.
68 RCIRCSA, bk. 1, 472.

animal,"[69] "evil Jezebel,"[70] "garbage," "blackie," "camp dogs,"[71] "Number nine,"[72] "Antichrist,"[73] and "whore."[74] Such descriptions suggest contamination, dehumanization, and depravity; mirror ways that children have been perceived within religious institutions; and echo language used about children in Western theology.[75] Underlying negative beliefs about children were shown to strongly influence the behavior toward those children by those charged with their care:[76] "Christian views of sin and punishment were used to rationalize the repressive character of the care that many of these institutions provided: The guilt and sin of Catholic doctrine, the dour antipleasure ideology of the evangelical Protestants—Methodists, Presbyterians, Salvationists—and the chilly austerity of the Anglican Church all found expression, in Children's Homes, in a practice that had little to do with love or comfort and much to do with the repression of all feeling."[77] The idea of total depravity, which relates closely to the idea of "original sin," has also influenced the way children think about themselves in relation to God. Berryman notes that connecting particular cognitive development structures and the logic of doctrine can stall a child's theological thinking. He calls this process *interlocking*.[78] During early childhood, he proposes, self-centrism and magical thinking can interlock with the doctrinal logic of original sin. The child can be convinced that when evil occurs, it has its origin within the child themselves. This belief was used by perpetrators to silence victims and survivors, who are encouraged to believe about themselves that, for example, "I was bad, that I

69 RCIRCSA, bk. 1, 545.
70 RCIRCSA, bk. 1, 470.
71 RCIRCSA, bk. 3, 52.
72 RCIRCSA, bk. 1, 319.
73 RCIRCSA, bk. 1, 402.
74 RCIRCSA, bk. 1, 496.
75 See Bunge, *Child in Christian Thought*.
76 RCIRCSA, *Religious Institutions*, bk. 3, 52–54.
77 RCIRCSA, bk. 1, 151.
78 Berryman, *Talking Theodicy with Children*, 2.

was evil and that I deserved what he did to me. He said, 'This is your fault.' I heard these words from him over and over and over."[79]

The Child in the Midst of Our Doctrine of Redemption

The image of a wrath-filled God whose very nature demands blood dominates the testimonies of victims and survivors in the RCIRCSA's final report. The use of humiliation and violent discipline was common and often associated with the language of "sin," "hell," and "redemption": "She told us that she lived in constant fear, as extreme physical and psychological violence from the priests and religious sisters was routine. She said the children were viciously flogged, forced to do hard manual labor, and told they would burn in purgatory for their 'sins.' 'We were so scared. . . . That's why I couldn't say anything to anybody,' she explained."[80] Within the doctrine of penal substitutionary atonement, the violence experienced by Jesus on the cross is seen as an essential component of the redemptive work of God. Victims and survivors report that within many religious institutions, this belief system facilitated the use of physical and emotional abuse as evangelistic tools. Children were punished for their "sins" so that their souls may be saved: "A number of survivors told us that they believed their treatment by Salvation Army officers was intended to 'break them' or 'break their spirits. . . .' Some told us they believed their treatment by The Salvation Army was intended to save or redeem them."[81] The ability to threaten a child with eternal damnation was frequently used by perpetrators to ensure compliance and nondisclosure. It utilized the child's existing belief that they are inherently sinful and added layers of fear and shame: "She told me never to mention this to anyone. I was a filthy girl that no one wanted, so

79 RCIRCSA, *Religious Institutions*, bk. 1, 470.
80 RCIRCSA, bk. 1, 319.
81 RCIRCSA, bk. 3, 52.

no one would ever believe me anyway."[82] It is here that the risks associated with the doctrines of created order, original sin, and penal substitutionary atonement align. A child who is embedded in a culture that gives certain individuals unquestionable moral authority is then told that they are inherently sinful and that to be saved from hell, they must obey the teachings of religious authority figures. These authority figures are thus empowered to use fear, shame, and violence to facilitate conviction or punishment of sin for the purpose of repentance because they deem the soul of the child to be more important than any harm caused to that child's body. Such people are then granted unquestioned and unsupervised access to the child by families and congregations who trust this individual implicitly. If a perpetrator gains access to this space, the results are horrific.

Conclusion

I have been asked on numerous occasions if intergenerational ministry poses a lower risk to children. My answer is always this: we don't know. Embedding a child in an environment with flat egalitarian leadership structures, where questioning and discussion are normalized faith practices and where children have the opportunity to develop healthy, positive relationships with a wide group of adults committed to their care, appears to be more protective. However, many of the intergenerational ministries I have observed continue to function using hierarchical leadership models. Often, the shift toward an intergenerational ministry model merely involves reintegrating children into adult-centric activities. This can expose children to complex theological content that they are ill-equipped to interpret without the opportunity for collective discernment.

Religious communities can no longer ignore the fact that certain theological and doctrinal beliefs and religious practices

---

82 RCIRCSA, bk. 1, 546.

have had unintended consequences that have increased the risk of abuse—spiritual, physical, emotional, and sexual. It is imperative that churches and other faith organizations consider the ways their own beliefs, even cherished ones, could potentially impact the children in their care. Such organizations cannot continue to deceive themselves, proclaiming abuse within religious institutions to be an issue of the past or limited to particular denominations. Abuses of moral authority and religious power also need to inform broader conversations taking place in such organizations about things like formational programs, liturgical practices, and wider public engagement. The moment such organizations or individuals decide that the life of one child is not enough to warrant systemic reform, history has shown that no number of lives will ever be enough. In such cases—and these are not a few—institutions and those in power have chosen to protect themselves instead of the child.

The church's own scriptures recount Jesus's promise to those who had believed in him: "Then you will know the truth, and the truth will set you free" (John 8:32). The RCIRCSA's report is a testimony to the truth of things. It represents an invitation toward the possibility of life unmarked by harm—for itself and for the children in its midst, those to whom "the kingdom of God belongs" (Luke 18:16).

Are we willing to wrestle with the complex questions of how and why theology is embodied in damaging ways? Will we hear the voice of the child in our midst?

> "For there is nothing hidden that will not be disclosed, and nothing concealed that will not be known or brought out into the open." (Luke 8:17)

Bibliography

Berryman, Jerome. *Talking Theodicy with Children without Arresting Their Theological Thinking*. Houston: Center for the Theology of

Childhood, 2007. https://old.religiouseducation.net/proceedings/TalkingTheodicywithChildren-READraft.pdf.

Bunge, Marcia, ed. *The Child in Christian Thought*. Grand Rapids, MI: Eerdmans, 2001.

Catterton Allen, Holly. *InterGenerate: Transforming Churches through Intergenerational Ministry*. Abilene, TX: Abilene Christian University Press, 2018.

———. *Nurturing Children's Spirituality: Christian Perspectives and Best Practices*. Eugene, OR: Cascade Books, 2008.

Catterton Allen, Holly, and Christine Lawton. *Intergenerational Christian Formation: Bringing the Whole Church Together in Ministry, Community and Worship*. Downers Grove, IL: InterVarsity, 2012.

Chi-Kin Lee, John. "Children's Spirituality: Personal Reflections on International Journal of Children's Spirituality (IJCS)." *International Journal of Children's Spirituality* 26, nos. 1–2 (2021): 1–8. https://www.tandfonline.com/doi/full/10.1080/1364436X.2021.1879504.

Commission to Inquire into Child Abuse. *Final Report of the Commission to Inquire into Child Abuse*. Dublin: Irish Government, 2009. http://www.childabusecommission.ie/rpt/.

Committee on the Rights of the Child. *Concluding Observations on the Second Periodic Report of the Holy See*. Geneva: United Nations, 2014. https://www.refworld.org/docid/52f8a1544.html.

Cornwell, John. *The Dark Box: A Secret History of Confession*. New York: Basic Books, 2014.

Csinos, David M. "From the Ground Up: Cultural Considerations in Research into Children's Spirituality and Theology." *International Journal of Children's Spirituality* 23, no. 1 (2017): 53–66.

Denton, M. L., L. D. Pearce, and C. Smith. *Research Reports Number 1–9*. Notre Dame, IN: National Study of Youth and Religion, 2008. https://youthandreligion.nd.edu/research-findings/reports/.

Department of Children, Equality, Disability, Integration and Youth. *Final Report of the Commission of Investigation into Mother and Baby Homes*. Government of Ireland, 2020. https://www.gov.ie/en/publication/d4b3d-final-report-of-the-commission-of-investigation-into-mother-and-baby-homes/.

Hirschberger, Gilad. "Collective Trauma and the Social Construction of Meaning." *Frontiers in Psychology* 9, no. 1441 (August 10, 2018). https://doi.org/10.3389/fpsyg.2018.01441.

Human Rights and Equal Opportunity Commission. *Bringing Them Home: Report of the National Inquiry into the Separation of Aboriginal and*

Torres Strait Islander Children from Their Families. Sydney: Commonwealth of Australia, 1997. https://humanrights.gov.au/sites/default/files/content/pdf/social_justice/bringing_them_home_report.pdf.

Independent Inquiry Child Sexual Abuse. *Safeguarding in the Church in England and the Church in Wales: The Anglican Church and the Roman Catholic Church*. London: Crown, 2020. https://www.iicsa.org.uk/document/anglican-church-safeguarding-church-england-and-church-wales-investigation-report.

Kaufman, Keith, and Marcus Erooga with Kelly Stewart, Judith Zatkin, Erin McConnell, Hayley Tews, and Daryl Higgins. *Risk Profiles for Institutional Child Sexual Abuse: A Literature Review*. Sydney: Commonwealth of Australia, 2016. https://www.childabuseroyalcommission.gov.au/sites/default/files/file-list/Research%20Report%20%20Risk%20profiles%20for%20institutional%20child%20sexual%20abuse%20-%20Causes.pdf.

Kinnaman, David. *You Lost Me: Why Young Christians Are Leaving Church . . . and Rethinking Faith*. Grand Rapids, MI: Baker, 2011.

Lovejoy, Arthur O. *The Great Chain of Being: A Study of the History of an Idea*. Cambridge, MA: Harvard University Press, 2001.

National Library of Australia Collection. "James Cook's Secret Instructions," ca. 1768. Cited in Justice Jargot, *The Rule of Law and Reconciliation: Opening Address to the Law Society of New South Wales Young Lawyers' Conference*. Accessed January 5, 2022. https://www.fedcourt.gov.au/digital-law-library/judges-speeches/justice-jagot/jagot-j-20171020.

Office of the Attorney General. *Report I of the 40th Statewide Investigating Grand Jury*. Pennsylvania: Commonwealth of Pennsylvania, 2018. https://www.attorneygeneral.gov/report/.

One Hundred Tenth Congress. *Legacy of the Trans-Atlantic Slave Trade: Hearing before the Subcommittee on the Constitution, Civil Rights, and Civil Liberties of the Committee on the Judiciary House of Representatives*. Washington, DC: US Government Printing Office, 2008. 39–707. https://www.govinfo.gov/content/pkg/CHRG-110hhrg39707/pdf/CHRG-110hhrg39707.pdf.

Penner, James, Rachael Harder, Erika Anderson, Bruno Désorcy, and Rick Hiemstra. *Hemorrhaging Faith: Why and When Canadian Young Adults Are Leaving, Staying and Returning to Church*. Canada: EFC Youth and Young Adult Ministry Roundtable, 2011. https://hemorrhagingfaith.com.

Pope Alexander VI. "Demarcation Bull Granting Spain Possession of Lands Discovered by Columbus Rome, May 4, 1493." Gilder Lehrman

Institute of American History. Accessed January 19, 2022. https://www.gilderlehrman.org/sites/default/files/inline-pdfs/T-04093.pdf.

Powell, Kara E., and Chap Clark. *Sticky Faith: Everyday Ideas to Build Lasting Faith into Your Kids*. Grand Rapids, MI: Zondervan, 2011.

Royal Commission into Institutional Responses to Child Sexual Abuse (RCIRCSA). *Final Report: Executive Summary*. Canberra: Commonwealth of Australia, 2017. https://www.childabuseroyalcommission.gov.au/preface-and-executive-summary.

———. *Final Report*. Vol. 16, bks. 1–3, *Religious Institutions*. Canberra: Commonwealth of Australia, 2017. https://www.childabuseroyalcommission.gov.au/religious-institutions.

Secretary of the Interior Deb Haaland. *Memorandum: Federal Indian Boarding School Initiative*. Washington, DC: Department of the Interior, 2021. https://www.doi.gov/sites/doi.gov/files/secint-memo-esb46-01914-federal-indian-boarding-school-truth-initiative-2021-06-22-final508-1.pdf.

Senate Community Affairs References Committee. *Forgotten Australians: A Report on Australians Who Experienced Institutional or Out-of-Home Care as Children*. Canberra: Commonwealth of Australia, 2004. https://www.aph.gov.au/parliamentary_business/committees/senate/community_affairs/completed_inquiries/2004-07/inst_care/report/index.

Senate Standing Committee on Community Affairs. *Lost Innocents: Righting the Record—Report on Child Migration*. Canberra: Commonwealth of Australia, 2001. https://www.aph.gov.au/parliamentary_business/committees/senate/community_affairs/completed_inquiries/1999-02/child_migrat/report/index.

Shand, John. *Central Works of Philosophy*. Vol. 6, *Ancient and Medieval*. London: Taylor & Francis, 2004.

Truth and Reconciliation Commission of Canada. *Honouring the Truth, Reconciling for the Future Summary of the Final Report of the Truth and Reconciliation Commission of Canada*. Manitoba: Government of Canada, 2015. https://irsi.ubc.ca/sites/default/files/inline-files/Executive_Summary_English_Web.pdf.

United States Office of Indian Affairs. *Fifty Seventh Annual Report of the Commissioner of Indian Affairs, for the Year 1888*. Accessed August 4, 2021, https://digicoll.library.wisc.edu/cgi-bin/History/History-idx?type=turn&entity=History.AnnRep88.p0018&id=History.AnnRep88&isize.

CHAPTER 13

Accompanying Children and Teens through Loss

Lacy Finn Borgo

The Boy, the Mole, the Fox and the Horse by Charlie Mackesy is a popular graphic novel about life, loss, and friendship. Near the end of the book, after the Mole and the Fox have offered their answers to the Boy's expression of loss and pain, an illustration captures the core message. Mackesy's use of black ink on a white background focuses and simplifies the image. In the illustration, the large head of the Horse hovers over the smaller, more fragile head of the Boy, a gesture of tenderness as the soft muzzle seems to caress the wispy hair of the Boy. In that connective moment, the Horse says to the Boy, "Life is difficult—but you are loved."[1]

We human beings need this kind of presence and message when we are in seasons of suffering and loss. As children and teens encounter loss and travel through the stages of grief, they need to know they are safe and loved. Think back to a loss that you experienced when you were a child or a teen. Who reminded you that you were safe and loved? Learning how to hold both love and the difficulty of life together is the challenge for all of us, and it will take a lifetime to discover. We begin this discovery as children.

---

1 Mackesy, *Boy, the Mole, the Fox and the Horse*, 43.

Expressions of Loss

Loss for children and teens naturally stirs a whirlwind of questions. The questions themselves are signposts of profound longing for love and safety. Some questions are practical, like, What happens to bodies when they die? Others are deeper questions at the core of human existence, like, If we are loved by God, then why do bad things happen? and, How can I know I'm safe?

The COVID-19 virus began to spread globally in early 2020, and since then, the world has become more acutely aware of the losses endured by children and teens. They have experienced the loss of stability, school experiences, friendships, family connections, and even hope. Children and teens also experience the everyday losses that come from increased freedom and the natural process of growing up. Loss is part of living and can be integrated into one's whole life with God. Loss can be a conduit for a deeper relationship.

Children and teens express loss in various ways and perhaps differently from how we adults might expect. They might be withdrawn or sullen; they might express big feelings or have no visible feelings. They might act out in ways that are not related to the loss itself. For children, grief comes in spurts. It might come to the surface for just a bit and then pop back down below. They may express their sadness and, in the next breath, ask if they can go swimming with a friend. A child's capacity for consciousness is wide. While the adult has a focused experience of the world, its pain, and its Creator, in contrast, a child has a wide and spacious experience. They will take in the loss alongside their love for ice cream with sprinkles.[2]

Children might reenact the event itself using toys or role-play the circumstance. They may revert to their older ways of being or ask deep questions at seemingly random points in time. Loss

---

2 Two excellent resources on children and grief are D'Arcy and Ford, *Helping Children Grieve*; and Goldman, *Life and Loss*.

is unique to each person. One thing seems common though: loss stirs longing in children and teens. They become acutely aware of their need for love and their inner wiring for safe connections. Their wonderings about God and God's love come to the surface.

Cultivating a Listening Heart

Younger children can't always articulate the questions they have, but this doesn't mean they don't have questions or need to express the feelings and thoughts stirring within them. Accompanying children and teens through loss begins by cultivating listening hearts within us—the adults. Adults can provide a safe space for children and teens in seasons of loss, but it takes a little work on the part of the adult. The soul of a child is like a wild animal—not as in feral, but as in requiring safety in order to come out of hiding and be vulnerable.

Being people of safety means that we have done our own inner work around loss. Do we let our losses come to the surface, and do we bring them into God's tender care? Have we come to the place of knowing that life is indeed difficult and that this difficulty exists in the same realm of God's generous love? Have we let great love and great loss transform us into people who have little need for easy answers or quick fixes? Are we willing to let children speak their feelings and their questions without the compulsion to belittle their experience or try to make it better? You might want to write the above questions in a journal and live with them for a while. Bring them to your conversations with God, and be attentive to what unfolds. You might notice that your own losses could use some tender, loving care. Finding a spiritual director, counselor, or compassionate listening friend can be part of cultivating your listening heart for children and teens.

Recognize

Once we give even a bit of our attention to intentionally cultivating a listening heart, we are ready to accompany children and teens through loss. There is no arrival point for readiness to listen but only a beginning. If we are faithful listeners to children and teens, we will live with them in the questions all of our lives.

With open hearts, we listen to their stories. We help them recognize how they feel and what they think. We become tender witnesses to what is stirring within. Sometimes, children are willing and very ready to share their feelings. They might begin to share when driving in the car, when cooking dinner together, or just before going to bed at night. Sometimes conversation opens naturally; other times, a variation of this question can help: "Would you like to tell your story about feeling sad, mad, or afraid?"

Children and teens may not have the feeling-language or inner articulation to put words to how they feel. Using colors, shapes, and even animals to represent feelings can be helpful. During COVID-19, Jimmy described his feelings of loss after his class went back to learning from home: "I'm like a sloth and can barely move." His sister Jenny described her experience as feeling "like a tiger ready to roar." After a community tragedy, a wise teacher led her class through an expression of feelings using color. She gave each child a blank piece of watercolor paper and a set of watercolors. Using the color wheel, she walked through the different possible colors as representations of feelings. Then they were invited to create paintings expressing their felt losses.

Making space for the sharing of losses within daily life can be helpful. Parents and teachers can literally set aside space for expressing loss. It might look like a journal where children can record their feelings, it might be a memorial space where children remember what or who they miss, or it might be a space of silence or even play where what needs to be expressed is too big for words.

It might look like children writing their memories of a classmate on rocks and placing them in the school garden. It might look like a "Jesus Journal," where members of a family are encouraged to share their sorrows with Jesus through written words and drawings. It can look like a bench, seat, or pillow that signals to everyone else that silence is needed. Praying the Examen with children and teens before bed is a good ritual for sharing our losses.[3]

The Examen has five movements:

1. Become aware of God's presence: Become aware of God's presence by using a bodily expression of our love and connection to God. That could be kneeling or the sign of the cross, a group hug, or a fist bump. Let your family get creative with bodily expressions of God's presence.
2. Look for the graces: Then review the day in chunks. Think back through your day and look for the graces. When did you experience goodness, beauty, truth, love, joy, peace, patience, or kindness? We look back for what was good and of God.
3. Look for the growth: Next, we look back through our day for the growth. What didn't go as we'd hoped? What felt hard or sad? When did we choose unkindness rather than kindness, and when did we choose to work against goodness? This can be a time to say, "I'm sorry," or ask for forgiveness.
4. Talk with Jesus: Pause for just a moment to talk with Jesus about the graces and the growth. It's important for us to hold a loving image of Jesus as we talk with him.
5. Think about tomorrow: As we look toward tomorrow, where do you anticipate that you'll need Jesus's help? Ask for that help now. Then conclude your prayer with your bodily sign of God's presence.

Children and teens can push behavioral boundaries when they are in seasons of loss. Their behavior expresses what they feel but cannot say. Gentle but clear boundaries can go a long way toward

---

3 For further teaching, see Borgo, "Examen-for-Families."

helping a child or teen feel safe. Structure and stability answer the child's unspoken questions around their sense of being safe. Having an adult listening companion with various tools of expression at the ready can be helpful in those moments of behavioral challenge. When a child or teen acts out, a caring question might be, "I wonder if you are feeling sad about something? I am here and willing to listen."

Presence and Listening

When stories of loss are being told, it is the adult's job to be present and listen but not interfere. We certainly are praying internally and listening to the guidance of the Holy Spirit. In our listening, we will feel the tug to make things better for this little one who is suffering, as if we could. It's important for us to know that our platitudes and "fix it" phrases—like "God just needed your mama in heaven" or "Aren't you happy that . . ."—do not help. While it is true that God can work all things for the good of the child, it is little, if any, comfort to hear so when a child's heart is breaking.

When we overstep our listening, we step in between the child and the Holy Spirit, who is the Divine Comforter. We take over with our goodwill and poor timing and squeeze God out of a possible encounter. We are speaking to our own struggle and not the struggle of the child. It is best to listen and listen and then listen more. Ask questions like "Can you say more about that?" and "How was it for you?" Invite the child or teen to express themselves through the creative arts or through playing with toys. I have watched children build hospital rooms and vaccine labs out of plastic bricks as expressions of their loss. These are sacred moments where we adults are invited to witness the pain of the child or teen; with the ears of Jesus, we listen to them in disclosure and connection.

Bodies and Meaning Making

Young children carry grief in their bodies.[4] Their feeling vocabularies are limited, so they will need to move their muscles to work through it. One mother tells the story of signing her two young sons up for tae kwon do after their father died. She needed a break, and they needed to break something. Years later, they shared with her how having a place where they could kick and hit helped them express how angry and sad they were. Children grieve in windows of time. They will not always be sad and, in fact, can go from very sad to giddy in a matter of seconds. This is God's kindness to them, as their capacity for grief is limited. If we want to be safe listeners for children, we will need to keep pace with their feelings in the moment. Not forced or frustrated but flexible, able to meet them where they are.

Children and teens will search for meaning in their loss. We are meaning-making creatures, and in our tender state, we will not care if the meaning we make is true. This can lead to feelings of guilt and shame around loss. Children and teens may blame themselves for what has occurred, even when it is far beyond rational to do so. When children and teens unearth their feelings of guilt, it is important for the adult listener to speak the truth in love—quite literally. The adult may need to speak the loving truth over and over and over again until the child or teen can listen themselves into freedom. Over and over, I have reminded children that they didn't bring COVID-19 into their families or country. COVID-19 is not their fault. Stating a simple truth, with just the details needed, is a grace.

If we think of our experiences as stopping points on a spiral staircase, we touch the experience over and over again as we go up and down, and each touch means revisiting old wounds until they are healed. The adult listener will need to be patient as the

---

4 D'Arcy and Ford, *Helping Children Grieve*.

child or teen touches their wound and continuously needs to hear the words of freedom anew.

Through listening to both the child and the Holy Spirit, we create space for a gently offered invitation. Our losses are sacred. Let that sink in for a moment. They are not trivial or moments that we must muscle through and get over. Often, our losses mark our love lost. A child or teen who is experiencing loss needs a way to mark what is no more. Ritual can be a helpful tool for marking our losses. Candles, memorials, prayer walks, and local expressions of activism are all ways that children can mark and honor their losses. Amanda walked a five-kilometer breast cancer event each year all throughout middle and high school to mark the loss of her mother to breast cancer. When Jeremy's pet hamster died, he got his parents' permission to paint a memorial on a wall in his bedroom, and they participated. Teens often keep their old and worn-out stuffed animals as memorials of their childhood.

Using Picture Books

Children's picture books are some of my favorite tools for walking through loss. Thoughtful words and intentional images mixed with color can create a background to project thoughts and feelings upon. This is true for all of us at any age. However, for children and teens, reading a picture book together offers one other gift—physical proximity. One of the most acute feelings children and teens experience in seasons of loss is isolation. They feel separate and alone when trying to process and make meaning out of pain.

When we gather with a child or teen to engage with a children's picture book together, our bodies come closer. We smell each other's smells, hear each other's breath, and with safe touch, we can gather each other into our arms. Safe touch is a powerful connector, reminding us without the use of words that we are not alone. Entering the story, engaging with the images, and noticing shape, color, and movement can help us both recognize and respond. Children and teens may find words for their loss and colors for how they feel. They may discover a hope that wasn't present before.

I have included a longish list of children's books at the end of this chapter. When you gather to engage together, be sure that you have space to linger over the images. Take time not only to follow the story but to enter it. Ask the child or teen what pictures they like or don't like, what color is their favorite or least favorite, and if the images or story remind them of how they feel. This might lead to the desire to write and illustrate a book of their own, sharing their story and their feelings through pictures. Blank copy paper and a box of crayons can be tools for healing.

Giving God Access

God longs to encounter children and teens through their losses. They can be invited to give God access to their painful stories through different prayer practices. When we assume that God knows everything and therefore wonder why we should tell God our stories, our intimate relationship becomes limited. This faulty line of thinking seeps into children and teens' thinking and robs them of intimate lives with God. Yes, God is all knowing, but God also respects our boundaries and will not trespass on our tender hearts. God wants to hear and have access to that which brings us pain. God longs to be actively with children and teens in their most painful moments.

We can offer children and teens a simple invitation to share their stories and feelings with God. Again, that can be done through playing out the story, creating art, or any number of expressions. Prayer becomes prayer simply through attention being directed to God. There are many ways to bookend listening with an act of awareness and attention. A few ideas might be the sign of the cross, a reverential bowing of the body, or even a simply spoken, "God, I know that you are with us and that you are listening too." During the pandemic, one teen I know composed songs on the piano expressing her loss. Each song began with "God, do you hear me?" Another created a playlist of collected songs that expressed how he was feeling. After listening, the teen recorded thoughts and God's response in a prayer journal. Each of these is prayer, giving God access to feelings and thoughts of loss.

In the response, there is an embedded invitation to also listen to how God replies. We can help children and teens listen and discern God's personal communication to them. Some things that God says to us are for us alone and might not be for other ears, but in general, children and teens are willing to share what they sense. Often, children and teens report hearing God say, "I love you" and "I am with you." When they cannot hear God—and sometimes, grief is so loud that we cannot—we can use our words and tender presence to speak just what they need to hear: "Life is difficult, but you are loved."

Listening to God requires discernment. The adult listener should keep in mind our loving God's characteristics as laid out by Paul in 1 Corinthians 13. Since God is love (1 John 4:7–12), God's response to the child will be patient and kind. It will not show a hint of envy or arrogance. God will not insist on God's own way or be irritable or resentful. God's response will bear all the sorrow and pain, believe the very best about the child or teen, and provide hope and resiliency for the present and future.

Teens and Big Questions

Teen loss has a unique fingerprint. During the adolescent years, the social context of the self becomes more active. Teens' peers become main avenues for engagement with the world around them. Perhaps you can see why their losses during COVID-19 have been so acute. In addition, the work of building and discovering identity gets most of their attention. Due to these developmental processes, loss looks a bit different than it did in childhood. Teens may be worried about how their peers see them after their loss. They may feel isolated and wonder if they are the only ones who have experienced such pain. Teens may struggle with how to reconcile their loss with who they are.

For every human being, our knowing of self is intimately tied to our knowing of God. This is what makes the adolescent spiritual life full of wonder and discovery and sometimes pain and tumult. Teens may kick against the God they knew when they were young as they process and reconcile their loss and pain. Keep in mind, God is not fragile. God is tender but not fragile. They can bring their pain and anger to God.

In anger, a teen who has been very connected to God in the past might declare that they no longer believe in God. This declaration can upset parents and pastors alike but not God. These honest moments can be channeled into prayer that keeps the anger from hardening. It might require a deepening trust on the part of the adult to stay tender and nonjudgmental. In that way, we get to represent God's love and acceptance—what an incredible honor. We can say to the teen that they don't have to believe in God to express their anger; our listening takes the heat out and gives anger a place to flow. It is part of their process, their faithfulness. Hold center, dear loving adult—your listening, welcome presence is needed.

Here is one reminder: anger is never a cause for harm. In anger, children and teens are capable of harm to both themselves and others. When we hold space for anger, we can also usher in the practice of healthy expression and hold a firm boundary around anger that harms.

Walking Alongside

When children are heard and encouraged, they feel loved. It is an expression of self-giving love to pause what we are doing, empty our heads and hearts of to-do lists and distractions, and listen deeply and well. This is what love looks like, and there are times when our listening presence will not be enough. A child or teen may need professional help to work through their loss. It is expected that normal routines and ways of being will be disrupted in a season of loss, but if those disruptions continue, seek help beyond your listening presence. Helping a child or teen connect with a professional is also what love looks like.

Mathew, Mark, and Luke all record Jesus saying, "Let the little children come to me" (Matt. 19:14; Mark 10:14; Luke 18:16). Each of the children who came brought their losses, and Jesus knew it. Matthew and Mark record a physical touch of some kind, and all three record a sharp reprimand to the adults who would impede the encounter. When we accompany a child or teen as they experience loss, we in fact clear the way for them to come to Jesus. They are invited to bring their sorrow, pain, and anger to him. It is mind-blowing to me that in those moments, we get to embody the listening presence of the living God. With all the courage and comfort of the Holy Spirit flowing through us, we get to say without saying, "Life is difficult, but you are loved."

Bibliography

Borgo, Lacy Finn. "Examen-for-Families." Renovaré. Accessed November 5, 2022. https://renovare.org/messages/examen-for-families.

D'Arcy, Paula, and Khris Ford. *Helping Children Grieve*. DVD. Brewster, MA: Paraclete, 2009.

Other Recommended Resources and Children's Picture Books

Bender, Mike. *The End Is Just the Beginning: A Book of Endless Possibilities*. Illustrated by Diana Mayo. New York: Crown Books for Young Readers, 2021.

Borgo, Lacy Finn. *All Will Be Well: Learning to Trust God's Love*. Illustrated by Rebecca Evans. Downers Grove, IL: InterVarsity Kids, 2022.

Doerrfeld, Cori. *Goodbye, Friend! Hello, Friend*. Illustrated by C. Doerrfeld. New York: Dial Books, 2019.

Eland, Eva. *When Sadness Is at Your Door*. Illustrated by E. Eland. New York: Random House Books for Young Readers, 2019.

Feinberg, Heather Hawk. *Crying Is like the Rain: A Story of Mindfulness and Feelings*. Illustrated by Chamisa Kellogg. Thomaston: Tilbury House, 2020.

Goldman, Linda. *Life and Loss: A Guide to Help Grieving Children*. 2nd ed. Oxfordshire, UK: Routledge, 1999.

Goring, Ruth. *Isaiah and the Worry Pack*. Illustrated by Pamela C. Rice. Downers Grove, IL: InterVarsity Kids, 2021.

Hutchison, Roger. *My Favorite Color Is Blue. Sometimes: A Journey through Loss with Art and Color*. Orleans, MA: Paraclete, 2017.

Linn, Matthew, Dennis Linn, and Sheila Linn. *Making Heart Bread*. Mahwah, NJ: Paulist, 2006.

Luyken, Corinna. *My Heart*. Illustrated by C. Luyken. New York: Dial Books, 2019.

MacBeth, Sybil. *Praying in Color: Kids Edition*. Illustrated by S. MacBeth. Brewster, MA: Paraclete, 2009.

Mackesy, Charlie. *The Boy, the Mole, the Fox and the Horse*. San Francisco, CA: HarperOne, 2019.

Mundy, Michaelene. *Sad Isn't Bad: A Good Grief Guidebook for Kids Dealing with Loss*. Illustrated by R. W. Alley. Annotated ed. Saint Meinrad, IN: Abbey, 2006.

Ryland, Cynthia. *Life*. Illustrated by Brendan Wenzel. San Diego: Beach Lane Books, 2017.

———. *The Stars Will Still Shine*. Illustrated by Tipanie Beeke. New York: HarperCollins, 2005.

Sanna, Francesca. *Me and My Fear*. Bilingual ed. London: Flying Eye Books, 2018.

Zweibel, Alan. *Our Tree Named Steve*. Illustrated by David Catrow. London: Puffin Books, 2007.

CONCLUSION

Practical Guidance for Implementing Best Practices in Real-Life Ministry

Robin Turner, editor

We considered titling this conclusion "How to Get This Book off Your Shelf and into the Crazies of Real-Life Ministry." The reality is that good research and practical examples of ministry can feel both inspiring and overwhelming for children's ministry leaders. Perhaps the most overwhelming part of reading a book like this, with a broad array of topics and a number of practical suggestions, is knowing how to prioritize what changes to begin to lead. Too often, our intentions for having thoughtful spiritual moments with children are eclipsed by printer jams, last-minute volunteer scrambles, and responding to parents' emails. As a current full-time director of children's ministries, I am painfully aware of the phenomenal books and resources that sit inches from my desk and how often I get to the end of a week feeling like I spent my office hours navigating logistics or earning an honorary degree in diplomacy rather than nurturing the spiritual formation of children in my congregation. So what does it look like for those of us in the trenches to implement the tools and resources provided in this book?

Implementing change and cultivating creative ministry approaches take both bandwidth—space and time to think, collaborate, and try new ideas—and the freedom to lay an idea to rest and try something new. Similarly, seeking God's direction in leading a ministry means setting aside time and energy to intentionally listen to the guidance of the Holy Spirit, especially through Scripture, prayer, and wise counsel. This kind of bandwidth often sounds like a luxury for children's ministry leaders, who are often so occupied with coordinating tasks and people that they can no longer embrace their roles as ministers and leaders. This section of the book will turn to focus on tools for creating bandwidth, refocusing on ministry rather than mere logistics, prioritizing where to lead change, and building networks of collaboration.

Creating Bandwidth: Building Sustainable Ministries

Perhaps the first priority for children's ministry directors is to evaluate whether they have a sustainable children's ministry model and what they can do to relieve the consistent areas of pressure and frustration in their ministries. In a sustainable children's ministry, creating bandwidth might look like letting a program go on hiatus during school breaks, choosing a lower-prep curriculum for a few weeks each year, or streamlining tasks to take place on a schedule rather than on demand.

For an underresourced children's ministry—whether from a lack of finances, volunteers, space, or something else—these small adjustments cannot relieve the pressure points enough to adequately bring the ministry area out of triage mode and into a space for innovation and formation. Working with children and volunteers has an inherent level of unpredictability, but ministries do not need to be marked by chaos. One phenomenal resource for evaluating a children's ministry for sustainability and creating systems for greater personal bandwidth is *Sustainable Children's Ministry: From Last-Minute Scrambling to Long-Term Solutions* by ministry architects Mark Devries and Annette Safstrom. In this book, they offer resources to evaluate the sustainability of a ministry and practical tools to address common issues that lead to burnout and frustration.

In many churches, there are just a few unsustainable habits or systems that might need to be addressed to relieve common bandwidth issues. Batching tasks, keeping dedicated supplies together, and streamlining communications are all ways that ministry leaders can free themselves up from logistics for greater ministry capacity. Here are a few examples:

- I dedicate one drawer next to my desk to all our "welcome baby" gift materials, including cards, stamps, and gifts, which means sending a gift to a family in our church now takes me less than ten minutes and can be taken care of as soon as I find out the news.
- We look at our soon-to-expire background checks and child safety clearances once quarterly and email all the volunteers who need renewals at the same time rather than check on a weekly or even monthly basis.
- We plan our major event calendar a year in advance and hand it out to families at both the start of the school year and the start of the calendar year, which allows busy families to mark their calendars before event logistics can be communicated. I don't enter the fall wondering what events

we should plan, since they were announced the previous January.

Finally, ministry leaders can prioritize allocating portions of their schedules to specific ministry tasks rather than letting things like managing logistics take all their available hours to the detriment of time spent on collaboration, creative engagement, or spiritual formation. Blocking out a morning a month to spend with other ministry leaders, prioritizing time each week for prayer and Bible study, and scheduling time for reading or other forms of further education can help ministry leaders maintain priorities. In the event of a true emergency, these things might be canceled, but the time is allotted to priorities rather than running errands or responding to emails.

Refocusing on Ministry

Every ministry setting includes a certain amount of necessary logistics management, and keeping a ministry running smoothly rather than letting it devolve into chaos can be the ministry gift of many administratively minded people, but the means of logistics cannot become the end goal of the ministry. Ministry leaders can be encouraged to refocus on how those tasks lead to an ultimate end of drawing children to Christ. The most smoothly run, well-resourced children's ministry department can lose sight of being a space marked by God's presence and love if its focus becomes logistics, childcare, or entertainment. The problem, of course, is that many families and children are easily satisfied with safe, smoothly run, fun children's programs. Ministering to and with children is about welcoming the work of the Holy Spirit, growing in knowledge and understanding of God's love, and seeking how to build the Kingdom of God together.

Expecting God to be at work in the life of a child and the community of children is a key element of planning formation-focused children's activities. God is not at a loss for how to connect in developmentally appropriate ways with children, but sometimes children's ministry activities focus so much on occupying children that they overlook opportunities to help them listen to God or reflect on where God is at work in their lives. By creating ministry rhythms that regularly build this reflection into children's lessons, the design of the program can consistently point to spiritual formation rather than entertainment or mere Bible-based activities.

Unfortunately, many people seem to associate formation or reflection exclusively with quiet and solitude. While quiet and solitude can be good and beneficial gifts to people of all ages in their spiritual formation, other community-based formation that engages children in meaningful ways can include activities that nurture fellowship, discovery, and creativity. Here are a few examples of engaging, active, and fellowship-based formative activities:

- Create a group art project for display at the church, such as a set of images that depict the stations of the cross for Holy Week or a collection of tissue paper butterflies to hang on Easter Sunday as a symbol of the resurrection.
- Take a nature walk either with intentional conversation about where children see God through creation or with intentional silence to listen to God in the quiet of nature.
- Create a wall of questions and wonderings where children can share with the community by writing the things they are seeking to know more about regarding God's character, specific Bible stories, or other life questions. Similarly, create a group gratitude list where the community of children can record their praise to God.
- Build a scene from a Bible story out of cardboard, LEGO, or blocks with careful attention to details in the story or the historical context. This is a particularly good activity for understanding details about the tabernacle, temple, or city of Jerusalem. Many children prefer using materials like LEGO for reflection to traditional art responses.

- Enjoy a fun meal and playtime together during a time set aside specifically for fellowship. While this might be inappropriate during a traditional worship service or Sunday morning setting, many churches and ministries recognize the importance of facilitating fellowship and new friendships. Dedicating a Sunday lunch or evening gathering to the sole purpose of forming fun memories together with fellow believers is its own form of spiritual formation!
- Engage in sneaky-service opportunities as a group, serving the church or ministry without seeking recognition or thanks. Things like picking up trash, watering or weeding the church garden, or preparing snacks for the church family to enjoy together are all ways children can serve.

In many instances, the same activity can take place with a different framing to make it more intentionally formation focused. Perhaps in a lesson on Psalm 23, the curriculum encourages preschool-age children to glue cotton balls onto each of the sheep on a coloring page. While this could be merely a preschool-friendly sensory experience, the activity leader might reframe it by saying something like "Look at how clean and cared for this sheep is; she must have a good shepherd! I wonder how many things might get stuck in a sheep's coat without a good shepherd. I wonder how our Good Shepherd cares for us?" This reframing of the activity leads the child into deeper consideration of God's character while creating art. The page is no longer just a reminder of the story to take home; it's a moment of reflection on the child's relationship with God.

Prioritizing Where to Lead Change

Once there is extra bandwidth in the ministry leader's schedule created by setting up more sustainable rhythms, what needs to be addressed first? These are questions best considered in the contexts of community and prayer.

When considering people in the community to invite to voice their input on potential change, look for wise and humble leaders rather than the loudest voices or even the most committed volunteers. Many people approach invitations for input on children's ministries as ways to voice their own desires or felt needs rather than work to carefully discern what the ministry as a whole might need the most. Seek input from those who are able to look at the ministry area holistically, who display a level of humility in putting the needs of others first, and who care deeply about the formation of children.

When looking at any vision or goal statements for the church or ministry as a whole, the voices of the broader community and past community can give input too. For instance, considering a prior written vision statement for the children's ministry might put in perspective the strengths that the ministry area intentionally developed over the years and the areas that were deemed priorities in the past but have become less so over the years. A ministry may have included a clause about the value of the church family and intergenerational friendships but focused intentionally on equipping nuclear families. Perhaps this congregation is called to realign some of its energy toward building relationships across generations! Another congregation might have strong intergenerational friendships but need to refocus energy on serving their broader community, building biblical literacy, or caring for children who are working through grief or suffering. By gathering wise counsel to prayerfully consider where God is calling them to grow and adapt, ministries and congregations can intentionally begin to implement small changes led by the Holy Spirit.

Building Networks of Collaboration

Along with building a sounding board within the ministry, children's ministry leaders benefit from having partners in ministry outside of their immediate contexts. Both internal support from a children's ministry leadership team and external support from a network of other local children's ministry leaders can help buoy a ministry leader through encouragement, support, and camaraderie. Children's ministry leaders often experience loneliness and isolation, which can compound typical frustrations into overwhelming situations. Even with demonstrated support from a senior pastor and other church leadership, children's ministry leaders often feel segregated from other ministry areas or solo in their endeavors. There are benefits to both local geographic networks and more distant denomination or tradition-based networks of children's ministry leaders.

I attend a monthly meeting with local children's ministry leaders representing a variety of traditions, church contexts, and backgrounds. We trade books, collaborate on best practices for things like child safety, share local tips for supplies or vendors, and pray for one another. The spectrum of traditions sometimes opens opportunities for me to consider new approaches to ministry and occasionally affirms that my congregation's approach to a ministry situation is the best fit for our particular theological perspective. Having a sounding board completely outside of my church and denominational context also offers some helpful objectivity to various ministry questions.

Email communication with children's ministry leaders within my theological tradition, whether local or long-distance, provides some encouragement for situations that are more particular to the theology or culture of my congregation. For instance, I have benefited from collaborating and sharing resources with them for teaching children about the sacraments of Communion and baptism or the liturgical calendar, all topics where I share more in common with my tradition than with my local ministry colleagues.

Finally, I have a list of mentor-colleagues whose ministry experience and skills offer wisdom and perspective on my current context. Their years of experience are helpful in navigating difficult interpersonal situations, hot-button issues, and other potentially emotionally charged ministry dilemmas. While the curveballs of ministry can feel overwhelming in the moment, they are rarely entirely new situations, and the encouragement and input of those who have successfully navigated similar circumstances over the years help keep things in perspective.

Conclusion

There is no one right path for applying the research and innovations presented in this book to the context of ministry. Instead, there's an invitation to partner with God's already-present work in your context equipped with recent research, best practices, and innovative ideas. As the apostle Paul writes in 1 Corinthians 3, we are invited into partnership with God as fellow workers, and it is God who provides growth according to the grace founded on Christ Jesus. This grace and God's presence can compel us forward in partnering with God's work in our ministry contexts, as it relieves us from undue pressure to trust in our own performance or perfection, instead encouraging us to seek thoughtful, intentional, God-led ministries.

Bibliography

DeVries, Mark, and Annette Safstrom. *Sustainable Children's Ministry: From Last-Minute Scrambling to Long-Term Solutions.* Downers Grove, IL: InterVarsity, 2018.

Contributors

Lacy Finn Borgo teaches and provides spiritual direction for Renovaré, the Companioning Center, and Mercy Center, Burlingame. She has a spiritual direction ministry for adults and provides spiritual direction for children at Haven House, a transitional facility for families without homes. Her recent books are *Spiritual Conversations with Children: Listening to God Together* and the children's book *All Will Be Well*.

Jared Patrick Boyd is a pastor, spiritual director, and founder of the Order of the Common Life, a missional monastic order for the twenty-first century. He pastors the Abbey, a contemplative church in the city of Columbus, Ohio. Jared is the author of *Imaginative Prayer: A Yearlong Guide for Your Child's Spiritual Formation* and *The Freedom of Constraint*. He and his wife have four girls and live in the west-side neighborhood of Franklinton in Columbus, Ohio.

Joseph P. Conway ministers with the Acklen Avenue Church of Christ in Nashville, Tennessee. In addition, he serves as an affiliate faculty member in the College of Bible and Ministry at Lipscomb University. He's the author of *Broken but Beautiful: Why Church Is Still Worth It*. He and his wife, Beth, enjoy life with three daughters.

Heather Ingersoll joined the Godly Play Foundation as the executive director in the fall of 2020. She earned a PhD in education from Seattle Pacific University and an MA in family life education from Concordia University. Before joining the Godly Play Foundation staff, she worked for several Christian churches supporting children's ministry programs, served as a professor of early childhood education, and taught courses in child development, positive psychology, spirituality in schools, and children's ministry.

Kevin Johnson serves as the director of children's ministries for Discipleship Ministries, United Methodist Church. He is an ordained elder in the United Methodist Church. Kevin holds a master's of divinity from Louisville Presbyterian Theological Seminary and a doctor of ministry in homiletical leadership from Phillips Theological Seminary. He is married to Jennifer and has three children, Braden, JonMarie, and Will.

Dana Kennamer is a professor of early childhood education at Abilene Christian University. Her publications include *Along the Way: Conversations about Children & Faith*. Despite Dana's busy life as an academic, you can find her on Sunday mornings and Wednesday evenings with the children of her church, who know her simply as "Teacher Dana."

Karin Middleton has served with an international mission agency for twenty years. She has led children's ministries in large churches and church plants in California and Colorado across a broad spectrum of Christian traditions. She also served in children's ministries in Scotland and London and conducted children's ministry research in Germany and France. She holds an MEd from Azusa Pacific and an MA in theology from Fuller Seminary.

Suzetta Nutt serves as a children's minister and the director of communications at Highland Church of Christ in Abilene, Texas. For the past thirty-seven years, her passion has been listening to children and wondering about the mystery of God together with them as they share the lifelong journey of faith. She and her husband, Bob, have three children, Lauren, Ryan, and Tabby.

Contributors

Trevecca Okholm (editor) began her professional life as a children's and family pastor for over a quarter century before moving into academics. She has spent nearly a decade teaching practical theology at Azusa Pacific University. She also serves churches as a ministry consultant and trainer for worship and wonder approaches to ministry with children. Trevecca has served on the board of the Children's Spirituality Summit since 2014. Her books include *Kingdom Family: Re-envisioning God's Plan for Marriage and Family* and *The Grandparenting Effect: Bridging Generations One Story at a Time*.

Anthony Peterson has designed and facilitated diversity workshops since 2004. He has led workshops in corporate, academic, and community settings. His degrees in psychology (BA, Willamette University) and Christian education (MA, Scarritt Graduate School) inform his perspective on diversity and inclusion. Anthony's diversity discussions took a personal turn in 2014 when he began documenting conversations with his White grandchildren regarding race, and his relevant TEDx talk has reached thousands. He hopes that those conversations serve as invitations for others to tell their own racial stories.

Robin Turner (editor) currently serves as the director of family ministries at All Saints Dallas, having spent the last decade working in children's ministries in North Carolina, Pennsylvania, and Texas in Anglican contexts. She studied Christian formation and ministry for her BA and MA at Wheaton College, and in 2019, she earned her doctor of ministry in leadership and spiritual formation from Portland Seminary. Her dissertation addressed leading change in congregations to value children's spiritual formation for the sake of the whole church body. She loves spending time with her husband, Sam, and their two young sons, Davy and Jack.

Edwin M. (Ed) Willmington is the director of the Fred Bock Institute of Music at the Brehm Center for Worship, Theology, and the Arts and composer-in-residence at Fuller Theological Seminary. Ed's recent compositional projects include "Reconciled in Christ," the music for the opening and closing ceremonies of the Third Lausanne Congress on World Evangelization, held in Cape Town, South Africa, in October 2010, and "Consolation for the Suffering," a musical work written to highlight the issue of Christian persecution. He also has a special interest in encouraging the creativity of musical artists and has developed Jubal House Publications (http://www.JubalHouse.com) as a means of sharing new works as tools for worship planning. Ed has a BA in church music and conducting from Bethel University in Minnesota and an MM and DMA in composition—both from the University of Arizona. Ed and his wife, Mary Lou, have two married daughters, Nicolette Kay and Cami Ferreira; two sons-in-law, Timothy Kay and Gus Ferreira; and four wonderful grandchildren.

Stacey Wilson works as a ministry consultant, facilitating the processes of reflection and culture change that enable churches to flourish as intergenerational communities of faith. A passionate advocate for diversity, inclusion, and trauma-informed care, Stacey develops practical, evidence-based resources and training for ministry practitioners. She has held leadership positions in three intergenerational faith communities over the last fifteen years and spends too many hours at her local café drinking coffee.

Esther L. Zimmerman serves as chair of the Church and Ministry Leadership Department at Lancaster Bible College / Capital Seminary. Previously, she served for twelve years as the international children's ministry director for a global mission organization. Her heart is to see every child in every community around the world have someone who can help them know, love, and obey God for a lifetime.

A call for the church—the whole church—to enter into a serious conversation about our children and their faith development

ALONG THE WAY

Conversations about Children and Faith

RON BRUNER and DANA KENNAMER PEMBERTON

ISBN 978-0-89112-460-3

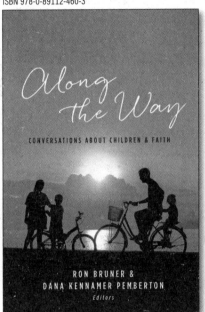

Conversations about children and faith draw us close to the heart of God, and the authors of *Along the Way* lead everyone in the church—parents, grandparents, teachers, friends, ministers, and leaders—into a careful, honest dialogue about nurturing children spiritually. Along the way, readers will rediscover how each child's walk with God is a unique journey of discovery. Readers will also realize that sharing these paths with children can change and bless not simply the children, but their own lives as well.

"*Along the Way* focuses on helping parents and church leaders to bring up children in Christian faith. It is a well-crafted, easily accessible book that reads like friends dialoging about how to nurture children. A beautiful outcome of reading this book would be for adults and children to continue these conversations as they walk together 'along the way.'"
—**SCOTTIE MAY**, Associate Professor, Christian Formation & Ministry Emerita, Wheaton College

"The subtitle says it all, "Conversations about Children and Faith." Rather than reading about children, faith, and ministry, this book reads like you are sitting among colleagues in dialog with one another about a matter that matters most to all of you. Well-balanced, it integrates insights from theology, tradition, research, and experience, with attention given to the often-overlooked Stone-Campbell Movement. I found this book to be insightful and a benefit to all who minister to and with children, as well as those of us who prepare others to do so."
—**JAMES ESTEP**, Professor of Christian Education, Lincoln Christian University

1-877-816-4455 toll free
www.acupressbooks.com

"Youthworkers who don't pay attention to families are like farmers who don't pay attention to the soil. *Owning Faith* is a welcome tool for those wise youthworkers who realize that nurturing and enriching the soil of families is one of the surest ways to impact the fruit of real life youth ministry."

—DUFFY ROBBINS,
Professor of Youth Ministry, Eastern University

OWNING FAITH

edited by **Dudley Chancey and Ron Bruner**

ISBN 978-0-89112-476-4

Today's adolescents face an uphill climb as they seek to own their faith. *Owning Faith* is an accessible guide into the adventure-filled, spiritual journey of adolescents. If you would like to learn how to be a wise and compassionate companion who can make an eternal difference in the lives of youth, *Owning Faith* will show you how.

LEAFWOOD
PUBLISHERS
an imprint of Abilene Christian University Press

www.leafwoodpublishers.com | 877-816-4455 (toll free)

LISTEN AND MAKE ROOM

Joining God in Welcoming Children

HAROLD SHANK

ISBN 978-1-68426-360-8

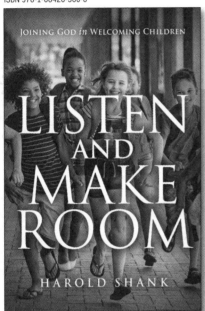

Listen for the cries of the vulnerable and welcome the children for whom Jesus made room.

When Jesus made room, the vulnerable came for prayer. He treated their ills. He fixed what was broken. Jesus gave sight to the blind, made the lame walk, and welcomed the little children, creating space for those who had been excluded. Then, he listened to those who often had no voice. Today, those people are often children.

We rarely listen to those who have small voices in our world. Instead, we fill up all the space ourselves, leaving no room for those who have little ability to acquire a spot. *Listen and Make Room* uses the example of Jesus to show us that children are at the core of God's mission.

"This is a must read to reawaken our hearts for the little ones in society who are ignored or unheard. There is no room for them. Convicting and compelling, Shank reminds us of Jesus's deep compassion for society's marginalized."
—**LYNN MCMILLON,** Distinguished Professor of Bible, Oklahoma Christian University

"The way of Jesus seems upside down in our broken world. Listening to and making room for the vulnerable is not the way to get ahead in this life. But Shank demonstrates that this upside-down way of living is, in fact, exactly what this world needs."
—**DR. KENT BRANTLY,** Ebola survivor and coauthor of *Called for Life*

1-877-816-4455 toll free
www.acupressbooks.com